Making Sense of Research

To the memory of Elaine's husband and
Patrick's father, Richard T. McEwan (1929-1990).

Elaine K. McEwan
Patrick J. McEwan

Making Sense of Research

What's Good, What's Not, and How to Tell the Difference

Foreword by Henry M. Levin

CORWIN PRESS, INC.
A Sage Publications Company
Thousand Oaks, California

For information:

Corwin Press, Inc.
A Sage Publications Company
2455 Teller Road
Thousand Oaks, California 91320
www.corwinpress.com

Sage Publications Ltd.
6 Bonhill Street
London EC2A 4PU
United Kingdom

Sage Publications India Pvt. Ltd.
B-42 Panchsheel Enclave
Post Box 4109
New Delhi 110 017 India

Printed in the United States of America

Library of Congress Cataloging-in-Publication Data

McEwan, Elaine K., 1941-
Making sense of research: What's good, what's not, and how to tell the difference/ Elaine K. McEwan, Patrick J. McEwan.
    p. cm.
Includes bibliographical references and Index.
ISBN 0-7619-7707-4
ISBN 0-7619-7708-2 (pbk.)
    1. Education—Research United States. 2. School improvement programs—United States. I. McEwan, Patrick J. II. Title.
LB1028.25. U6M39 2003
370'.7'2—dc21

                                    2002156706

This book is printed on acid-free paper.

03 04 05 06 07 7 6 5 4 3 2 1

Acquisitions Editor:	Robert D. Clouse
Editorial Assistant:	Erin Clow
Production Editor:	Denise Santoyo
Copyeditor:	Marilyn Power Scott
Typesetter:	C&M Digitals (P) Ltd.
Cover Designer:	Tracy E. Miller
Production Artist:	Sandy Sauvajot

Contents

Foreword

Educational decision makers are constantly confronted with challenges for improving educational outcomes. They are bombarded with stories in journals and newsletters that herald new educational breakthroughs in curriculum, instructional strategies, teacher qualifications, and technology that have been "shown" to raise student test scores. They are assailed with the recommendations of consultants and experts who begin their sentences with the authority of three words: "Research shows that...." But, they also know that these words are used very loosely in education, often to promote approaches to which the advocate is committed. Only rarely is the researcher required to provide documentation that substantiates the research findings. Even worse, what is often called research in education would not pass muster as rigorous evidence in any of the sciences or social sciences. Educational experimentation is difficult to undertake, and educational researchers often lack the specialized training that is required for systematic inquiry.

What is an educational decision maker to do under such circumstances? Can research claims be trusted? How can one understand the differences between solid research findings and mere claims that "Research shows that...." Recently, the stakes have risen. The *No Child Left Behind Act of 2001* mandates that decisions using federal funding must be made on the basis of "scientifically based research." Presumably, state and local decision makers using federal funds must limit the choice of educational interventions for improving instruction to those that are scientifically validated. Yet, most policy makers and decision makers are not likely to be able to distinguish among interventions according to this criterion. Advocates of educational interventions have historically placed findings of questionable validity into scientific-appearing formats such as graphs and histograms, assertions of "significant" results, and journal citations. All of these are designed to confer the manifestations of "scientificism" on claims of educational effectiveness. Often these devices are used for marketing purposes. Unfortunately, the vast majority of research claims in education have been found to be suspect in terms of the validity of the evidence. Only a few are solidly supported by systematic research, but which few?

Making Sense of Research by Elaine and Patrick McEwan is the most effective attempt that I have seen to assist decision makers in sifting through scientific claims about educational interventions. The book takes readers through a comprehensive set of principles regarding the evaluation of research claims and applies these to a set of case studies of prominent reforms. The collaboration of a noted educator and a highly regarded economist provides insights and understanding into both the strengths and weaknesses of education research. These insights are applied directly to prominent educational reforms and the analysis of the quality of research underlying them. Educators owe a debt of gratitude to the McEwans for their clarity in presentation and penetrating guidance. Without question, this book will serve as the standard work in assisting educators and decision makers to assess the validity of research claims in education as they determine how to improve student outcomes.

—Henry M. Levin
William Heard Kilpatrick Professor
of Economics and Education,
Teachers College, Columbia University and
David Jacks Professor of Higher Education
and Economics, Emeritus,
Stanford University

Preface

The dictionary defines research as "careful, patient, systematic, diligent inquiry or examination in some field of knowledge, undertaken to establish facts or principles" (McKechnie, 1983, pp. 1538-1539). When Webster's definition of *research* is paired with the word *education* the results seem almost oxymoronic. Educators often make decisions at the last minute, under extreme pressure, and with more regard for what is popular or innovative, than for what is established, factual, or truthful. For many educators, any consideration of the rigors of research ended when they sold their statistics books to the used bookstore—grateful that they would never again have to "crunch numbers" or decipher data. Unfortunately, they regarded research as an obstacle to surmount on the way to an advanced degree, not an essential aspect of informing their day-to-day practice. Research was for the ivory tower types—not for "down-in-the trenches" practitioners.

We can no longer afford this shortsighted approach. One word has changed the educational landscape—*accountability*. Now that educators are increasingly accountable for the outcomes of their efforts, the decisions they make regarding instruction and curriculum have taken on more gravity. Good intentions and hard work no longer count. Politicians, parents, and the press want results and research can help us get them. Make no mistake; research cannot provide recipes or prescriptions. Schooling is far too idiosyncratic to respond to simplistic formulas. However, when carefully read and thoughtfully considered, quality research can inform, enlighten, and provide direction to practitioners that will save us time and money, but more importantly enhance the effectiveness of our schools and increase the opportunities for our students.

We, the authors of *Making Sense of Research*, are related to one another, as you may have already surmised. We are a mother-son team—an unusual writing combination to be sure. But we think you will find that our unique blend of training and experiences provides a helpful perspective as you attempt to make sense of education research. If you have not already done so, take a moment to skim our biographies in *About the Authors*. We bring the best of two worlds to the writing of this book—the "real" world where education is practiced daily and the "research" world where the "disciplined search for knowledge" (Smith & Glass, 1987, p. 6) is ongoing. Ideally, these two worlds would be well-connected with the key findings regarding educational policies and practices making their way straight from the pages of refereed journals to the in-baskets of education's principal stakeholders and decision makers. However, as one writer pointed out, "The [education] research-to-practice pipeline has sprung many leaks" (Miller, 1999, p. A17). We aim to put our collective fingers in those leaks.

In our experience, the relationship between education researchers and practitioners is a tenuous and occasionally nonexistent one. Researchers are often guilty of shutting down practitioners with esoteric arguments, while practitioners are no less guilty of putting up their own smoke screens to defend their distrust of data. "When was the last time *you* were in a classroom? You ought to get out into the real world," they assert. The authors have certainly been guilty of engaging in these arguments from time to time—even with each other. In a way, our authorship is a metaphor for the larger questions: How can education research improve practice? How can educators make sense of the complexities and even incongruities of research? Conversely, how can researchers tap into the rich knowledge base of educators regarding the implementation of research in authentic settings?

THE GOALS OF THIS BOOK

Our mission is set forth in the book's title: *to equip our readers with the conceptual understandings they need to make sense of education research.* This is not merely an academic exercise, however. Our ultimate goal is that you would use research findings to inform decision making and practice in your classroom, school, or district. Making sense of research is not just about reading and understanding research done by others. In our opinion, making sense of research is also about doing your own site-specific, user-driven research as a way of sustaining school improvement, keeping the vision alive, and attaining your mission.

If your eyes glaze over whenever you read a research study because you lack the tools to comprehend what it means, then you are being held hostage to someone else's interpretation of the findings. If you read only the introduction and the conclusion to a research study, ignoring everything in between, you may as well not read it at all. By the time you finish reading *Making Sense of Research,* you will be able to judge the quality of research for yourself and have confidence in your judgment.

WHO THIS BOOK IS FOR

We have written this book for educators and educational stakeholders who want to be informed and active participants in discussions regarding curriculum, instruction, and policy. This book is for those who make decisions—from the seemingly smallest teacher-made decision regarding time allocation during reading instruction to major statewide policy decisions such as reducing class size. The following individuals will find *Making Sense of Research* to be helpful:

1. Concerned and conscientious teachers who recognize that their efforts are not bringing about the desired results and want to be more effective in their classrooms

2. Principals who feel increasing pressures to bring students to mastery of national, state, or local achievement standards and are frustrated by the often haphazard way in which program decisions are made

3. Teams of teachers and administrators who are charting school improvement initiatives and need the tools to make quality decisions

4. District administrators who are faced with large-scale budgetary and curricular decisions and need direction in the allocation of resources.

5. University professors who want their students to become well-informed and knowledgeable consumers of education research.

6. Educational consumers and policymakers such as parents, school board members, or legislators who want to base their decisions on sound research.

WHAT THIS BOOK IS NOT

Making Sense of Research is different from other books you may have purchased or read about education research in the past. It is not a book that explains how to *do* research. Neither does this book methodically summarize research findings regarding a laundry list of educational innovations, instructional practices, or well-known reforms so that you won't have to do any thinking for yourself. You have listened to the "experts" for too long. It is time to do your own thinking. While we do provide a variety of interesting examples, illustrations, and case studies from current research findings, we do not provide recommendations about the *best practices* or the *proven methods.* Books of this nature become outdated very quickly with the appearance of newer programs and additional research.

Actually, one of the most important lessons we can learn from research is that all-purpose solutions do not exist. What may work for one set of students and teachers in a particular setting may not be as applicable or effective in another classroom or school. It is our belief that educators are intelligent enough to read the research for themselves, evaluate its trustworthiness as well as applicability in their own setting, and then make informed decisions. Our goal is to empower you to be confident and accountable regarding your instructional, curricular, and policy decisions in a variety of settings and job roles.

OVERVIEW OF THE CONTENTS

Chapter 1 introduces five broad questions that should change the way you read and think about research:

1. The causal question: Does it work?

2. The process question: How does it work?

3. The cost question: Is it worthwhile?

4. The usability question: Will it work for me?

5. The evaluation question: Is it working for me?

To better illustrate the first four questions, we will discuss research findings in four controversial areas: class size reduction, reading instruction, private-school vouchers, and whole-school reform. While of interest in their own right, the cases will provide a platform for illustrating the concepts and tools of education research. The fifth and final question will be discussed in the context of doing site-specific, user-driven research. Before we tackle the questions, however, Chapter 2 provides a quick tour of the world of education research— a behind-the-scenes look, if you will, at how the research "industry" works.

Chapters 3 and 4 explain how to find answers to the first big question: *Does it work?* This question has preoccupied researchers in every branch of the social sciences for many years. Their ingenuity has led to the development of numerous methods to determine whether there are *causal* effects of a specific treatment or policy on the students, teachers, schools, or districts (or even states and countries) in which it was tested and observed. The best of these methods are referred to as experimental, and they are described in Chapter 3.

Other methods, loosely referred to as quasi- or non-experimental, are examined in Chapter 4.

Chapter 5 looks at the second big question: *How does it work?* To answer this question, which concerns *process* rather than *outcomes*, we will turn our attention to qualitative data. Whereas there is no doubt that quantitative data (e.g., achievement test scores) are an essential aspect of results-based decision making, we will demonstrate that education research is not an either-or endeavor. We must also value, integrate, and use information that is collected through observations, interviews, and the analyses of documents (e.g., memos, letters, vision statements, student work samples, or teachers' journals).

Chapter 6 takes on the fourth question: *Is it worthwhile?* Though frequently ignored in debates about education research, the costs of research-based decisions must be considered. Do the costs of a program or policy render it infeasible? Is there another, less costly means of accomplishing the same goals?

In Chapter 7, we examine the fourth big question: *Will it work for me?* Just because a method or program is shown to have an effect on a group of students or schools in an experimental study, that is no guarantee that it will work for you. We explore how you can determine the generalizability of research to your unique setting using a series of rules of thumb.

In Chapter 8, we consider the last, but by no means the least, question: *Is it working for me?* Although published research is an essential guidepost for practitioners, it cannot provide all of the answers once you have made a decision to act upon those research finding. The methods that characterize good research by academics are also powerful tools for investigating the causal effects of locally developed curricula or evaluating purchased programs or reform models. User-driven research can aid in answering the question: *Is it working for me?*

A FEW WORDS OF EXPLANATION

As authors, we debated the necessity of including chapters that define and explain (yet again) research and statistics. We have chosen to steer clear of this "kitchen sink" approach to writing about research methods. Our suspicion is that these chapters are rarely read with the attention they deserve. When they are read, the forest is completely lost for the trees by beleaguered students who scramble to memorize obscure formulas. The message of this book is not that statistics and other research methods are unimportant—quite the contrary. They are exceedingly important, but they are nothing more than tools to be marshaled in answering the five critical questions. If the questions are poorly understood or imprecisely formulated, then understanding a set of methodological tools (or not) is of little consequence. As a compromise, however, we include intuitive discussions of techniques used by education researchers—or tools that we wish were used by education researchers. These are complemented by short sections at the end of every chapter with suggestions for additional reading.

As you read, you will note the use of the term *education research* rather than the more commonly used *educational research*. Although the majority of authors who have written on this subject use the designation *educational research* in their book titles and texts, we prefer the example of Lagemann (2000) and Lagemann and Shulman (1999). We must further acknowledge our tremendous intellectual debt to the methodological writings of Shadish, Cook, and Campbell (2002). The newest edition of the Cook and Campbell (1979) classic has alternately inspired, encouraged, and challenged us with its crisp writing, coherent explanations, and thought-provoking questions. The reader who is intrigued by our discussion would do well to consult these volumes.

ACKNOWLEDGMENTS

Winston Churchill captured the essence of what it means to write a book when he said, "Writing a book is an adventure. To begin with, it is a toy and an amusement; then it becomes a mistress, and then it becomes a master, and then a tyrant. The last phase is that just as you are about to be reconciled to your servitude, you kill the monster, and fling him out to the public" (Gilbert, 1991, p. 887). Before we fling our joint effort out to the reading public, we must acknowledge the contributions of others to our efforts.

I (EKM) am grateful to Patrick McEwan for writing a book with his mother. It isn't every son who would have the patience with and faith in his mother to undertake a project such as this. I am proud of his scholarship and commitment to excellence. I also owe an enormous debt of gratitude to James Heald, my academic mentor and long-time friend. Without his confidence in me, aided by a positive recommendation to an editor friend, my educational writing career might never have been launched. Most especially, I offer my heartfelt thanks to my husband and business partner, E. Raymond Adkins, for his support, encouragement, and honest appraisal of my work.

I (PJM) am indebted to Elaine McEwan, who constantly prodded me—whether she realized it or not—to link my research endeavors to the "real world" of education practice (every education researcher should have an award-winning principal handy to ask the all-important question: "So what?"). I also am deeply grateful to my colleague and mentor, Henry M. Levin, who thoughtfully combines research and practice in education—and who unstintingly shares his lessons with others.

Last, we both appreciate the frequent readings of this manuscript by our daughter and sister, Emily McEwan-Fujita. Although engaged in personal research and writing, she always took the time to offer helpful comments and suggest excellent alternatives.

In addition, Corwin Press gratefully acknowledges the contributions of the following reviewers:

Dr. Jim Duncan
Director of Schools
Wilson County Schools
Lebanon, TN

Linda S. Mueller,
Aces High School
Principal/Administrator
Everett, WA

Eleanor Perry, ASC Professor
Arizona State University
ASUW College of Education
Tempe, AZ

Carolyn S. Ridenour, Professor
University of Dayton
Department of Educational Leadership
School of Education and Allied Professions
Dayton, OH

Steven A. Schmitz, Professor
College of Education and Professional Studies
Department of Curriculum and Supervision
Central Washington University
Ellensburg, WA

About the Authors

**Elaine K. McEwan** is an educational consultant with The McEwan-Adkins Group offering workshops and consulting services in instructional leadership, school improvement, and raising reading achievement K-12. A former teacher, media specialist, principal, and assistant superintendent for instruction in a suburban Chicago school district, she is the author of more than 30 books for parents, children, and educators. Some of her titles include *The Principal's Guide to Raising Reading Achievement* (1998), *The Principal's Guide to Raising Math Achievement* (2000), *Raising Reading Achievement in Middle and High Schools: Five Simple-to-Follow Strategies for Principals* (2001), *Ten Traits of Highly Effective Teachers: How to Hire, Mentor, and Coach Successful Teachers* (2001), and *Seven Steps to Effective Instructional Leadership, Second Edition* (2002). She was honored by the Illinois Principals Association as an outstanding instructional leader, by the Illinois State Board of Education with an Award of Excellence, and by the National Association of Elementary School Principals as the National Distinguished Principal from Illinois for 1991. She received advanced degrees in library science (MA) and educational administration (EdD) from Northern Illinois University. Visit Elaine's Web site at http://www.elainemcewan.com, where you can contact her, read excerpts from some of her books, or learn about available on-location or online workshops.

**Patrick J. McEwan** is Assistant Professor in the Department of Economics at Wellesley College in Wellesley, Massachusetts, and an affiliate of the David Rockefeller Center for Latin American Studies at Harvard University. Previously, he taught in the Department of Educational Policy Studies at the University of Illinois at Urbana-Champaign and served as Assistant Director for Research at the National Center for the Study of Privatization in Education at Teachers College, Columbia University. He completed his PhD in education at Stanford University, in addition

to master's degrees in economics and international development. His published books (with Henry Levin) include *Cost-Effectiveness Analysis: Methods and Applications, Second Edition* (2001) and *Cost-Effectiveness and Educational Policy: 2002 Yearbook of the American Education Finance Association* (2002). He is the author of numerous journal articles, book chapters, and reports, and he has consulted on education policy and evaluation at the Inter-American Development Bank, RAND, UNESCO, and the ministries of education of several countries. His recent research (with Martin Carnoy) has evaluated the impact of Chile's national voucher plan on the effectiveness and efficiency of primary education.

**CORWIN
PRESS**

The Corwin Press logo—a raven striding across an open book—represents the happy union of courage and learning. We are a professional-level publisher of books and journals for K-12 educators, and we are committed to creating and providing resources that embody these qualities. Corwin's motto is "Success for All Learners."

1

Asking the Right Questions

Does education research have any impact on the instructional practices, curricula, and policies in your classroom, school, or district? Probably not, if you are like many educators we know. You may even secretly believe that your own common sense and experience are far more trustworthy than the experiments and observations of researchers. We all know individuals who wouldn't dream of buying a new car or choosing a treatment for a medical condition without researching the options. Yet on the job, they will commit hundreds of thousands of dollars of their schools' or districts' budgets to an innovative or supposedly exemplary program without carefully evaluating the available research findings.

One elementary school principal explained the problem this way: "We tend to move from one fad to another in order to demonstrate that we are 'state of the art' even though most of the activities have little impact. There is big money in selling education programs and consultants use 'research says' to sell programs that purportedly can fix just about anything. Most . . . teachers and administrators can't differentiate viable research from poor research" (Walker, 1996, p. 41).

One can certainly understand why some practitioners dismiss education research as irrelevant to their daily lives and continue to "do their own thing." Even insiders concede that there are problems with it: poor research designs and sloppy statistics (Cook, 1999), divisive bickering (Gage, 1989; Snow, 2001), and petty politics (Shaker & Heilman, 2002). Others are more optimistic about the potential of education research to inform practice: "Research is the most powerful instrument to improve student achievement—if only we would try it in a serious and sustained manner" (National Educational Research Policy and Priorities Board, 2000a, p. 1).

This statement serves as a challenge to both researchers *and* educators. Researchers have an obligation to produce useable knowledge for practitioners, but educators are no less accountable for applying what is already known to the practice of schooling. We bear an additional responsibility as well—that of holding publishers, curriculum developers, and consultants accountable for evaluating their products and models using rigorous research techniques and then making that research available to practitioners.

WHAT IS *OUR* APPROACH TO MAKING SENSE OF RESEARCH?

Before proceeding, it is important to clarify some fairly broad assumptions that we will make about research: (a) that one *can* frame a meaningful question related to educational practice, (b) that one *can* develop a hypothesis related to that question, (c) that one *can* design a study—whether quantitative, qualitative or ideally a skillful combination of both—and collect data to assess the hypothesis, (d) that one *can* assess whether the data support the hypothesis with some degree of certainty (or uncertainty), and (e) that one *can* apply this knowledge, within reason, to inform decision making, whether at the classroom, school, district, state, or national level.[1]

Even if research appears to follow the preceding steps, one must be circumspect about accepting the "facts" that it purports to establish. In the manner of Sherlock Holmes, we have to sift through research evidence to determine what it is really saying. The issue of causality is a good example, one that receives particular emphasis in this book. Life in schools—and, indeed, life in general—is rife with causal statements: "Our test scores went up *because* of the new reading program." "Teachers are leaving the school in droves *because* of low salaries."

If this book accomplishes nothing else, it aims to convince the reader that causal statements cannot be made in a cavalier fashion. Schools are complex and multifaceted. Causal links are difficult to establish with certainty, if only because there are usually alternative—and sometimes equally plausible—causes for that which we seek to explain. For example, it may be that test scores went up not because of a new reading program, but *because* of an influx of well-to-do students or a sudden exclusion of low-achieving students from the testing. Or it may be that salaries, low as they are, have nothing whatever to do with the mass exodus of teachers. They are leaving *because* the principal makes their lives

> Causal links are difficult to establish with certainty, if only because there are usually alternative—and sometimes equally plausible—causes for that which we seek to explain.

miserable. Although establishing clear causal links is a daunting assignment, the task is easier if one pays close attention to rules-of-thumb (to be introduced throughout the book) that have been developed and refined by generations of social scientists. This book will repeatedly emphasize that identifying "good" research hinges on understanding—and critiquing—the causal underpinnings of that research.

FIVE QUESTIONS ABOUT RESEARCH

Our district has tried numerous strategies: we lifted a school day; we increased time on-task; we increased the graduation requirement; we mandated exit testing; and we put in a no-driver's-license-if-you-drop-out provision. Many other school boards have tried instituting similar enhancement policies. Locally we try to deal with attendance and discipline rules, but these measures alter the nature of the system without addressing the root causes of the problem. We have audited our rules for compliance purposes. What needs to be examined now is the unhappy consequence of these efforts: there have been no significant improvements in student achievement patterns. These innovations have failed to eliminate poor instruction and ineffective and redundant curricula. This raises the question of exactly what our professional roles are going to be to help more students become prepared for a new century. (Dorn, 1995, p. 7)

You can read between the lines of this lament by a Florida high school principal. His superintendent and school board no doubt issued a mandate: "Raise student achievement." This is a tough assignment at the high school level, or at any other level for that matter. Principal Dorn and his staff seemingly tried every strategy, idea, and innovation they could think of and nothing has worked. His frustration is palpable as he raised a very critical question: "What exactly am I supposed to be doing as a principal?"

This book does not—it cannot—offer a single answer to Dorn or to others that share his goal of improving schools. In fact, we are deeply skeptical of consultants, salespeople, and project leaders who purport to provide such answers. Rather, it suggests five questions that Dorn and educators like him should ask of research. By presenting these questions, we do not aim to waffle (thus evoking Harry Truman's plea for a one-armed economist, so that he might never hear "on the one hand" and "on the other hand"). The questions simply acknowledge two hard realities about education research.

First, *all* authors think that their research is "good" and worthy of a receptive audience. How can the beleaguered practitioner separate the wheat from the chaff? Some quality-control mechanisms already exist, of course. There are academic journals with more rigorous quality standards than others (enforced by impartial and anonymous reviewers). A great deal of the worst research is never published at all. Yet even good journals publish studies with overstatements, misstatements, and downright fabrications. Further, the proliferation of sub-standard journals, self-published Web sites, and advocacy research organizations means that it is increasingly difficult *not* to find an outlet for publication. Education is full of well-intentioned, but occasionally ineffective, attempts to synthesize and communicate research findings (e.g., Berliner & Casanova, 1993; Zemelman, Daniels, & Hyde, 1998). At the end of the day, a practitioner's common sense may have to be the final arbiter of what constitutes "good" research. We firmly believe that every practitioner can become a more informed and critical consumer of research, if armed with the right questions.

> Even good journals publish studies with overstatements, misstatements, and downright fabrications.

The second hard reality is that most researchers have the relative luxury of not having to worry about the implementation of their findings in classrooms and schools. Unfortunately, research findings do not always translate easily to the ambiguities of educational practice. Thousands of victims of botched staff development or reforms gone haywire can attest to that. What works in one context may fail miserably in another. Thus, research cannot be analyzed solely on the basis of the hermetically sealed bubble in which it was conducted; it must be evaluated in light of the context in which the findings will be applied, whether a classroom, school, district, or state. Once again, practitioners are often in the best position to decide what might work for them, based on their informed reading of the research.

To aid practitioners in their quest for understanding, we offer five questions:

1. The causal question: Does it work?

2. The process question: How does it work?

3. The cost question: Is it worthwhile?

4. The usability question: Will it work for me?

5. The evaluation question: Is it working for me?

Apply the first four questions to research *before* you adopt or implement a program, method, or policy. For example, if you (and your team) are considering the implementation of "multiple intelligences" as a way to organize curricula and design instruction, or contemplating the use of block scheduling as a means of raising achievement in your high school, seek out every available research study—both quantitative and qualitative. Read them carefully to determine if *it* (i.e., multiple intelligences or block scheduling) actually works, how *it* works, if *it's* worthwhile, and if *it* will work for you. Ask these questions *before* you commit to adoption.

Once you have made the decision to adopt and actually begin implementation, ask the fifth and final question—is *it* working for me. Ask this question at several points *during* implementation (i.e., a formative evaluation to fine-tune the implementation process) and then ask it again *after* implementation (i.e., a summative evaluation to determine the overall effectiveness of the method or policy). Figure 1.1, Asking the Right Questions, shows how and when the five questions can be used to make sense of research.

How many times have you adopted a program and then hurriedly moved on to another priority, failing to investigate whether the program you *believed* would work based either on research or a glowing testimonial, is actually working? Question 5 can only be answered by going "on location" in your classroom, school, or district and conducting what we call *user-driven research*.

The Causal Question: Does It Work?

Many research studies in education, primarily those with a quantitative bent, test whether a causal relationship exists between interventions and outcomes.[2] The interventions are infinite, ranging from ability grouping to whole-school reform. The tested outcomes are equally diverse, although the biases of experimental researchers, as well as most

> The bottom line is whether the intervention being considered "causes" a particular outcome to change.

parents (Public Agenda, 2002), tend to favor some type of standardized measure of achievement.

The bottom line of these studies is whether the intervention being considered "causes" a particular outcome to change. For example, did added teacher training in a school district *cause* students' test scores to rise? Drawing this inference is rarely as simple as we would like to believe. Even if we observe that test scores rose shortly after teachers participated in training, we must immediately rule out *every other potential explanation* for the change in test scores. Only then can we credibly infer that a causal relationship exists between training and test scores. The range of alternate explanations (and whether they are remotely plausible) will depend on the particulars of the research context. Perhaps the school district enrolled a new group of wealthy (and high-achieving) students. In this instance, the rise in test scores would have occurred even in the absence of staff development.

Figure 1.1   Asking the Right Questions

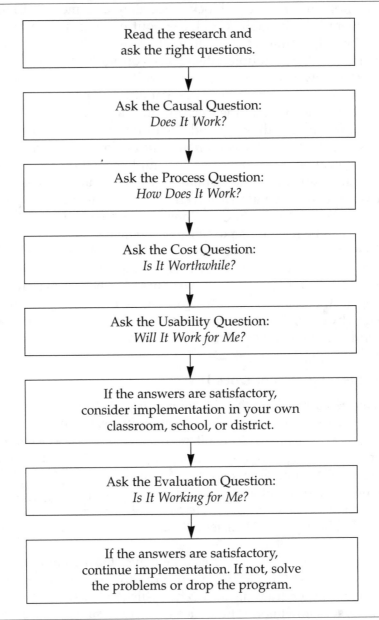

High-quality research in education can spare readers from this guesswork. It does so by adhering to tried and true elements of good research design. One of the best designs is the randomized experiment. There is a treatment group (of students, schools, or other units) that participates in an intervention. Likewise, there is a control group that does not receive the intervention. The sine qua non of an experiment, however, is randomized assignment to treatment and control groups. That is, the assignment of a particular student or school to either group depends on nothing more than chance (or, quite literally, the flip of a coin). If implemented properly, a good experiment allows the researcher to convincingly establish whether an intervention is the *only* plausible explanation for gains (or losses) in valued outcomes. Why? The answer lies in the fact that with randomized assignment we can be virtually certain that the only difference between the two groups is their exposure to the intervention. They were essentially identical at the outset of the experiment. Chapter 3 will define the elements of a randomized experiment in much greater detail, and describe why it is such a powerful means of obtaining strong answers to the causal question: Does it work?

> The sine qua non of an experiment is randomized assignment to treatment and control groups.

Unfortunately for those of us looking for more certainty, randomized experiments are often the exception in education research (though not in other fields, such as health). The fallback position of most education researchers is the quasi-experiment. This is a much-used (and abused) term that refers to research designs meant to replicate experimental conditions. Like experiments, quasi-experiments usually rely on comparing the outcomes of a treatment group that received an intervention to a comparison group that did not.[3] Unlike experiments, there is no randomized assignment to these groups—hence the prefix "quasi." You might already be imagining the pitfalls to be encountered in a poorly done quasi-experiment. Let's say we are trying to assess whether a new reading curriculum "works" by comparing the test scores of the students in a classroom that received the treatment (i.e., the new reading program) to the scores of students in another classroom who did not experience the new program. Suppose that the "treated" class is taught by a highly effective veteran teacher, whereas the other class is taught by an embittered, burnt-out one. Did the curriculum work? Any differences in outcomes between the two classes *might* be due to the reading program, but the quality of the instruction could also be the explanation for the higher scores.

Of course, a very good quasi-experiment would go to extraordinary lengths to rule out explanations besides the curriculum, thus deriving a strong "causal" conclusion. It would do so through careful matching procedures or sophisticated statistical techniques or any number of other methods. (Shadish et al., 2002). We will provide a sampling of these in Chapter 4, as well as some of the hazards in their application and interpretation.

The Process Question: How Does It Work?

Even if we succeed in uncovering a causal relationship, that knowledge does not tell us exactly *why* a relationship exists between a treatment and an effect. In other words, we do not know the possible classroom and school processes or interactions that may have mediated the causal relationship, or lack thereof. If reduced class size is found to improve achievement, for example, it presumably does not happen by magic. Something occurs in the instructional setting of smaller-size classes that produces higher student achievement: Teachers may devote more time to students with learning challenges, or smaller classes may promote a better disciplinary climate, or students may be more inclined to participate in a less crowded classroom. The "how" of this causal relationship may be a combination of all of these explanations—or none of them. The point is that causal description—evidence that something happened via an experiment or quasi-experiment—does not always imply or provide a causal explanation of how something happened (Shadish et al., 2002).

Yet understanding the processes that undergird a positive (or negative) causal finding can greatly enrich our knowledge. How was the intervention implemented and were there any significant setbacks or roadblocks? Was this implementation responsible, to some degree, for the observed outcomes? Were some elements of the intervention more effective than others, and might these be profitably emphasized in subsequent implementations? And how, exactly, did the intervention succeed in altering the outcomes?

Researchers may find such information helpful in testing and even refining the theory that led them to conduct the research in the first place. Even more germane from this book's perspective is that practitioners may find it useful as they evaluate the relevance of a research study for their own purposes. Knowledge of such processes can be vital in deciding whether and how the findings of a research study might be replicated—or improved upon—in an alternate setting.

> The "thick descriptions" necessary to understand processes can often be obtained from research with a more qualitative bent.

The "thick descriptions" necessary to understand processes can often be obtained from research with a more qualitative bent (although the best quantitative studies will also gather information on processes). A variety of techniques—ranging from case studies to ethnographies—fall into this category. Chapter 5 will describe some of these and show how they can be a useful means of answering perplexing questions about *how* education interventions work.

The Cost Question: Is It Worthwhile?

Teachers, principals, and even superintendents often perceive costs as an issue for someone else—the district business manager or accountants. Even most books on education research and evaluation take up the issue of costs as an afterthought, if it is given any consideration at all. In contrast, we think the issue of costs is central for all practitioners, particularly when they are contemplating new programs or policies. How many schools, for example, have introduced a whole-school reform package, only to discover that it stretched their personnel to the breaking point and caused other important priorities to be shelved? How many districts have enthusiastically pursued class size reduction, only to find that limited space has consigned students and their newly hired teachers to converted janitorial closets?

> Teachers, principals, and even superintendents often perceive costs as an issue for someone else—the district business manager or accountants.

These are precisely the conundrums faced by schools that act upon research findings—however glowing the "causal" findings— without considering the cost implications of decisions. You will discover that our definition of costs is broader than the average accountant's. To be sure, it includes typical resource costs like expenditures on salaries, instructional materials, and facilities; salaries are especially important in the labor-intensive work of education. However, it also includes costs that never pass through an accountant's balance sheet. Imagine a policy that is apparently "costless"— say, the implementation of a mandatory period of sustained silent reading for all students in an elementary school. No new teachers are hired and no money exchanges hands. And yet, teacher and student time is now occupied in silent reading that would have been devoted to other activities like tutoring, studying, and grading. Unless these tasks were *entirely* unproductive, something was sacrificed by reallocating the time of teachers and students. The value of this lost opportunity is a cost—perhaps difficult to quantify—but a cost nonetheless. It should clearly factor in to the decisions of practitioners.

Chapter 6 will introduce two general approaches to considering costs: cost-feasibility and cost-effectiveness. They are familiar enough concepts in everyday life, but somehow they have become estranged from decision making in the educational arena. Cost-feasibility corresponds to the essential question: Can we afford it? In other words, what are the monetary (and nonmonetary) costs of a particular intervention, and is it feasible for our district (or school or classroom) to bear those costs?

Cost-effectiveness corresponds to a broader and *comparative* question: Is there a less costly means of accomplishing the same thing? Suppose that a particular intervention has been shown to be effective across a wide range of schools, including yours. And yet, it comes with a hefty price tag. We might legitimately ask, can the same effects be obtained via another intervention at a lower cost? Or reversing the question, does another intervention, costing the same amount, provide even larger effects? In short, what intervention will give us the most "bang for our buck"?

The Usability Question: Will It Work for Me?

Let's suppose that you do find a research study that credibly demonstrates that an intervention "works," succeeds in describing why, and is worthwhile in terms of both cost-feasibility and cost-effectiveness. Consider, as an example, an after-school tutoring program that has been shown to increase mathematics achievement. Do those results automatically imply that the program will work everywhere? More to the point, do the results imply that it will work in *your* school or district? The answer is often "no," which won't surprise practitioners who are occasionally the willing or unwilling victims of "proven" reforms.

Let's consider several hypothetical instances in which the positive results from the after-school program research study may not apply to your school. Imagine that the research study was conducted in schools that enroll mostly upper-middle-class students. Your student body, on the other hand, contains students from poor and working-class backgrounds, many of whom receive free-and-reduced lunches. These students have after-school obligations, ranging from child care for their younger siblings to part-time jobs. Targeting and retaining them in such a program in your school would be difficult.

In addition, the tutoring in the research study was done by a group of trained parent volunteers, many of whom were given release time from jobs at the local university. In your community, parent volunteers are in short supply due to the economic constraints just cited. Instead, your tutors will be drawn from the ranks of local high-school students who will receive only an abbreviated orientation. You suspect that the altered version of the treatment might work, though with a diminished impact on mathematics achievement.

Last, the research study only examined the impact of mathematics achievement, using a special test instrument developed by the researcher, aligned with that school's curriculum. You plan to evaluate mathematics achievement using a very different instrument—the one mandated by your school district. And although mathematics achievement is certainly a focus of your school's efforts to improve, there are also great concerns about raising reading achievement. You wonder if the tutoring program might have ancillary benefits for students' reading, particularly given the text-intensive approach to teaching mathematics that is favored in the tutoring program.

The preceding example suggests that caution is warranted when generalizing the causal conclusions of a particular research study, whether quantitative or qualitative, to your context. Perhaps the student populations are different. Or the treatment will undergo modifications. Or different outcomes are considered. This bad news is compounded by the undeniable reality that you will *never* find an exhaustive description of precisely where and how the research would be most applicable.

All is not lost, however. Many researchers are quite careful in evaluating the conditions under which their findings might be generalized. While a single study might provide only a few clues—perhaps limited by the scope of its data—you can often locate wide-ranging summaries of the available research on a given topic that use a group of statistical techniques known as meta-analysis. In doing so, one can learn a great deal about whether causal conclusions hold across a wide range of students, treatment variations, and outcomes. And even in the absence of firm evidence about generalizability, there are common sense rules for answering the question, Will it work for me? Chapter 7 will describe them.

The Evaluation Question: Is It Working for Me?

Education research is often—and unnecessarily—confined to the rarefied atmosphere of academia. There, highly trained intellectuals often focus on very narrow or particular aspects of schooling. They often zero in, whether quantitatively or qualitatively, without regard for the problems or possibilities inherent in replicating or implementing what they have researched. Once the findings are disseminated, practitioners are left "on their own" to figure out how what is purported to be a fabulous instructional innovation or a breakthrough in learning can make a faithful leap from the drawing board to the classroom.

We believe that the implementation of such "research-based" programs must be accompanied by practitioner-initiated and site-specific research that never stops asking the question, Is it working for me—in my classroom, school, or district? Posing *this* question means applying the questions we have previously asked with regard to actual research studies in the context of your own

> We believe that the implementation of "research-based" programs must be accompanied by practitioner-initiated and site-specific research that never stops asking the question, Is it working in my school or district?

setting. First, you will seek to know *if* a program is actually doing what it is supposed to be doing; then, determine *how* it is doing it; next, investigate its costs; and last, consider whether it makes sense to modify, sustain, or even expand these efforts.

Answering these questions need not dictate that districts will design their own randomized experiment (although they certainly could, and even should if a program's effects are uncertain). Nor does it necessarily mean that teachers will prepare case studies of their own implementation experiences (although they might and could even receive some type of credit or stipend for doing so). Chapter 8 will provide examples of user-driven research that you can adapt for your own use.

Four Case Studies of Education Research

The four case studies introduced in this section will appear again in Chapters 3 to 7, not only to illustrate key concepts about the kind of research under discussion but also to demonstrate how to ask and find answers to the first four questions using actual studies. The bodies of research that we have chosen are somewhat controversial in nature. There are nearly equal numbers of scholars and researchers on either side of these issues—both claiming to know how the research should be interpreted and what it means for practitioners. We submit that you needn't rely exclusively on the opinions of these researchers. Instead, you can use the five questions to make sense of these debates and disagreements for yourself.

CASE STUDY   Class Size Reduction: Does Size Matter?

Ask any parent whether they prefer to have their child in a small class or a large one, and you might be greeted with a look of disbelief. Among many, it is almost an article of faith that reducing class sizes will improve student outcomes, by virtue of allowing teachers to spend more time with individual students. Apparently, many politicians agree with this logic. Legislatures in more than 20 states have decided to spend large amounts of money on lowering class sizes, usually with the expressly stated goal of improving student performance.[4] One of the most well-known examples of class size reduction occurred in California. In 1996, an education budget was approved by the California State Legislature, part of Establish CSR Program Bill of 1996, that allowed local districts to receive state funds for class size reductions in the early grades (Johnston, 1996). As of 2000-2001, districts received $850 for each K-3 student enrolled in a class of 20 or fewer students (Stecher & Bornstedt, 2002).

You might assume that that an avalanche of high-quality research on class size reduction has swiftly followed these investments—but you would be wrong. It is true that some states have devoted more resources to research than others; California, Tennessee, and Wisconsin are good examples (Jacobson, 2001). But in the vast majority of cases, it is *assumed* that class size reduction is producing benefits for schools and students. In Nevada, for example, "officials at the state education department still have little proof that the long- running initiative is really improving student achievement," despite four previous evaluations (Jacobson, 2001).

Yet most proponents of class size reduction still claim to have research on their side. That research is drawn from just a few states, with findings from Tennessee occupying center-stage. You have likely heard of the Tennessee STAR project. In 1985, the Tennessee legislature funded an experiment in 79 schools in which students were randomly assigned to "regular" classes (22-26 students) and "small" classes (13-17 students). Ignore for the moment the fact that some teachers would trade their planning period for what constitutes a regular-sized class in Tennessee. The experiment showed that standardized test scores rise because of attendance in smaller classes and that these differences seem to persist (Grissmer, 1999).[5]

Predictably, there are researchers who dispute the rosy conclusions of the Tennessee STAR experiment. Stanford University economist Eric Hanushek is one of the most prominent voices of dissent. He has published influential reviews of the education "production function" literature, in which authors use statistical methods to search for the correlation between school resources and student achievement. He concludes from these non-experimental studies that the "evidence does not suggest that any substantial achievement gains would accrue to general class size reduction policies of the type recently discussed and implemented in various jurisdictions around the United States" (Hanushek, 1999, p. 144). Hanushek's opinions are oft repeated by opponents of class size plans, and Hanushek himself has testified in a wide array of court cases where the effectiveness of school resources is at issue.

So who is right? As you might have surmised by now, we think this is the wrong question—or at least an incomplete one. From the vantage point of the decision maker or practitioner, the evidence on class size needs to be subjected to the questions described earlier. Does class size have a *causal* relationship to outcomes? If so, why does this relationship exist? How much will it cost, and is this expense justified? Even if research shows a causal relationship, will it necessarily carry over to *my* school or district?

CASE STUDY   Phonics: Can It Teach Them All to Read?

There are few more contentious curricular forums than that of reading.[6] In no other instructional arena, save perhaps math or bilingual education, are the issues as hotly debated. Given that the ability to gain meaning from the printed page is one of the most important building blocks of academic success, making sense of the reading debate is essential for educators at every level.

Phonics (a method for teaching students how to decode or sound out words) and *whole language* (an instructional philosophy variously interpreted by teachers and academics but usually centered on learning to read using a whole-word approach in the context of reading literature)[7] are the terms that have characterized the debate in the past. Most recently, the debate has revolved around studies sponsored by the National Institute of Child Health and Human Development (NICHHD; e.g., Foorman, Fletcher, Francis, Schatschneider, & Mehta, 1998)[8] and a report on reading instruction from The National Reading Panel (2000). The Houston Study (Foorman et al., 1998), named after the school district in which the research took place, is the most controversial of the NICHHD research studies; it compared classroom reading instructional methods containing three types of phonics instruction—explicit, embedded, and implicit. It concluded that an advantage exists for reading instructional approaches that emphasized explicit instruction in the alphabetic principle (phonics) for at-risk children.

Barbara Taylor, Richard Anderson, Kathryn Au, and Taffy Raphael (2000), respected and high profile reading academics, vigorously critiqued the study and condemned the way it was "overly promoted by the media and misused by some policy makers and educational leaders to support a simple solution to the complex problem of raising the literacy of young children in high-poverty neighborhoods" (p. 16). Taylor and her colleagues took issue with what they believed were four erroneous assumptions on the part of Foorman and her colleagues (1998): (a) reading is simply a matter of reading words as opposed to gaining meaning, (b) reading difficulties occur because students are deprived of instruction and also suffer from lack of home preparation in understanding the alphabetic principle, (c) instructional methods equal teaching, and (d) "training" teachers in a specific methodology equates with professional development. The critics seemed less concerned with the research design or its findings about the effectiveness of phonics instruction than with the publicity the study had received and the associated political fallout for researchers whose agendas were not experimental or quasi-experimental in nature.

Foorman, Fletcher, Francis, and Schatschneider (2000) issued a lengthy rebuttal, and reinforcements for the phonics forces arrived in the form of a meta-analysis regarding the effects of systematic phonics instruction compared to nonphonics instruction on learning to read (Ehri, Nunes, Stahl, & Willows, 2001). Researchers concluded, based on 66 treatment-control comparisons derived from 38 experiments and quasi-experiments that "phonics instruction proved effective and should be implemented as part of literacy programs to teach beginning reading as well as to prevent and remediate reading difficulties" (p. 393). How can teachers and principals develop a balanced literacy program, if reading researchers can't agree? *Is* phonics necessary for every child? What are the implications of the phonics research for instruction in your school?

CASE STUDY   Vouchers: Are Private Schools in the Public Good?

For most of the 1990s, the merits of private-school vouchers were debated by politicians and on editorial pages. A voucher is simply a coupon that is redeemable for tuition at private schools. Some proposals would make vouchers available to all children; in others, they would be limited to disadvantaged children. In some, private schools that accept vouchers would be subject to state regulations about curriculum and personnel; in others, private schools would be subject to minimal regulation.[9]

In its various permutations, the concept of vouchers has existed for quite some time. Thomas Paine (as cited in West, 1967) suggested a kind of voucher plan in *The Rights of Man*, and Nobel-Prize-winning economist Milton Friedman (1955) made a forceful case for vouchers in the 1950s. The recent furor over vouchers and similar reforms was spurred by the polemical writings of John Chubb and Terry Moe (1990), who argued that America's public schools are effectively "broken," their effectiveness hamstrung by a dysfunctional bureaucracy.

For all the debate surrounding the "ideal" voucher plan, the implementation of vouchers has been limited to a few high-profile cases. For many years parents in Maine and Vermont have been eligible to receive state-funded vouchers, but only in areas without sufficient public school coverage. In the 1990s, the cities of Milwaukee and Cleveland began distributing vouchers to low-income children. A much-heralded statewide program in Florida offers vouchers to students in public schools that are judged to be persistently failing. An even larger number of programs in New York, Washington, DC, and elsewhere offer privately funded vouchers— essentially scholarships—to low-income children in public schools.[10] In some cases, like California and Michigan in the fall elections of 2000, referenda on vouchers have been rejected by state voters.

No matter what a voucher program looks like, it typically rests on an important assumption: private schools are more effective than public schools at improving student outcomes. Or to phrase it in the manner of this book, attending a private school (instead of a public school) *causes* student outcomes to improve. Since the early 1980s, researchers have produced reams of evidence that purports to test that assertion.

Perhaps not surprisingly, they have a hard time agreeing, even when they are assessing the same program. For example, John Witte, the state-appointed evaluator of Milwaukee's voucher program found "no consistent differences" in test scores of voucher recipients and a comparison group (Witte, 1998, p. 241).

Harvard professor Paul Peterson and his colleagues (as quoted in Olson, 1996) countered that Witte's work is "so methodologically flawed as to be worthless." Their own work, conducted after Witte's, finds uniformly positive results (Greene, Peterson, & Du, 1998). However, a third study by Princeton professor Cecilia Rouse found yet another set of results that appeared to split the difference. She found that voucher recipients in Milwaukee experienced gains in math achievement but not in reading (Rouse, 1998). Similar controversies have dogged the voucher debate in other contexts, including evaluations in Cleveland, Florida, New York City, and elsewhere.

A cynic might chalk it all up to politics; we have a different view. At the core of researchers' disagreements, there usually lies a clear disagreement—over research methods and data. It is hard to know which side to believe unless one possesses an appreciation of these issues. It is even harder to decide if research might have something useful to say about one's own school, district, or state. In subsequent chapters, we will explore the multiple layers of the research debate over private-school effectiveness, and assess how its findings can be used to answer the questions posed in the previous sections.

CASE STUDY   Whole-School Reform:
Greater Than the Sum of Its Parts?

Traditionally, efforts to improve schools have proceeded in a piecemeal fashion. Once problems were identified, they were addressed with a bewildering and not always coherent array of "solutions" that have waxed and waned in their popularity. These have ranged from block scheduling to cooperative learning to computer-assisted instruction. In the 1980s, a new approach began to take hold. Partisans of "whole-school" reform suggested the only means of obtaining large and sustained improvements in schools was to drastically change the way schools operated, rather than simply grafting policies onto existing institutions (Levin, 2002).

The Northwest Regional Educational Laboratory (2001) has produced a catalog that lists more than 28 models for whole-school reform. Some of the most recognized include James Comer's Comer School Development Program (2002), the Success for All approach developed by Robert Slavin (Slavin & Madden, 2001), and the Accelerated Schools Project of Henry Levin (National Center for Accelerated Schools, 2002a). Although they all qualify as "whole-school" reforms, they sometimes recommend vastly different strategies and goals (Levin, 2002). For example, the School Development Project (SDP) emphasizes the improvement of the interpersonal relationships and social climate in a school. Success for All relies upon a prescribed curriculum to improve early-elementary school reading proficiency. The Accelerated Schools Project relies upon a constructivist learning theory in which schools

have great latitude to determine their strategies for improvement.

Whole-school reform initiatives received some important boosts in the 1990s. A nonprofit organization called New American Schools provided funding to some whole-school reform models. Some school districts, such as Memphis, required schools to choose among the varied reform packages (although Memphis abandoned its initiative in 2001). And since 1997 the federal government has provided millions of dollars to support "comprehensive school reform."

In light of so much agreement on the need for whole-school reform, one might presume that a strong research base exists that can aid in discerning which models are most effective. In fact, the amount of high-quality research is not large, especially compared with the surfeit of program models and the long line of willing sponsors of whole-school reform. There are only a few randomized experiments, all conducted on Comer's School Development Project (Cook, Habib, Phillips, Settersten, Shagle, & Degirmencioglu, 1999; Cook, Murphy, & Hunt, 2000). There is a voluminous amount of quasi-experimental research conducted on the Success for All program, and a growing research base on other projects such as Accelerated Schools and the models included in New American Schools (Barnett, 1996; Bloom et al., 2001; Levin, 2002). In subsequent chapters, we will place some of these studies under the microscope, and assess whether they can provide answers to the vital questions delineated in this chapter.

FURTHER READING

If you are interested in pursuing any of the case studies independently, the Resource section provides a complete listing of the pertinent references in Chapters 3 through 7, grouped by topic.

NOTES

1. Our assumptions may well evoke strong reactions from two types of readers. Many quantitative researchers will take exception to our statement that qualitative research *can* test hypotheses and play a role in uncovering or confirming causal relationships. They believe that qualitative research by its nature is incapable of hypothesis testing and that uncovering causal relationships between interventions and outcomes is the sole prerogative of quantitative research. On the other hand, many qualitative researchers will find all of our assumptions to be suspect. We refer readers to King et al., (1994, pp. 3-9) and Shadish et al. (2002, pp. 478-484) for discussions of these issues from both qualitative and quantitative perspectives.

2. We caution the reader that although qualitative research *can* test causal relationships, it is only when the methods and logic of qualitative research are made explicit and when qualitative data are collected very systematically, that causal inferences (albeit imperfect ones) can be made based on observational data.

3. A common convention is to refer to "control groups" when assignment is randomized and "comparison groups" when it is not.

4. For an overview of current state initiatives, see the following class size advocacy Web site: http://www.reduceclasssizenow.org/state_of_the_states.htm.

5. Later chapters will review these findings in greater detail. Much of the recent debate over the Tennessee STAR experiment is contained in the Summer 1999 issue of the *Journal of Educational Evaluation and Policy Analysis*.

6. Jeanne Chall and Marie Carbo debated phonics in the pages of *Phi Delta Kappan* in the late 1980s (Carbo, 1988; Chall, 1989). Carbo, however, later backed off her antiphonics position (1996). Gerald Coles and Reid Lyon took up the debate in the late 1990s in *Education Week* (Coles, 1997; Lyon, 1997).

7. For a complete discussion of this debate, see McEwan, E. K. (2002).

8. See the discussion at http://cars.uth.tmc.edu/debate.htm.

9. For a review of different approaches, see Levin (1991).

10. For an early review of these programs, see Moe (1995).

2

Behind the Scenes in the World of Education Research

Education research has been termed both "an elusive science" (Lagemann, 2000), and "a black hole" (Miller, 1999). These are not terribly complimentary terms for a body of work that educators are being told should drive their decision making and practice. With a reputation said by some to be "awful" (Kaestle, 1993), can we trust what education research has to say? Consultants, publishers, and various gurus frequently intone the phrase, *the research says*, whether to impress audiences with their knowledge or to put a scientific spin on what they are selling, but the phrase has become so ubiquitous as to be a bad joke in some circles. Whatever else you may think about education research, you will no doubt confess in a moment of truth that it often just doesn't make sense. We hope that Chapter 1 has begun to illuminate your thinking regarding some of the more hands-on aspects of understanding research, but the purpose of this chapter is to give you an overview or behind-the-scenes look at the world of education research. What is it? Who does it? Can you trust it? Does education research really matter?

THE WORLD OF EDUCATION RESEARCH

The first assignment for a novice when tackling a new discipline is to learn the lingo. Like any specialized domain of knowledge, the field of research, and more particularly education research, has its own unique vocabulary. If all you needed were a few simple definitions, we would point you to a dictionary and be on our way to the next chapter. The world of research, however, thrives on specialized terminology, and putting it into context will help you make sense of research, as well as this book, more quickly.

Imagine the "big" world of research as a collection of individuals who are each fascinated, even obsessed, by a particular body of knowledge—biology, anthropology, or education, for example. These individuals are so intrigued by their disciplines that they want to know as much as they can about the broad rules and structures that organize and govern these domains. Biologists yearn to unravel the genetic code; anthropologists seek to define the culture and language of tribal peoples, and educators are searching for the best means of helping students to reach their academic potential. Whatever their fields, researchers are highly curious about and extremely focused on some narrow sub-specialty within their disciplines. Most dedicate their careers to exploring, organizing, and explaining this particular area of interest by means of research. If you were to attend commencement at a major university where doctoral degrees are conferred and listen to the dissertation titles that are read aloud while hoods are placed over the graduates' heads, you might scratch your head regarding some of the topics and ask, "Who cares?" Researchers do. Despite their shared passions for learning, however, their worldviews, methodologies, and purposes are not always the same.

The Worldviews of Researchers

There are many templates one might use to subdivide the world of education research. We will consider three. The first template that is useful for understanding research, or more precisely for understanding education researchers, relates to their worldviews. One camp views educational problems as ripe for the application of the scientific method, a simple version of which was elucidated in Chapter 1, in which hypotheses about educational problems are weighed against data. Another camp is skeptical of this approach. Their critiques are manifold, but they often arise from a discomfort with the notion that a scientific approach can yield a single, value-free assessment that is sufficient to guide action.

We are not unsympathetic to this critique, although we do feel that it is often used in an overly simplistic fashion to dismiss arguments. We are inclined to agree with Phillips (2000) who argues that "There are substantial reasons for believing that all effective thinkers, across a very broad range of disciplines—including the humanities—use similar intellectual methods. Whether these are called the 'scientific method' or the method of 'effective thinking' is a matter of personal preference. . . . Basically, effective thinking, in science and elsewhere, involves the identification and clarification of problems, the formulation of tentative solutions, and the practical (or theoretical) testing of these and the elimination of those that are not successful in resolving the original problem" (p. 167).

Research Methodologies

The second template posits methodology as the organizing feature. There are two basic methodological approaches used to research a question or problem: quantitative and qualitative. Quantitative research uses statistical methods to show relationships between variables, whereas qualitative research relies on observation and written description. The qualitative researcher deals primarily in words and pictures while the quantitative research uses numbers and statistics. In our view, these two methodologies should not be thought of as adversarial, but rather as complementary. Both methodologies are employed for the purpose of making inferences based on data that has been gathered. For example, a quantitative researcher whose primary interest lies in determining a causal relationship between a treatment and outcome (the does-it-work question) might administer multiple pretests and posttests to see if an instructional approach causes achievement to rise. However, the same researcher might also videotape teaching sessions, interview parents, and talk to students to tease out important qualitative information about *how* the method actually accomplishes what it does. Conversely, qualitative researchers seeking to tease out causal explanations (the how-does-it-work question) might conduct numerous case studies in which the same treatment is studied with various types of students and then present their observational data in a tabulated and quantified format.

> Quantitative research uses statistical methods to show relationships between variables, whereas qualitative research relies on observation and written description.

The ongoing discussion regarding which methodology is "best" is a moot one as far as we are concerned. The crucial question is the degree of rigor brought to bear by the researcher. We concur with King, Keohane, and Verba (1994) who assert that "neither quantitative nor qualitative research is superior to the other, regardless of the research problem being addressed" (p. 6). The critical question is the degree to which precise rules or research procedure and inference are applied to the design of the study and interpretation of the data.

The Purposes of Research

A third possible template for considering the world of research has to do with its purposes. There are two broad reasons for doing research: (a) to discover something new or make a contribution to a field of knowledge (i.e., knowledge for its own sake), or (b) to "illuminate a societal concern" (Patton, 2002, p. 213) and then test a method, program, or policy for possible recommendation to practitioners as a useful practice to solve that problem.

The first category is called *pure research* and the second, *applied research*. Both types are needed in education (or any other field), but we are most interested in applied research because of its potential for informing decision making. There are many researchers, both in and out of the field of education, who are currently calling for more applied research in education—the generation of more useable and practical knowledge to solve specific problems (Lagemann, 2000; Shavelson & Towne, 2002).

> There are many researchers who are currently calling for more applied research in education—the generation of more useable and practical knowledge to solve specific problems.

The distinction between pure and applied research in education is not a definitive one, but generally there are two principal types of applied research: evaluation and action. Evaluation research is generally conducted to judge the overall worth or value of a program. It can be done "after the fact" to judge the worth of textbooks, curricula, computer software, policies like vouchers and class size, whole-school reforms, or the effectiveness of an entire school or district, or it can be done in a formative way as a means of ironing out problems during the implementation of a program.

Action research is a second type of applied research in which practitioners attempt to solve a specific site-based problem. Chapter 8 describes our version of action research, user-driven research, and shows how you can become a researcher in your own setting.

Our perspective, which you may already have surmised, focuses on applied research that is based roughly on a scientific approach and utilizes both quantitative and qualitative methods. We use the word *roughly* to describe our position, because although we favor a scientific approach to finding out what we would like to know, we do concede that there is no *absolute* certainty regarding any causal description or explanation we obtain from experimental research. As Shadish et al. (2002) note, "the experiment is not a clear window that reveals nature directly to us" (p. 29). Experiments and other research endeavors, while necessary and of great benefit when choices of practice must be made, are not perfect.

Although there are many perspectives, often conflicting, on how to theorize and study the problems of education (and an equal or greater number of definitions of "good" research or "scientific" research), the following evaluative questions, based on King et al.'s (1994) description of scientific research, apply equally to qualitative and quantitative research: (a) Does the research seek to make descriptive or explanatory inferences on the basis of empirical information about the world? (b) Are the research procedures explicit, codified, and obvious so that the reliability of the research can be assessed? (c) Does the researcher deal with the issue of uncertainty by not only avoiding sweeping causal statements, but also by providing a thoughtful estimate of the degree of uncertainty present in the causal inferences that are made? d) Does the research adhere to a set of rules of inference?[1] (pp. 7-9).

WHO DOES EDUCATION RESEARCH?

Broadly speaking, there are three groups that produce education research in the United States. First, there are academics in schools of education. It's fair to say that generalizations will fail about this group. Within these schools, there is tremendous variation in academic backgrounds, theoretical preferences, and methodological approaches. These scholars are grouped in departments with names such as "teaching and learning," "curriculum and instruction," "policy," "educational psychology," "leadership and administration," and an infinite variety of others.

> Within these schools, there is tremendous variation in academic backgrounds, theoretical preferences, and methodological approaches.

Second, there are academics in more traditional departments who cross over into education research, such as anthropologists who do ethnographies in schools, economists who do cost-effectiveness studies of educational programs, or psychologists who do experimental research on specific aspects of cognition. These academics tend to be strongly wedded to the theories and methods espoused by their own disciplines, although they frequently hold joint appointments in schools of education.

Third, there are professional researchers who are employed by think tanks that contract with the federal government and other entities to conduct large-scale research studies. Some of the best known of these organizations include the RAND Corporation, Mathematica Policy Research, the American Institutes for Research (AIR), and the Manpower Demonstration Research Corporation (MDRC). All of these organizations have Web sites where their research reports are available.[2] Innumerable smaller firms, both for-profit and not-for-profit, also conduct education research, usually under contract to government or private organizations.

WHO PAYS FOR IT?

Education research costs money to conduct. Funding comes from two principal sources: foundations and government agencies. The Spencer Foundation, the Ford Foundation, and the Smith-Richardson Foundation are major funders in this arena.[3] However, a large portion of the money comes from the government. The political climate, economy, and agenda of a given administration often dictate how much money is available and to whom and for what type of research it will be given.

Currently, four major federal agencies disseminate research funds competitively from their budgets, which are approved yearly by Congress: the Office of Educational Research and Improvement (OERI) and the Office of Special Education Programs (OSEP), both under the umbrella of the Department of Education; NICHHD, under the umbrella of the National Institutes, which funds health-related research; and the National Science Foundation (NSF), an independent agency governed by a 24-member board and a director appointed by the President. Its mission focuses on research in science and mathematics education (NSF, 2002). In an effort to coordinate and focus federal education research efforts, these four agencies have formed the Interagency Education Research Initiative (IERI) to improve education in mathematics, reading, and the sciences (IERI, 2002).

OERI is a vast and sprawling conglomerate of education research activities (five of them centered on topics like early childhood and at-risk students); research initiatives (of which the IERI is one); national research and development centers; and regional educational laboratories. In an attempt to focus and prioritize the federal research agenda, the National Educational Research Policy and Priorities Board (NERPPB) was formed in 1995. A primary goal is to "review synthesize, and interpret knowledge related to educational theory, practice, and policy" (NERPPB, 2000b, p. 1). Funds to support OERI and its research agenda flow through the Education Department's budget. Although the money spent annually on education research in the United States is a minuscule percentage of the overall federal education budget and represents far fewer dollars than those committed to medical research, there *is* money for education research.[4]

WHERE IS IT PUBLISHED?

Education research is likely to be published in three sources: (a) academic journals, (b) books, and (c) a broad category of reports and working papers. By themselves, these categories cannot tell you much about whether the research is useful and informative. There are, however, some general guidelines.

Academic journals are typically edited by university professors who are particularly knowledgeable in the fields being studied. Most of these journals rely on peer review to ensure that published articles meet the highest standards of the field. Articles that are submitted for publication are usually sent anonymously to other professors who recommend revisions before they are accepted for publication or rejected. When the process works well, which is quite often, it ensures a high level of quality. When it misfires, peer review can function as little more than a rubber stamp for the friends of the editor.

> When it misfires, peer review can function as little more than a rubber stamp for the friends of the editor.

The former is almost always true at the best journals, which receive many more submissions than they can publish. For example, the American Educational Research Association publishes several journals, including *Educational Evaluation and Policy Analysis* and the *Review of Educational Research*, that attain a high level of quality. However, education journals multiply faster than rabbits, and there are numerous journals on the "second tier" or even the "third tier" of quality. There are so many, in fact, that one would be hard-pressed not to find *some* outlet for publication—all the more reason for assuming a critical posture towards research conclusions.

Scholarly books are another category. The best of them are usually authored rather than edited volumes. An edited volume is a collection of articles authored by various individuals and then assembled with an introduction by an editor. These papers often undergo a less thorough peer review than journal articles. Cynical academics view these collections as "dumping grounds" for papers the authors were unable to publish elsewhere or as places to rehash or summarize old papers. Perhaps the best evidence in support of this view is that most universities are unwilling to place much importance on book chapters when deciding to promote professors to tenure; they are more likely to value peer reviewed journal articles. That said, some edited collections do undergo thorough review, but that is often at the discretion of the editor. Authored volumes must usually meet a higher standard of quality. At the best presses, these volumes undergo a thorough prepublication review by outside experts.

Technical reports and working papers are a mixed bag. In many cases, they are scrutinized more carefully than journal articles. At the RAND Corporation, for example, final reports are reviewed by experts within and outside the organization. At other organizations, particularly those with strong political agendas, reports and working papers typically face less scrutiny. It is not uncommon to read a newspaper article that trumpets a new research finding only to discover that it journeyed directly from the author's computer to the published page—with little in the way of outside critique.[5]

> It is not uncommon to read a newspaper article that trumpets a new research finding only to discover that it journeyed directly from the author's computer to the published page—with little in the way of outside critique.

This situation is partly abetted by the widespread availability of research databases like ERIC (which you may have used in your own research). It compiles abstracts on educational research studies, including journal articles as well as unpublished working papers and research reports. Usually, the latter have undergone no outside review, and it is up to the practitioner to make determinations of quality.

CAN YOU TRUST EDUCATION RESEARCH?

The investigative process you undertake prior to making program decisions or purchases for your classroom or school is not all that different from the research you might do prior to buying stock or deciding where to retire. You use common sense, read between the lines, research the issue as carefully as you can, and then make a decision. Obviously, if your stockbroker is selling shares in a company you know is owned by his brother-in-law, you might question whether this is a good investment. Likewise, if the land you plan to build your retirement home on is underwater when you arrive to inspect it, you will question the accuracy of the sales brochure. Always begin your investigative process by asking the questions introduced in Chapter 1. However, it also pays to ask the question that police detectives often ask when trying to determine motive: Who stands to profit?

> It pays to ask the question that police detectives ask when trying to determine motive: Who stands to profit?

There is plenty of profit to be made in the world of curriculum, schoolwide reforms, staff development, and educational publishing.[6] A given piece of research may be less than objective if those who have conducted it or paid to have it done stand to benefit from the research findings, monetarily, professionally, or politically. It is worthwhile to determine what agency, think tank, university, or foundation funded a particular piece of research, if possible. Research funded by government agencies usually requires an acknowledgment of that fact on any print dissemination. Research is not necessarily tainted or suspect just because it's been done or funded by a particular advocacy group, educational publisher, or curriculum developer, but it would be wise to evaluate it particularly carefully.

In 2002, Scholastic released a report on its READ 180 technology-based reading improvement program—no doubt, in anticipation of the legislative mandate that educators base decisions on "scientifically-based-research" (Olson & Viadero, 2002; Viadero, 2001). The READ 180 research was conducted by Policy Studies Associates (2002) in Washington, DC. The unnamed researchers who prepared the report maintained a modicum of credibility with their caveat that "while it seems clear that READ 180 students made positive gains [the study covered a 1-year time frame], it is sometimes difficult to know with confidence how these gains compared to what gains would have occurred without READ 180, what other factors might have contributed to these gains, and what the READ 180 intervention actually looked like from one school to the next" (p. 8).

Their credibility took a nosedive, however, when they turned around in the summary and said just the opposite: "Early research and evaluation are unequivocal in their findings that the implementation of READ 180 results in solid gains in student reading scores [over a one-year period]" (Policy Studies Associates, p. 9). Be sure to read the fine print and consider the source of each and every research study you use as a basis for costly decisions. Who paid for the study? Who will benefit from its publication? Whose agenda is being promoted?

A combination of desperation to solve vexing educational problems, exuberant claims regarding a program's effectiveness, and a careless reading of available research can lead to ill-advised decisions.

A combination of desperation to solve vexing educational problems, exuberant claims regarding a program's effectiveness, and careless reading can lead to ill-advised decisions. For example, some school districts around the country (e.g., Baltimore Public Schools, Miami-Dade Schools, and Memphis Public Schools) took Robert Slavin's research evaluating the efficacy of Success for All (SFA) at face value and have been disappointed in their results (Edmondson, 2001; Ruffini, 1992; Urdegar, 1999). In a paper presented to the conference of the American Education Research Association, Slavin, a developer of the SFA program, reported that the results of evaluations of 19 SFA schools in nine districts in eight states clearly showed (a) that the program increased student reading performance, (b) that SFA students learned significantly more than matched control students, and (c) that there were unequivocal benefits for SFA students (Slavin & Madden, 1995).

Developers of the program consistently reported "success for all"—especially for those students who were in the bottom 25% at the outset (Slavin, Madden, Dolan, & Wasik, 1996), but they failed to note that their definition of "success" was based on the SFA schools performing better than the control schools on a test selected by the program developers, *not* on students performing at or above grade level on a nationally normed standardized achievement test. Eager for any intervention that would improve literacy levels for their at-risk students, administrators either unable or unwilling to critically assess the problems[7] apparent in Slavin's research rushed to sign up their schools for SFA. Currently, SFA is being implemented in about 2,000 schools, serving more than one million children (SFA, 2002).

Approach education research with a healthy skepticism. Carefully examine all studies, but especially those conducted by developers and publishers. Beware of any program that purports to be a one-size-fits-all panacea or "a proven intervention that turns lives around" (Scholastic, n.d.). There are no "big and final" answers to the problems facing educators. Any research or program that makes grandiose promises to that effect must be carefully evaluated.

> Approach education research with a healthy skepticism. Carefully examine all studies, but especially those conducted by developers and publishers.

WHAT DOES THE FUTURE HOLD FOR EDUCATION RESARCH?

The reauthorization of the Elementary and Secondary Education Act, officially known as the No Child Left Behind Act of 2001 (2002), contains more than 100 references to the term *scientifically based research*.[8] This legislated definition of what constitutes reliable research has generated a flurry of books, panels, meetings, organizations, hearings, and reports for the purpose of debating, discussing, and defining exactly what constitutes scientific inquiry (Brookings Institution, 1999; Campbell Collaboration, 2001; NERPPB, 2000a, 2000b; Shavelson & Towne, 2002; Snow, Burns, & Griffin, 1998; U.S. Department of Education, 2002).

In addition, numerous independent organizations and government-funded bodies are gearing up (yet again) to identify what works for practitioners. In the past, similar initiatives, both governmental and private, were based largely on testimonials and non-experimental research. This time around, the recommendations are supposed to be based on the experimental research standard set forth in the No Child Left Behind Act of 2001 (2002) legislation (National Clearinghouse for Comprehensive School Reform, 2002; Strategic Education Research Partnership, 2002; What Works Partnership, 2002).

Many researchers from other disciplines advocate for what is called "evidence-based" decision making to become the norm in education. During the past decade, the global medical community has implemented such a model (Donald, 2002), which has attracted the attention of social scientists. Evidence-based medicine is defined

as a decision-making framework that facilitates complex decisions across different and sometimes conflicting groups. It involves considering research and other forms of evidence on a routine basis when making healthcare decisions. Such decisions include clinical decisions about choice of treatment, test, or risk management for individual patients, as well as policy decisions for groups and populations . . . Because it involves routine use of research evidence, evidence-based medicine was literally impossible before the advent of large electronic databases of research in the early 1990s. In addition, evidence-based medicine provides clinicians with practical information and tools for assessing best practice in relation to individual patients that until recently were simply unavailable. (Donald, 2002, sec. 2)

The guiding force behind evidence-based medicine was a British epidemiologist by the name of Archie Cochrane, who conceived the idea of compiling all of the experimental research findings on specific conditions and their treatments and then distilling them into succinct reports on which physicians could base their diagnoses and treatments. Headquartered in the United Kingdom, Cochrane's brainchild was established in 1993 and is known as the Cochrane Collaboration. It regularly summarizes the findings from randomized experiments in health care for practitioners and makes them available via a computerized database.

A group of researchers at the University of Pennsylvania is spearheading the same kind of initiative for social science research, to include education. The Campbell Collaboration (2001), named in honor of the social scientist Donald Campbell, includes a worldwide representation of governments, social agencies, universities, research organizations, foundations, and non-profit and for-profit organizations. The aim of the collaboration is to join the various social science disciplines (including education) in the way that the Cochrane Collaboration brought together medical research to improve public policy and enhance evidence-based decision making. Various researchers will be tapped to do "Campbell reviews" for the

Collaboration using meta-analysis (see Chapter 7) to synthesize social science research on various topics. The prospects are exciting, if only practitioners can be persuaded to trust the evidence instead of undertaking what Philip Davies, cochair of

> If only practitioners can be persuaded to trust the evidence instead of undertaking . . . "faith-based initiatives."

the Collaboration's education panel, calls "faith-based initiatives" (Davies, as quoted in Viadero, 2002, p. 8).

We are optimistic, although cautiously so, about the prospects for more useful and rigorous education research in the next decade. Increased attention and funding by the federal government, the reorganization of the OERI, and the establishment of the Campbell Collaboration are all signs that education research may be about to bloom.

DOES EDUCATION RESEARCH REALLY MATTER?

Education researcher Diane Ravitch (1998) departed from her usual scholarly treatises when she described her hospitalization for a pulmonary embolism in an *Education Week* essay: "What if Research Really Mattered?" Although most of us would no doubt have been traumatized by such an experience, Ravitch's mind was running on two tracks as she lay in intensive care. One track was listening to a group of specialists explaining the diagnosis and treatment of her possibly life-threatening condition to a crowd of doctors, residents, and interns gathered around her bed. The other track was thinking about the world of education research; her thoughts were not particularly positive. She reports, "As I lay there, listening to them discuss my condition, I had a sudden insight: I was deeply grateful that my treatment was based on medical research, and not education research" (1998, n.p.).

Ravitch (1998) imagined what education researchers would be saying in a similar situation, and the picture was not a pretty one:

Among the raucous crowd of education experts, there was no agreement, no common set of standards for diagnosing my problem. They could not agree on what was wrong with me, perhaps because they did not agree on standards for good health. . . . I was almost completely convinced at that point that the discord among the experts guaranteed that I would get no treatment at all, but then something remarkable happened. The administrator of the hospital walked in and said that she had received a large grant from the government to pay for treatment of people who had my symptoms. Suddenly, many of those who had been arguing that nothing was wrong with me decided that they wanted to be part of the effort to cure me. But to no one's surprise, the assembled authorities could not agree on what to do to make me better. (n.p.)

Ravitch's (1998) essay is humorous on the one hand and down-right depressing on the other. *Does* education research really matter? *Does* it offer anything of worth to inform the decisions and policies of practitioners? We believe that it does. We believe that well-conceived and rigorous research is essential to the practice of our craft and the achievement of our students.

We concur with Gage (1989), who in a speech to the American Education research Association said,

> Education research is no mere spectator sport, no mere intellectual game, no mere path to academic tenure and higher pay, not just a way to make a good living and even become a big shot. It has moral obligations. The society that supports us cries out for better education for its children and youth—especially the poor ones, those at risk, those whose potential for a happy and productive life is all too often going desperately unrealized. Therefore, even as we debate whether any objectivity at all is possible, whether "techni-cal" [scientific] research is merely trivial, whether your paradigm or mine should get more money, we must remember that the pay-off inheres in what happens to the children, the students. That is our end concern. (p. 149)

FURTHER READING

Ellen Condliffe Lagemann's (2000) very fine historical treatment of education research is must reading for anyone wanting a long-term perspective on the growth and evolution of the field. We also recommend Mosteller and Boruch (2002), a recent collection of articles—most focusing on randomized experiments—that pleads for more systematic research endeavors to guide decision making in education.

NOTES

1. These rules of inference as applicable to qualitative research can be found in King et al. (1994).

2. See http://www.rand.org, http://www.mathematica-mpr.com, http://www.air.org, and http://www.mdrc.org.

3. See their Web sites at http://www.spencer.org, http://www.fordfound.org, and http://www.srf.org.

4. Although federal budget figures are almost impossible to pin down exactly, the FY2002 Approved Budget for OERI was about $200 million and the budget request for FY2003 (which assumes a completed reauthorization of the primary federal education research program is just over $400 million). NICHD received an estimated $252 million in FY 2002 and is budgeted to receive in excess of $275 million for FY2003.

5. For whatever reason, this seems to be much less likely to occur in health. Newspaper articles on new developments in these fields are likely to begin with the phrase, "Tomorrow's issue of the *New England Journal of Medicine* will publish a peer reviewed study that suggests. . . . "

6. For an overview of the growing education industry, see http://www.eduventures.com.

7. The following methodological and implementation problems have been noted by independent evaluators who are not connected to or employed by the SFA organization: (a) students are not assessed using a nationally normed reading test; (b) there is a lack of information regarding how researchers selected the schools to be matched to the experimental schools; (c) claims for success are based on experimental groups outperforming control groups, as opposed to experimental groups reaching a grade level standard; (d) there is a sharp drop-off in reading performance after first grade (Jones, Gottfredson, & Gottfredson, 1997; Ruffini, 1991; Urdegar, 1998; Venezky, 1998).

8. "The term scientifically based research (a) means research that involves the application of rigorous, systematic, and objective procedures to obtain reliable and valid knowledge relevant to education activities and programs and (b) includes research that: (1) employs systematic, empirical methods that draw on observation or experiment involves rigorous data analyses that are adequate to test the stated hypotheses and justify the general conclusions drawn, (2) relies on measurements or observational methods that provide reliable and valid data across evaluators and observers, across multiple measurements and observations, and across studies by the same or different investigators; (3) is evaluated using experimental or quasi-experimental designs in which individuals, entities, programs, or activities are assigned to different conditions and with appropriate controls to evaluate the effects of the condition of interest, with a preference for random-assignment experiments or other designs to the extent that those designs contain within-condition or across-condition controls; (4) ensures that experimental studies are presented in sufficient detail and clarity to allow for replication or, at a minimum, offer the opportunity to build systematically on their findings; (5) has been accepted by a peer reviewed journal or approved by a panel of independent experts through a comparably rigorous, objective, and scientific review (Olson & Viadero, 2002, p. 14).

3

The Causal Question

Does It Work? (Part I)

A recent editorial in *USA Today*, bemoaning mediocrity in teacher education programs, summarized a research study for its readers in an accompanying sidebar: "Dallas researchers tracked groups of children with similar reading scores starting in fourth grade. Half were assigned highly rated teachers for 3 years; the other half were given low-rated teachers" (Editorial, 2002, p. 14A). The results, depicted in a bar graph, indicated that students assigned to the highly rated teachers scored at the 76th percentile in reading at the end of the 3 years, whereas the students assigned to the ineffective teachers scored at the 42nd percentile (Jordan, Mendro, & Weerasinghe, 1997). In essence, the editorial board pronounced that the "good-teacher treatment" worked.

The findings of this study confirm what many of us believe about teachers and their impact on students. But without reading the study yourself, it is impossible to determine whether the treatment in this particular study actually *caused* reading achievement to go up. The minute you encountered the word "assigned" in the editorial, a red flag should have gone up. *How* were the students assigned to the highly rated and the lower-rated teachers? Were their names picked out of a hat? Were "good" teachers allowed to choose their own classrooms, perhaps opting for the students with the fewest disciplinary problems? Answering these questions is not just important. It is *vital* to determining whether it was really the treatment that was responsible for test score gains.

This example is hardly an isolated one. At the heart of almost every debate about improving schools lies a causal question. Does a new reading curriculum *cause* students to read with greater comprehension? Does attending a full day of preschool *cause* students to be more successful in elementary school? Much of education research is devoted to unearthing answers to these causal questions—to assessing whether some program or policy "works" in the manner that it is intended to work. And almost every parent, politician, and voter—in short, everyone who has been a student—is inclined to make judgments about cause-and-effect relationships in schools.

Identifying a causal relationship is a difficult but not insurmountable task. This chapter will argue that one of the best ways to do so is with a randomized experiment, first mentioned in Chapter 1. Even when experiments are not available—and they are admittedly rare in education research—they still provide a powerful framework for critiquing almost any study that attempts to answer a causal question. Before describing experiments in more detail, however, it is useful to think more carefully about the basic requirements for inferring that a causal relationship exists.

> Identifying a causal relationship is a difficult but not insurmountable task.

THE CAUSALITY CONUNDRUM

We would like you to become more skeptical in your evaluation of research that purports to establish causality. Think of yourself as both judge and jury in a very important case. Rather than determining an individual's guilt or innocence, however, you will bring all of your intelligence, common sense, and background knowledge to bear on the facts of a case to determine whether a specific treatment is responsible for the effects that have been observed. The research study is the evidence.

Making a decision is more challenging than we commonly assume. To see why, think for a moment about the following causal claim: "Attending preschool results in higher reading achievement at the end of first grade." This statement presumes that we can determine the reading achievement of students in first grade who attended preschool—an easy enough task. However, it also presumes that we know how the same students *would have fared* on achievement tests, *had they not attended preschool*. In this case, the causal claim implies that students who enjoyed the benefits of attending preschool score higher than their "unattended" selves would have scored. Social scientists commonly refer to the latter condition as a counterfactual, because it refers to a condition that is, quite simply, contrary to the facts.[1] In fact, the students *did* attend preschool. And yet, causal statements rely vitally upon "what-if" questions about counterfactuals.

What if those same students had not attended preschool? Would their achievement have been lower or higher?

When we say that a program "caused" test scores to increase, we are saying that test scores increased by more than they *would have* in the absence of the program. Knowing these two states of the world—the real and the counterfactual—is the key to estimating the causal impact of preschool. But wait a minute, you might be saying to yourself. How is it possible to simultaneously observe two different states of the world *for a single group of students?* It is, of course, a logical and practical impossibility. There are many teachers who qualify as miracle workers, but even they would be hard-pressed to defy the laws of time and space.

Instead, we try to "create reasonable approximations to this physically impossible counterfactual" (Shadish et al., 2002, p. 5). What exactly is a reasonable approximation? It turns out that our intuition provides a very useful guide. Most of us would try to find a second group of students that is similar in most every respect, *except for their exposure to preschool.* A key dilemma for the researcher is ensuring that both groups of students are truly similar. If they are not, then counterfactual reasoning breaks down. It then becomes difficult—even impossible—to discern whether the differences in reading achievement between the two groups are because of the causal impact of preschool, or because the groups were not that similar in the first place. Perhaps one group of students has more involved parents than another, which might contribute to higher reading scores. Or perhaps one group is acquiring English as a second language making it more difficult to learn to read in English. For causal inference to work smoothly, we cannot compare apples to oranges.

> The randomized experiment provides the most powerful means of ensuring that the two groups of students are similar.

As this chapter describes, the randomized experiment provides the most powerful means of ensuring that the two groups of students are similar—that one group, in other words, will adequately represent the counterfactual. Before describing the experimental approach in more detail, it is helpful to see how and why some other approaches are less suited to answering causal questions.

SIMPLE (MINDED) METHODS OF ESTABLISHING CAUSALITY

All of us are under pressure to draw causal conclusions about our actions. Maybe your school district is implementing a new higher-level thinking skills program based on your recommendation, or you are utilizing cooperative learning for the first time in your classroom. Did these initiatives "work" in the manner intended? The fact is, most of us have a ready answer to that question, and it is frequently positive. To arrive at these answers, we often use informal varieties of research to assess causality. The two most common are (a) the before-and-after approach and (b) the comparison group approach. In fact, they are examples of weak quasi-experiments, a topic that is fully addressed in the Chapter 4. For now, our purpose is not to suggest that these approaches are entirely "incorrect." Quite the contrary, they can provide valuable insights into causal questions if their findings are viewed with an appropriately critical eye, because they illuminate some of most common pitfalls to obtaining believable answers to causal questions, and they set the stage for our discussion of experiments.

The Before-and-After Approach

It is a rare principal, teacher, or even parent who has not indulged in an informal version of before-and-after research. Usually, it goes something like this: (a) the school implements a new policy—mandatory school uniforms, for example; (b) the principal notices that reports of disciplinary problems decline from one year to the next; and (c) the staff and parents presume that the introduction of uniforms "caused" discipline to improve. Certainly, the introduction of uniforms is a reasonable explanation, but there may be other explanations that are equally plausible. A natural question to ask is whether something else happened at the same time as

> The before-and-after approach often makes it quite difficult to establish whether a program *or* some element of history is responsible for an outcome.

the introduction of uniforms that also affected student behavior. Perhaps a schoolwide security policy was implemented, including the use of security guards to patrol the hallways. In this case, it is hard to tell whether uniforms, security guards, or something else was responsible for the improved discipline. Collectively, we refer to these outside events, occurring at the same time as the program or intervention, as *history*. The before-and-after approach often makes it quite difficult to establish whether a program *or* some element of history is responsible for an outcome.

The before-and-after approach has other pitfalls. To illustrate these, let's use another example: (a) a school district adopts a new instructional approach to mathematics, based on a popularly recommended reform; (b) students who participate in the program have higher test scores—higher, at least, than the previous year; and (c) everyone believes that the new approach "caused" test scores to improve. Again, it is entirely possible that the reform did produce its intended consequences. But it is important to ask whether that is the *only* reason that test scores rose. If it is not, it can hardly be said that the observed association has a fully causal interpretation.

Between one year and the next, it is plausible that students' test scores rose because of a natural process of maturation that bears little relation to their classroom experiences. Alternatively, the first round of testing may have given students practice in taking a particular test. Not surprisingly, their success on the second round is partly an artifact of such testing procedures. In some districts, it is not uncommon that students who receive novel curricula are identified as those most in need of help. Sometimes, it is the lowest-scoring students who are targeted for assistance. When these students are retested, it is quite common for their scores to rebound upward because of a statistical phenomenon called *regression to the mean*. Similarly, initially high-scoring students tend to experience declines in subsequent measurements. These changes are easily confused for causal effects of classroom instruction. And as in the previous example, it is plausible that an important element of history—occurring at the same time as the reform—affected test scores.

The Comparison Group Approach

Has your district ever contemplated the introduction of a program that motivates students to read? It may have used a wide range of (expensive) resources: lots of books and supplementary materials, innovative computer software for every student, and a full-time staff member. Perhaps the superintendent wanted to make sure that the program would actually get results, given its substantial cost and suggested that implementation should proceed in only one of the district's two middle schools. Then, at the end of the year, the implementing school's reading achievement would be compared to the other school's. Higher achievement, on average, would indicate that the program "worked," or so it was reasoned.

The approach relies on counterfactual reasoning. The implementing school provides a natural estimate of how student outcomes are affected by the program. In a perfect world, we would like to know what the same students' outcomes *would have been* in the absence of their participation in the program. Obviously, we cannot do so without the benefit of a time machine. But as an alternative, we can use students in the comparison school to approximate the counterfactual.

> In a perfect world, we would like to know what the same students' outcomes would have been in the absence of their participation in the program.

This approach has some shortcomings, however, and they are potentially quite severe. They revolve around the omnipresent possibility that the comparison school is different in some unknown way from the treated school. Imagine, for example, that the super-intendent asked for a volunteer school to "test" the reading program. The principal who volunteered his school has a stated building goal of improving reading achievement, whereas the other principal is more focused on the affective aspects of schooling. Eventually, the program school scored higher than the comparison school. One might ask whether it was due to the effects of the program or because of a more motivated teaching staff, a stronger instructional leader, and the benefits of several contemporaneous reading improvement initiatives.

Or imagine that the school district allowed a degree of parental choice among schools within the district. In the summer before implementation was to begin, a group of motivated parents got wind of the reading program and decided to transfer their children out of the comparison school. Again, was increased achievement due to the program or because of an influx of students from highly motivated families?

Both scenarios are examples of selection, one of the most common and pernicious dilemmas in social science research. It is also frequently referred to as selection bias, self-selection, or selectivity. It occurs when unobserved characteristics that influence selection into a specific treatment or program—such as staff or family "motivation"—also influence program outcomes. Without appealing to sophisticated statistical methods, and even *with* such methods, selection makes it difficult to determine whether outcome differences between two groups of schools or students are because of a specific program or methodology or because the two groups were not very similar in the first place.

> Selection makes it difficult to determine whether outcome differences between two groups of schools or students are because of a specific program or methodology or because the two groups were not very similar in the first place.

Internal Validity

In the examples above, we showed how simple approaches to answering causal questions can end up giving us the wrong answers, or at least ambiguous ones. That is the case because they do not succeed in *credibly* establishing whether an association between a program and outcome has a causal interpretation. When this causal interpretation is lacking, it is common to say that a research study lacks internal validity.[2] The internal validity of a study can be thrown into question for a variety of reasons discussed above—history, testing, maturation, and especially selection. Collectively, these factors are known as threats to internal validity.

Some are more plausible and some are less plausible, depending on the nature and context of the research study. However, it behooves every educator to carefully consider whether such threats—and not the program or policy being studied—provide a reasonable explanation for the pattern of results.

The very best way of ruling out threats to internal validity, and ensuring a believable set of conclusions, is to design a good study. In the absence of well-designed experimental research, usually the case with popular programs being sold to increase achievement, educators must become insistent in their demands for rigorous research and more diligent in their interpretation of the research that *is* available. As we suggested in the introduction to this chapter, randomized experiments are one of the best designs for making sure that a program, method, or policy actually works.

> Educators must become insistent in their demands for rigorous research and more diligent in their interpretation of the research that is available.

THE ELEMENTS OF AN EXPERIMENT

The word *experiment* is used quite loosely in everyday language, even by education researchers, to connote some kind of innovation, tried or tested in an unspecified way: "We're experimenting with a new approach to dealing with the drug problem at our school." The mere mention of the term is evocative of scientific rigor. Nevertheless, that image is only deserved if the "experiment" in question fulfills two very specific requirements.

In a research-based definition, the word *experiment* can always be replaced by the phrase *randomized, controlled experiment*. The use of "controlled" implies that we are studying at least two groups: (a) a treatment group that participates in a program, policy, or intervention and (b) a control group that does not. However, a control group alone is insufficient to qualify a study as experimental. It is extremely important to know *how* the treatment and control groups are chosen. More specifically, it must be true that assignment to the two groups is randomized. Understanding this concept is essential to understanding the power of experimental research.

Why Random Assignment?

The use of a control group is based on the idea that it represents the counterfactual—that is, it approximates what the treatment group *would have* looked like in the absence of the treatment. This obviously requires that the two groups are similar at the beginning of the study, prior to implementing the treatment. If the groups are not similar, then any subsequent comparisons between them do not necessarily tell us that the method or treatment in question had a causal effect. Are later differences in group outcomes because of the treatment, or because the two groups were never similar in the first place?

A nearly foolproof means of ensuring that treatment and control groups are similar is via randomized assignment. To illustrate this, let's imagine we have identified a group of 2,000 high school students, a diverse mix of ability levels and family backgrounds. Our goal is to determine whether a drug education program has any impact on reducing the incidence of drug use among the students. We will treat about half the students and allow the others to serve as the control group. To randomly assign students, we simply flip a coin 2,000 times, assigning "heads" students to the treatment and "tails" students to the control. By definition, every student has a 50/50 chance of participating in the treatment. More carefully stated, each has an equal probability (0.5) of participation. We could have just as easily randomized by other means (e.g., the roll of a die or special computer programs).[3]

> A nearly foolproof means of ensuring that treatment and control groups are similar is via randomized assignment.

To verify that randomization creates similar treatment and control groups, it is common to compare them according to previously collected baseline data. We just mentioned that the original group of students contained a diverse mix of ability levels and backgrounds. Suppose that we had gathered two pieces of baseline data from each student: GPA (grade point average) and family income. Further imagine that we calculated the average value of these two variables for students in the treatment group, and then for students in the control group. We would anticipate that the average GPA and the average family income of each group is similar. Will they be *exactly* the same? This would be highly unlikely, because the vagaries of a random draw means that students in one group may have slightly higher or slightly lower GPAs or family incomes. In other words, any differences would be due to chance alone.

Once treatment and control groups are randomly assigned, the treatment is administered—in this case, the drug education program. At the conclusion of the treatment, data are collected on a specified set of outcomes—perhaps self-reported measures of drug use or numbers of drug-related incidents reported by the school security officer or the local police department. If the average incidence of

> We must be quite certain that differences between the two groups are results of a program effect and not chance alone.

drug use among students in the treatment group is lower, we are immediately tempted to infer that the program had a causal impact on drug use. But not so fast. We must determine whether the difference between the two groups is statistically significant. We must be quite certain that differences between the two groups are results of a program effect and not chance alone. (More about statistical significance later.)

What if randomized assignment had not been employed in assigning students to treatment and control groups? Instead, let's consider possible outcomes if students were allowed to volunteer for the program. Suppose that the volunteers, for whatever reason, are largely students with better grades, with the result that the treatment group has a higher average GPA than the control group. We might infer, based on experiences in our schools, that students with higher grades tend to have lower rates of drug use. After the program is implemented and we discover that the incidence of drug use among treated students is lower than among control students, we cannot say with any certainty that it is because the program "worked." The results could simply have been because students in the treatment group were less predisposed to use drugs. The phenomenon of selection bias makes it very difficult to discern.

In Chapter 4, we'll suggest that it is possible to use statistical methods to "control" for observed differences among students, such as GPA and family income. However, it is still possible that students who volunteered for the treatment are different in some unobserved and unmeasured ways. If these unobserved characteristics affect drug use, then selection bias is still present and the causal interpretation of the results is thrown into question. The fact remains that randomized assignment to treatment and control groups is the *best* means of obtaining credible answers to causal questions. And that is because it provides a convincing way of ensuring that the treatment and control groups are similar in observed and unobserved ways.

> Randomized assignment to treatment and control groups is the best means of obtaining credible answers to causal questions.

Units of Randomization

Until now, we have referred to instances in which *students* are randomly assigned to treatment and control groups. However, it is easy to imagine instances in which random assignment of students is not practical. Perhaps we would like to assess the impact of a new teaching technique on achievement. We could hardly assign students *within* a given classroom to receive or not receive the treatment. By definition, all students in a particular classroom are subject to the same treatment, because they share the same teacher. In these and other cases, it is often more feasible to randomly assign classrooms, schools, or even entire school districts.

The unit of randomization depends on the particular context of the study, including the nature of the treatment. It further depends, in no small measure, on who is conducting the study and how much control they possess over experimental conditions. In a highly centralized education system, such as one finds in some countries, it is likely that authorities can randomly assign 200 school districts to treatment and control groups with no resistance. In a highly decentralized system, similar to that found in the United States, it is difficult to imagine tens of thousands of individual school districts and their sometimes fractious school boards subjecting themselves to random assignment imposed by their states or the federal government. Even within school districts, the random assignment of schools might encounter obstacles. How many building principals or teachers relish being "assigned" to implement a treatment? Nonetheless, it can and does occur. A later case study will describe how entire schools were randomly assigned to participate in a whole-school reform in Illinois and Maryland (Cook et al., 1999; Cook et al., 2000).

Defining the Treatment, Outcomes, and Sample

To this point we have discussed experiments in rather generic terms, in order to emphasize the concept of randomization. However, there are three very practical questions that the confident consumer of education research must ask and answer when examining the findings of a randomized experiment. What is the treatment? What are the outcomes? What is the sample? If researchers do not offer clear and complete answers to these questions, then it will be difficult, if not impossible, to draw firm causal conclusions from such studies.

> There are three very practical questions that the confident consumer of education research must ask and answer when examining the findings of a randomized experiment: What is the treatment? What are the outcomes? What is the sample?

What Is the Treatment?

Research studies that administer a treatment to students or other subjects should clearly define the nature and extent of the treatment. This may seem obvious, but many research studies indulge in broad generalizations that make it difficult to understand what exactly a treatment entailed. In the hypothetical examples of previous sections, we certainly engaged in some overgeneralizations, and you may have done it yourself. It may be the case that treated students attended "small" classes, for example, and control students attended "regular" or even "large" classes. But how small is small, and how large is large? The answer should be made explicit to *you*, the reader. Similarly, it is not uncommon to see glowing references to studies about difficult-to-define concepts like *balanced literacy*, *active learning*, or *multiple intelligences.* Terms with vague and diffuse meanings, "unanalyzable abstractions" (Sarason, 1996, p. 38), must be defined regarding the specific conditions and situations under which they become operational. In order to determine causality with regard to a specific approach or method, you must be able to determine and understand how any general concept is made concrete in specific treatments. Without specific details, assertions about the causal impact of vaguely defined "treatments" tend to ring hollow. Furthermore, specific descriptions of treatments are vital in deciding whether a treatment is feasible or useful in one's own circumstances, an important theme of Chapter 7.

> To determine causality with regard to a specific approach or method, you must be able to determine and understand how any general concept is made concrete in specific treatments.

Even when a treatment seems to be described in detail, its description might not validly describe the treatment that actually took place. Experimental researchers have cataloged many instances in which this is the case.[4] For example, school personnel might rebel at the notion that treated students will receive resources that are denied to others. If additional resources are given to the control students in an effort to compensate, then this should—ideally—be included in the description of the treatment.[5] Similarly, it is possible that students who are randomly denied a treatment—and consigned to a control group—will feel resentful or discouraged (Fetterman, 1982; Shadish et al., 2002, p. 80). This itself is a kind of treatment administered to the control group, and it should be described if possible. Other cases are described by Shadish et al. (2002).

What Are the Outcomes?

It is equally important to describe the desired outcomes of the study, and how they were measured. Obviously, outcome measures should reflect the underlying objectives of the program or policy. If a program is designed to affect students' reading comprehension, then outcome measures should include a test of reading comprehension. However, be alert for overly broad descriptions of outcomes that provide few clues about what is actually being measured. For example, there are hundreds of possible tests that could be administered to measure "reading achievement." Some tests emphasize a broad range of knowledge, whereas others are tightly matched to a particular curriculum. Some emphasize simple word reading ability; others measure the ability to comprehend lengthy passages of text. The list goes on and on. You can easily imagine circumstances under which one

> You can easily imagine circumstances under which one outcome measure could yield positive findings in an experiment, whereas another would show no program effect at all.

outcome measure could yield positive findings in an experiment, whereas another would show no program effect at all.

Even when a program's objectives are adequately captured by outcome measures, it is important to consider outcomes that are not directly related to program objectives. Reading programs, for example, often require additional time to be spent on reading instruction during the school day. In doing so, the programs diminish the amount of time spent on other instructional activities, perhaps reducing achievement in other subjects like mathematics. This can only be ascertained if the researcher considers multiple outcome measures.

What Is the Sample?

All randomized experiments begin with a sample of students, classrooms, or schools. Members of this sample are randomly assigned to the treatment and control groups. To make sense of a research study, you must know how that initial sample was chosen.

To see why, think about a researcher who is evaluating the impact of a new staff development program in a large urban school district. She needs to gather a sample of schools to participate in her experiment, but she could proceed in different ways. One option is to assemble a master list of all city schools, and then draw a random sample of schools from the master list. These schools are then randomly assigned to treatment and control groups. Because the initial sample was randomly chosen from the population of schools, the results of the experiment can be generalized to all schools in the city.

What if the researcher had proceeded differently? Say it was impractical to draw a random sample from the entire group of city schools. For one thing, a large number of the schools' administrators simply did not want to participate. Instead, the researcher solicited many "volunteer" schools where the principals had indicated their interest in participating. From this sample of volunteers, she randomly assigned half to the treatment and half to the control. In this case, the results of the experiment are applicable to schools with similar elements of "volunteerism," but they cannot be easily generalized to all schools.

> It is common to use convenience samples that contain volunteers who have expressed a willingness to participate in research.

The latter approach is typical in the world of education research, where it is common to use convenience samples that contain volunteers who have expressed a willingness to participate in the research (this is also common in psychological and medical research). If the members of the convenience sample are randomly assigned to treatment and control groups, then the results are still internally valid—they have a causal interpretation. It is harder to generalize the results to other contexts because members of the sample are "special" in unknown ways. Yet every researcher needs to deal with these issues, because education experiments use convenience samples with great frequency. We will return to these issues in Chapter 7 when we ask the question, "Will it work for me?"

How the sample is chosen is not the only sampling question that needs to be addressed. Also consider how large the sample of a particular study actually is. At one extreme, you might imagine a case where we sample the entire population of interest. If we conduct an experiment to learn about elementary school children in Los Angeles, we might randomly assign about half of the city's children to a treatment and half to a control group. In this extreme case, we can easily generalize the results of the experiment to the population—this, for the simple reason that the experimental sample *is* the population.

At another extreme, imagine that we sampled only 100 students in Los Angeles, randomly assigning half to the treatment. In this case, the small sample size would mean that our estimate of the difference between treatment and control groups would include information about the treatment effect as well statistical noise, due to the vagaries of random sampling. This makes it more difficult to discern whether a difference between treatment and control groups is due to a real program effect or simply due to the "luck of the draw." It is especially difficult to detect program effects that are very small in magnitude. As a rule of thumb, a larger sample makes it easier to confidently establish whether the difference between treatment and control groups is due to the treatment.[6]

Analyzing Experimental Results

Experiments provide more convincing answers to causal questions than other research designs. And yet—in a wonderful irony—they require much less sophisticated methods to analyze their results. Consider how a typical experiment proceeds: (a) we identify a sample of students and collect baseline data, (b) we randomly assign students to treatment and control groups, (c) we apply the treatment, and (d) we collect data on outcome measures. To analyze the experimental data on outcomes, one compares the outcomes of students in the treatment and control groups. This can be as simple as computing the mean (or average) outcome of each group and calculating the difference between the two means. If the difference favors the treatment group, then there is a positive program effect.

> Experiments provide more convincing answers to causal questions than other research designs. And yet—in a wonderful irony—they require much less sophisticated methods to analyze their results.

We are typically interested in two aspects of the mean difference. First, does the mean difference between treatment and control groups have statistical significance? Statistical significance merely implies that a difference is, in all probability, not equal to zero.[7] If you think about it, statistical significance is not a terribly high bar to set. It is quite possible that the mean achievement of the treatment group is only slightly higher than the achievement of the control, but that the difference is still "statistically significant" (i.e., nonzero). This is especially likely if the size of treatment and control groups is quite large. Yet the criterion of statistical significance does not really tell us anything about whether the difference is big or small.

To determine that, we need to ask a second question: does the mean difference have practical significance? There is no unambiguous way of determining whether an effect is large or small—it depends on the unit in which the outcome is expressed and the context in which the results are being used. Frequently, differences in test scores will be expressed as effect sizes, or percentages of a standard deviation (i.e., an effect size of 0.2 is 20% of a standard deviation). On the SAT, for example, a standard deviation is 100 points, so an effect size of 0.2 is equal to 20 points. In this case, a small or large effect is in the eye of the beholder—especially for students on the cusp of getting into a university!

WHAT CAN GO WRONG WITH EXPERIMENTS?

Randomized experiments have received a glowing appraisal in this chapter—and deservedly so. But that doesn't mean they are flawless. Sometimes, experiments can go awry, making it more difficult to answer causal questions. Shadish et al. (2002) discuss the practical dilemmas of experimentation in a very lucid way. If you are interested in more details, see their Chapters 9 and 10, in particular. We will highlight just one problem that can occasionally

> Sometimes, experiments can go awry, making it more difficult to answer causal questions.

wreak havoc with experimental results: the case of the disappearing subjects—attrition from the treatment and control groups.

We have repeatedly emphasized that causal results hinge on the similarity of treatment and control groups. Indeed, randomized assignment guarantees such similarity, at least at the beginning of an experiment (this can be verified by comparing the baseline data of treatment and control group participants). But as an experiment proceeds, this can change markedly. In the unpredictable world of schools, it is common for children to move to another community, to be absent on the day that achievement tests are administered, or to simply withdraw from participation in a research study. These and similar phenomena are collectively referred to as *attrition*. It is not uncommon for 10% or more of the original sample to drop out of an experiment.[8]

Attrition is not a severe problem if the participants who drop out of a study are similar, on average, to those who remain. The treatment and control groups are smaller—and the statistical estimates of the treatment effects are less precise—but the groups are still comparable. Attrition *is* a problem if it makes the groups incomparable in observed or unobserved ways. For example, what if attrition only occurs among low-income students in the control group? Then, the remaining members of the control group are "different" in observed and even unobserved ways from the treatment group. This makes it difficult to determine whether the treatment is causing differences in student outcomes, or whether the groups were made incomparable by attrition. In fact, attrition is simply another variety of selection bias.

To guard against the ill effects of attrition, researchers should compare the baseline data of responding students in both the treatment and control groups. If the baseline data are similar across the remaining students, then it provides some measure of confidence that attrition has not compromised the causal validity of the results (although it is still possible that they differ in unobserved ways).

Why Are Experiments So Unpopular With Education Researchers?

A hefty volume called *The Digest of Social Experiments* (Greenberg & Shroder, 1997) summarizes more than 100 social experiments that have been conducted in recent decades. The experiments assess the impact of everything from job training programs to welfare assistance—but the field of education is surprisingly underrepresented. There are a few experiments that assess the impact of preschool interventions, and our case studies cite a number of examples in K-12 education.[9] However, the fact remains that experimentation is quite rare in education.[10]

Why is this so? In part this may be because experiments are perceived to create ethical dilemmas. For example, potentially beneficial treatments are randomly withheld from experimental participants (for an illuminating discussion of ethical issues like this, see Shadish et al., 2002). Of course, the same denial of service occurs with great frequency in health care research, but ironically this does not seem to prick the consciences of education researchers who disdain experimentation in their own field.

Another common critique is that experiments place undue emphasis on answering *causal* questions, perhaps at the cost of answering others. In many cases, for example, they cannot address the question of whether a treatment will "work" in a wide array of contexts. We treat this issue at greater length in Chapter 7, suggesting that these trade-offs are important to consider. Ultimately, we feel that obtaining credible answers to causal questions is a necessary (albeit insufficient) condition for bolstering efforts at school improvement.

> Obtaining credible answers to causal questions is a necessary (albeit insufficient) condition for bolstering efforts at school improvement.

Based on his long experience in the field of experimentation, Cook (1999) surmises that U.S. schools of education foster an intellectual culture that rejects experimentation out of hand. The culture is founded upon "multiple beliefs, any combination of which could sustain the (erroneous) conviction that randomized experiments are not worthwhile" (p. 54). He concludes that the fundamental warrant of the randomized experiment—its ability to answer causal questions—is still strong. We concur.

CASE STUDY   Does Class Size Reduction Work?

To assess whether being in a small class instead of a large class *causes* student outcomes to rise, a group of researchers in Tennessee initiated the STAR experiment.[11] Begun in 1985, the experiment randomly assigned students to large and small classes and measured whether a range of student outcomes were affected.

The experimental sample included 79 elementary schools in Tennessee that fulfilled some minimal criteria. First, the schools had to volunteer to participate in the experiment during four years, allowing data collection and site visits. Second, the schools had to enroll at least 57 children in a given grade (so that enough students were available in each school to randomly assign to different classes).

In 1985, the first year of the experiment, kindergarten students in each school were randomly assigned to three types of classes: (a) small classes (13-17 students), (b) regular classes (22-25 students) with a teacher's aide, and (c) regular classes with no teacher's aide. The first two classes were treatment groups, to be compared with the control group. Teachers were also randomly assigned to each type of class. During the next 3 years, entering kindergartners were randomly assigned in the same manner (older students continued in treatment or control groups until the third grade).

The results suggested that students in smaller classes score higher than students in regular classes on achievement tests—with effect sizes between 0.15 and 0.25 (Grissmer, 1999). These effect sizes tended to be higher for minority students than they were for others. Other researchers have continued to follow students even after the experiment had ended, to see whether these advantages persist. During Grades 4 to 7, students in the original treatment group scored higher than control students (with effect sizes of 0.11-0.2).[12] This occurred even though the treatment group began attending regularly sized classes after the third grade. Krueger and Whitmore (2001) followed the STAR students even farther along in their educational careers. They found that students in the original treatment group were considerably more likely to take the ACT or SAT tests (required for college admission) than control students.

Despite these results, the STAR experiment did suffer from some flaws, and it is important to ask whether those can explain the pattern of results. For example, there was attrition from the treatment and control groups because some students left the experiment or did not provide follow-up data. On average, however, the remaining students in the treatment and control groups were similar, at least according to observed characteristics (Grissmer, 1999).

The STAR experiment has received well-deserved attention as one of the few large-scale experiments in the United States that examines the causal impact of an education intervention. To some extent, however, the debate has given short shrift to other important questions. After all, we are not merely interested in whether class size "worked" among a group of students in Tennessee. We are also interested in why it worked, and whether the same results can be achieved in other contexts. And, as we are all aware, class size reduction is not cheap; it requires more teachers and more classroom space. So we also need to ask whether its costs are justified by its benefits. These issues will be treated in the next chapters.

CASE STUDY   Does Phonics Instruction Work?

Phonological awareness (PA), the ability to differentiate and manipulate words, syllables, and sounds, is a constellation of skills that are prerequisite to success in phonics instruction. In a three-year experiment, Torgesen et al. (1999) followed the reading progress of 180 students from kindergarten (mid-year) through second grade. The goal of the study was to assess whether PA instruction can diminish the prospects of reading failure among students with weak to nonexistent PA skills.

Students were selected for the study from a total kindergarten population of 1,436 students in 13 elementary schools using a two-part screening process. First, all students were given a letter naming task. Then, the students who scored in the bottom 30% on the task were screened with a battery of additional tests. A final sample of 180 students was selected. These students were randomly assigned within their 13 schools to one of four conditions—three treatment groups and a control group. The four groups of students had similar verbal IQs and other baseline measures before the treatment, suggesting that the randomization procedure worked well.

Students in the three treatment conditions received four 20-minute sessions of one-to-one instruction per week for 2½ years (88 total hours). The three treatment groups included a regular classroom support tutorial, a phonological awareness plus synthetic phonics tutorial, and an embedded phonics tutorial. The regular classroom support tutorials mirrored the regular classroom curriculum. The phonological awareness plus synthetic phonics tutorials used the *Auditory Discrimination in Depth* program (Lindamood & Lindamood, 1984), a highly explicit instructional methodology. In the embedded phonics tutorials, phonological awareness and phonics instruction were taught in the context of reading and writing whole words.

After the treatment, the students who received the phonological awareness plus synthetic phonics (PASP) tutorials had significantly stronger skills in phonological awareness, phonemic decoding, and word reading, than did their counterparts who had embedded phonics tutorials. When all groups are considered, students in the PASP group were stronger on word level reading skills than children in the control group and the classroom-support tutorial group. There was no significant difference in passage comprehension among the groups.

Less anticipated were the effects of the treatment on grade retention. The PASP group had significantly fewer students retained (9%) as compared to the control group (41%), classroom-support group (30%), and embedded phonics group (25%). This "retention effect"—although intriguing in its own right—did make it somewhat difficult to isolate the unique effects of phonics instruction. Part of the treatment effect may be due to the fact that PASP students are more likely to advance through the grades and receive second-grade instruction.[13]

The experiment was not without some challenges. During the 2½ year study, 23% of the original sample left the study, mainly because families moved out of the community. Attrition of this sort is not uncommon. However, the authors do not report whether the attrition led to any observable differences among the four groups on the baseline data, such as verbal IQ.

Nonetheless, the experiment provides fairly credible evidence that phonics instruction "works" in a narrowly prescribed way, if delivered in an intensive fashion to children at risk of reading failure. Important questions remain about *how* phonics instruction works, whether the results will hold for other students and settings, and whether the costs make such programs worthwhile. These issues are treated in later chapters.

CASE STUDY   Do Private-School Vouchers Work?

At the heart of the voucher debate lies a causal question: How are students' outcomes affected by attending private schools instead of public ones? Of course, we have no problem in measuring the outcomes of students who are observed to attend private schools. The more challenging problem is to measure the counterfactual. What if the same students had attended a public school? Would their achievement have been lower?

A good way of estimating the counterfactual is by conducting a randomized experiment. In 1997, Mathematica Policy Research did exactly that in New York City, collaborating with the School Choice Scholarships Foundation (Mayer, Peterson, Myers, Tuttle, & Howell, 2002).[14] The School Choice Scholarships Foundation announced that it would provide 1,300 scholarships for attending religious or secular private schools. To be eligible, children had to be entering Grades 1 through 5, to be attending a public school, and to have a low family income. The School Choice Scholarships Foundation received a large number of applications; this group constituted the convenience sample of students.

From this sample, students were randomly assigned to a treatment group (receipt of the scholarship) and a control group (no scholarship). Baseline data were collected from students and their families, including the Iowa Test of Basic Skills and detailed questionnaires about parental education, income, and other factors. The characteristics of the treatment and control groups were similar, on average, before the experiment began.

The "treatment" in question wasn't private-school attendance. Instead, it was the *offer* of a scholarship to students (who could then decide to attend or not attend a private school). In fact, about 78% of the treatment group attended a private school for at least one year.[15] Those who declined the scholarship may have done so because the scholarship did not cover the full amount of tuition (the median tuition in New York private schools at the time was around $2,000).

The researchers collected data on student outcomes at the end of the first, second, and third years of participation. The average test scores of treated students were no different than the average scores of control students (i.e., the means were not statistically different). Stated another way, the effect of *offering* a scholarship on student achievement was zero. This picture changed, however, when the researchers divided the students by race and ethnicity (most were African American or Latino). African Americans in the treatment group scored 5.5 percentiles higher than African Americans in the control group (an effect size of about 0.2). The difference was statistically significant, indicating that the result is probably not due to chance. Among Latinos, however, there was no difference between treatment and control students.

As in almost any experiment, there was attrition from the treatment and control groups. That is, no data was available for some students, most often because they simply did not attend the data collection sessions held by the researchers. For example, only 69% of the treatment group and 65% of the control group returned to take achievement tests after the third year of participation. By itself, attrition is not a problem unless it rendered the two groups incomparable. At least according to the baseline data, the two groups still look very much the same, which diminishes our concerns about attrition.

Some important questions are harder to address. What explains the impact of the treatment (or lack thereof, in the case of Latinos)? Can the experimental results provide useful clues about implementing a voucher program elsewhere? And are the expenditures on vouchers worthwhile? These issues are discussed in later chapters.

CASE STUDY   Does Whole-School Reform Work?

For all the ink spilled over the benefits of whole-school reform, there are only two randomized experiments that assess the impact of a particular reform model on outcomes. Both evaluations were conducted on the School Development Project (SDP) of James Comer (Cook et al., 1999; Cook et al., 2000). The SDP is based on the idea that "each school should determine its own academic and social goals. Specified are only the processes and structures needed to establish, monitor, and modify these goals" (Cook et al., 1999, p. 544). These processes and structures include three collaborative groups within the school: the School Planning and Management Team, the Social Support Team, and the Parent Team. The program relies strongly on the notion that schools need to improve the social climate of the interpersonal relations between staff, students, and parents. If test scores improve, it will be occur, in part, because the social climate has improved.

Thomas Cook and his colleagues conducted two randomized experiments in Maryland and Chicago to test whether the SDP yields such outcomes. The first experiment began with a sample of 23 middle schools in Prince George's County, Maryland, an ethnically diverse suburban community outside of Washington, DC (2 of the county's 25 middle schools did not participate). The schools were assigned to the treatment or control groups by the flip of a coin. The researchers studied three groups of students in each school: those who began seventh-grade in 1991, 1992, and 1993. Of these students, 77% agreed to participate in the study (consent had to be obtained

from parents). Despite the attrition, the participating students in the treatment and control groups still had quite comparable baseline data on test scores, absenteeism, and GPA.

In Chicago, the experiment was somewhat more complicated. The initial sample was composed of elementary schools in poor neighborhoods where the principal had indicated a willingness to participate. In Year 1, 8 schools were assigned to treatment or control groups by the flip of a coin. In Year 2, 12 additional schools were randomly assigned. However, 3 of the treatment schools in Year 1 dropped out of the experiment, and 1 of the control schools in Year 2 dropped out. Nonetheless, the baseline data revealed few differences between the characteristics of students in the treatment and control schools.

Using a wide array of outcome measures, the experiment in Maryland found the treatment schools did not have school climates or student achievement that differed from that of the control schools. In other words, there did not appear to be a program effect. In contrast, the Chicago evaluation found more positive results. The program caused positive changes in measures of standardized test scores as well as negative student behaviors.

Both experiments credibly established whether the program "worked" in improving outcomes—and they brought up some interesting questions. Why did the program succeed in Chicago but apparently not in Maryland? What do these programs cost, and are they worth it? And will the program succeed in other contexts?

FURTHER READING

Classic and eminently readable works on social experimentation include Campbell and Stanley (1963) and Cook and Campbell (1979). The latter has been comprehensively updated in Shadish et al. (2002), distinguished for its thorough and nontechnical explanations of the concepts introduced in this chapter. Readers who seek "nuts-and-bolts" guides to social experiments should consult Boruch (1997) and Orr (1999). The former provides many hands-on tips to the organization and conduct of an experiment. The latter is particularly helpful in describing the statistical tools used to analyze experimental data (although it requires an introductory statistics course to fully appreciate). Neither focuses exclusively on education, but many useful examples are provided from other fields.

NOTES

1. For a description of counterfactual reasoning, see Shadish et al. (2002).

2. This term was coined by Campbell (1957) and is used frequently in the social sciences. For a thorough explanation, see Shadish et al. (2002, pp. 53-54).

3. For some discussion of the mechanics of randomization, see Shadish et al. (2002, Chap. 8).

4. See especially Shadish et al. (2002, pp. 72-81). In their more technical language, treatments should possess construct validity. That is, the treatment that is described in a research study should bear a close resemblance to the treatment that was administered to participants.

5. Shadish et al. (2002, p. 79) refer to this as *compensatory equalization*.

6. There is a small caveat here: When the unit of randomization is the classroom, school, or higher unit, then larger numbers of students than usual are needed to attain the same degree of statistical precision in estimating program effects. For an explanation (that requires some grounding in statistics), see Orr (1999, p. 132-133).

7. Statistical significance is assessed using simple statistical tools, such as *t* tests, that are covered in introductory statistics courses; we won't be reviewing those tools here. For further details, the reader is advised to consult Orr (1999).

8. As a rule of thumb, Orr (1999) suggests that attrition of more than 30% should raise a red flag in an experiment.

9. These include the Perry Preschool Program and the Carolina Abecedarian Early Childhood Intervention (e.g., Barnett, 1996; Masse & Barnett, 2002).

10. Cook (1999) cites an array of evidence showing the rarity of experiments, including a finding that fewer than 1% of dissertations in education use randomized experiments. Also see Boruch, De Moya, and Snyder (2002).

11. Besides the additional research team, a wide range of independent researchers has analyzed the STAR experiment. In particular, see Mosteller (1995), Krueger (1999), and the citations therein.

12. See Grissmer (1999, p. 233). Also see Nye, Hedges, and Konstantopoulos (1999).

13. The authors of the study attempted to separate the effects of phonics instruction and grade-level instruction by creating subsamples of "matched" students. However, introducing quasi-experimental techniques casts some uncertainty on the causal findings.

14. In addition to the New York experiment, other randomized experiments with vouchers have been conducted in Dayton, Ohio, and Washington, DC (for a summary, see Howell et al., 2002). Other research has been conducted on Milwaukee's voucher program, where randomized assignment of vouchers occurred at the school level (e.g., Rouse, 1998).

15. The experimental design in this study is suited to answering the question, Did the *offer* of scholarship affect student outcomes? We are also interested in another, related question: Did actual *attendance* at a private school affect student outcomes? If all scholarship offers are accepted, then the answer to the two questions is identical. In this case, it is not, because around one quarter of scholarship offers were declined. To answer the second question is more complicated because it introduces elements of selection bias. Students who chose not to accept the voucher offer were different in observed and perhaps unobserved ways from other students in the treatment group. Addressing this thorny problem requires additional statistical methods (which are well described by Mayer et al., 2002). In any case, an important message to take away is that whenever we veer from the original experimental design—by not comparing *all* students in the treatment and comparison groups—experimental data are more difficult to analyze and interpret.

4

The Causal
Question

Does It Work? (Part II)

I f there is one thing that educators "know" for certain, it is that reading a lot makes one a better reader. There are programs that motivate students to read more at an appropriate level of difficulty and with accountability, like Reading Counts (Scholastic, 2002) and Accelerated Reader (Advantage Learning Systems, n.d.). There are books that show teachers how to develop SSR (sustained silent reading) programs in their classrooms (Pilgreen, 2000), and there are hundreds of principals around the country who have kissed pigs, eaten worms, and shaved their heads, all in the name of motivating their students to read more.

At first glance, the research appears to bolster our intuition. Results from the 1998 National Assessment of Educational Progress suggest that the students in three grades (4th, 8th, and 12th) who read more pages daily in school as well as for homework tended to have higher reading achievement than their classmates who read less (National Center for Education Statistics, 2001). In fact, there are dozens of correlational studies that show similar findings. Good readers read a lot. Poor readers don't read much. If you think about it, the causal interpretation of these findings is far from clear. One plausible explanation is certainly that reading causes achievement to rise. Another explanation, equally plausible, is that high-achieving students are simply more avid readers. Somehow, the latter explanation needs to be ruled out before it can be said that reading *causes* achievement to rise.

Chapter 3 extolled the virtues of randomized experiments, especially their ability to answer causal questions. But the simple reality is that randomized experiments are not that common in education; the example in the previous paragraph is but one illustration. There is no shortage of impassioned pleas for additional experimentation—ours can be added to the list—but there are few education researchers engaged in the day-to-day business of conducting experiments. As you have surely noticed, this does not prevent academics and pundits from prefacing their sound-bites about education policy with that well-worn chestnut: "research says."

> There is no shortage of impassioned pleas for additional experimentation—ours can be added to the list—but there are few education researchers engaged in the day-to-day business of conducting experiments.

If those statements rely on any research at all—sometimes, a doubtful proposition—they almost always refer to quasi-experimental or non-experimental research. Of course, this begs some important questions. If the research isn't experimental, what exactly is it saying? Can it *really* tell us whether a program, policy, or intervention works? The goal of this chapter is to help you answer these questions for yourself. Although it won't turn you into a statistical expert, it will provide you with some basic concepts to help identify and critique the causal findings of research studies that do not rely on randomized experiments.

QUASI-EXPERIMENTS AND NON-EXPERIMENTS

What They Are *Not*

When pursuing answers to causal questions, there are two broad alternatives to randomized experiments: quasi-experiments and non-experiments. As their prefixes suggest, both are defined in relation to their more respectable cousin, the randomized experiment. So it is natural to begin by emphasizing what they are *not*. Quasi-experimental and non-experimental research do *not* rely on randomized assignment to treatment and control groups.

If you read Chapter 3, this should produce a tinge of concern. Why? To reiterate, random assignment to treatment and control groups ensures that the only difference between the groups is their exposure to a treatment. Thus, the control group provides a good estimate of the counterfactual—of how the treatment group *would have* fared in the absence of the treatment. If there are any differences in outcomes between the treatment and control groups, they are almost certain to be *caused* by the treatment. They are probably not due to other factors, such as selection, history, and maturation—all threats to internal validity that were discussed in Chapter 3.

It is clear that any alternative to a randomized experiment needs to include a defensible means of estimating the counterfactual, if the researcher's goal is to answer a causal question. In most cases, this turns out to be a challenging task but not an impossible one. It is greatly facilitated by paying attention to some basic principles of research design, and by making good use of statistical techniques. We'll return to this topic in a later section, after we consider the general features of quasi-experiments and non-experiments.

> Any alternative to a randomized experiment needs to include a defensible means of estimating the counterfactual, if the researcher's goal is to answer a causal question.

What They *Are*

Beyond the lack of random assignment, what distinguishes quasi-experiments and non-experiments? In a quasi-experiment, the researcher exercises at least *some* control over the conditions of the treatment. This usually includes when, where, and how it is administered (i.e., a program was implemented during the 2001-2002 school year, in Edison Elementary School, using the Silver Bullet Reading Program). In this respect, a quasi-experiment is just like a randomized experiment. Moreover, the researcher's control in a quasi-experiment sometimes includes *who* receives the treatment, but this control never includes the ability to randomly assign the treatment (if it did, it would be a true rather than a "quasi" experiment).

In a non-experiment, the researcher exercises no control at all over the previous factors. He or she simply observes that a treatment of some kind has taken place and that some group of individuals participated. If you think about your own experiences, this is probably quite common. Most of us have been involved in some initiative where the decisions were made, the money was spent, and students were taught—well before the hurried calls were placed to do some "research" on whether the initiative actually "worked." Regardless of how well that research is done, it is broadly referred to as non-experimental.

The foregoing descriptions of quasi- and non-experimental research are pretty vague—purposely vague, in fact. This is unavoidable, because there is no *single* type of quasi-experiment or non-experiment. Quite the contrary; there are many, many variants of each approach. Some provide powerful means of answering causal questions—nearly as powerful as randomized experiments. Others tend to produce research studies that are best consigned to the bottom of a birdcage.

Yet it is common to find a study that "blithely pronounces itself to be a good cause-testing study just because a quasi-experimental design is being used. No cognizance is taken of the fact that some quasi-experimental designs are much stronger than others" (Shadish et al., 2002, p. 486). The authors of studies like these should feel a little sheepish. They are a bit like real estate agents intent on selling "quasi-houses." You wouldn't buy such a house without asking a few questions first. Are the quasi-walls made of Styrofoam or (hopefully) some more durable sub-stance? Does the quasi-roof admit a torrent of water? In short, does it perform the minimal functions that are expected of a real house?

The authors of studies like these should feel a little sheepish. They are a bit like a real estate agent who is intent on selling "quasi-houses."

When evaluating quasi- and non-experimental evidence, we need to apply the same critical test. The primary function of an experiment is to answer a causal question. This is only possible if the researcher identifies a counterfactual. Naturally, then, we must ask whether a quasi-experiment or even a non-experiment can believably perform that task.

THE RESEARCHER'S BAG OF TRICKS

What happens when researchers can't randomly assign students to treatment and control groups? They need to reach into their bags of tricks and find some other means—hopefully, convinc-ing—of estimating the counterfactual. This bag of tricks has two compartments, one reserved specifically for elements of research design. Think of these design elements, if you will, as the architec-tural blueprints for a research study. They specify, sometimes in exhaustive detail, how and when the treatment is to be allocated and administered and how its progress is to be measured. The other compartment in the bag is reserved for a variety of statistical techni-ques, the most important being regression analysis.

Design elements and statistical analysis can be combined in a wide—almost infinite—variety of ways to conduct different quasi-experimental and non-experimental research studies. Quasi-experi-mental research tends to lean more heavily on design, although it almost always includes, or should include, some thoughtful statistical analysis. Non-experimental studies rely almost entirely on statistical analysis. The next two sections will describe each of these in further detail, as a prelude to specific discussions of the most common quasi- and non-experimental approaches.

Design

Design elements are "something an experimenter can manipulate or control . . . to help address a threat to validity" (Shadish et al., 2002, p. 507). Chapter 3 already familiarized you with several design elements and how they address threats to validity. One of the most common elements, used in a wide variety of research studies, is a comparison group. The purpose of including a comparison group is to provide an estimate of the counterfactual—hopefully, a good one. Just how good is partly determined by how students, classrooms, or schools are assigned to the treatment and comparison groups.

In fact, the method of assignment constitutes one of the most important design elements. Random assignment ensures that the composition of the comparison group is similar to the treatment group. By definition, this design element isn't available in a quasi-experiment. The alternatives to random assignment are bracketed by two extremes.

> The method of assignment constitutes one of the most important design elements.

At one extreme, researchers explicitly control who participates in treatment and comparison groups (although the degree of control does not encompass random assignment). For example, the researcher might assign students—or other units—to a treatment group, and then identify "similar" students to serve as the comparison group (e.g., students with similar family characteristics). This kind of assignment is referred to as *matching*, and is discussed further later on.

At the other extreme, researchers have no control at all over who participates in the treatment and comparison groups. Group membership is driven entirely by self-selection—by the decisions of individual stakeholders. For example, parents and students may decide when and where to participate in a school program. If the program has too many applicants, schools and teachers may decide which of the applicants is eligible to participate. However the selection process works, the key point is that the researcher has little or no direct control over who receives the treatment.

When the researcher has no control over selection, it can cast doubt on the causal interpretation of a research study. In the very worst case, it results in treatment and comparison groups that are almost nothing like one another, both in ways that we can measure (e.g., family income) and also in ways that we cannot (e.g., student motivation). Who knows whether the groups are different because the treatment "works" or because the groups were never alike from the start?

> Even if treatment and comparison groups "look" similar, it is possible that unobserved differences lurk beneath the surface.

Our common-sense expectation is that by exercising some additional control over the design—perhaps by matching—the researcher can create treatment and comparison groups that are more comparable. This is probably true, but even this has its own pitfalls. Even if treatment and comparison groups "look" similar, it is possible that unobserved differences lurk beneath the surface. If these unobserved differences also affect outcomes, then selection rears its ugly head once again, and the causal interpretation of the results is thrown into question. All this serves as a good reminder of why randomized assignment is so powerful. It ensures that treatment and control groups are similar in *every* way, whether observed or unobserved.

There are many other design elements, and a full discussion would take us far afield (see Shadish et al., 2002, pp. 156-161 for a careful overview). However, it is worth mentioning just one more of these elements. In most cases, it is extremely helpful to administer a pretest to students in the treatment and comparison groups before the treatment is applied (the same advice can be applied to randomized experiments). The most obvious use of pretest data is to verify the existence of selection. If the treatment and comparison groups have very different pretest scores, on average, then it casts some doubt on whether the comparison group will provide an adequate counterfactual.

The thoughtful use of pretests can help in other ways as well. Sometimes, more than one pretest can be applied, perhaps during successive years prior to the implementation of the treatment. These measurements can tell the researcher if there is some preexisting trend in outcomes in that school, due to history, maturation, testing, or another factor. Prior knowledge of these trends can help ensure that they are not erroneously attributed to the "causal" effect of a treatment that is later applied. As helpful as pretests can be, they are not always given. This is often because of the added research costs, in both time and money.

Statistics

Chapter 3 suggested that it is quite easy to statistically analyze the results of a true experiment. One calculates the average outcome of the treatment group and then of the control group. And voilà—the difference between the two averages is a good estimate of the causal effect of the treatment. We usually anticipate that the treatment group will score higher based on what we have hypothesized. The statistical analysis is easy precisely because of the effort that was expended on implementing a powerful design element—randomized assignment. Zvi Griliches (1985), a well-known statistician and economist, said it best: "If the data were perfect, collected from well-designed randomized experiments, there would be hardly be room for a separate field of econometrics" (p. 196).

So what happens when the data aren't "perfect"—when they are obtained from quasi-experiments and non-experiments in which randomized assignment was not used? Let's consider an extreme case of an after-school mathematics enrichment

What happens when the data aren't "perfect"—when they are obtained from quasi-experiments and non-experiments in which randomized assignment was not used?

program in which selection is driven *entirely* by students. All treated students have chosen to attend the program, whereas comparison students have not. For the moment, assume that the parents of treatment students have higher levels of education, on average, than parents of comparison students. The reasons for this aren't all that important, but it might be because highly educated parents push their children to participate in additional activities.

What happens if we simply compare the average mathematics scores of treatment and comparison students? The scores are probably different, on average. But is it because of the treatment or because the treatment students have highly educated parents? A simple (and naïve) comparison of means makes it impossible to distinguish between two plausible explanations. Here is where additional statistical techniques can occasionally save the day.

Regression analysis is perhaps the most common tool of quantitative researchers. It is used in cases where a particular outcome measure—also referred to as a dependent variable—is thought to be determined by a number of independent variables. In the present case, we anticipate that mathematics scores (the dependent variable) are determined by two independent variables: (a) participation (or not) in the treatment and (b) the level of parental education. Regression analysis allows us to isolate the unique contribution of a particular independent variable to math scores, by holding constant or "controlling for" the other variable. For example, we can estimate the difference between math scores of treatment and comparison students, holding constant their levels of parental education. It is akin to conducting the following thought exercise: What if we only compared treatment and comparison students with the same amount of parental education? Would their math scores differ?

> Regression analysis is perhaps the most common tool of quantitative researchers.

By using regression analysis to control for parental education, we can more closely approximate the "apples and apples" comparison that we desire (in essence, an attempt to mimic a true experiment). But is our problem completely solved? That depends on whether there are unobserved and unmeasured variables that determine both math scores and treatment group selection. Imagine that we neglected to collect data on student motivation. Motivated students were more likely to participate in the treatment, and they were also more likely to have high scores on the math test. In this case, the problem of selection has been lessened by controlling for parent education but not eliminated. It is still possible that the difference in math scores between treatment and comparison students is due to motivational differences and not the treatment.

Most researchers anticipate this problem by measuring and controlling for a large number of variables—almost any variable they can anticipate that influences outcomes and treatment group selection. Call it the "kitchen sink" approach to regression analysis. But here's the catch: It only works if the researcher *perfectly* controls for *every* variable that determines both outcomes and treatment group status. Then and only then does the analysis provide a credible answer to the causal question.

This hard fact provides a simple illustration of why social scientists are inclined to say that "correlation is not causation." Actually, this statement is often used a little carelessly. In a randomized experiment, a correlation between the treatment and outcome measure *does* imply causation. And in a perfectly conducted regression analysis—that controls

> Social scientists are inclined to say that "correlation is not causation."

for all relevant background variables—correlation between the treatment and outcomes *does* imply causation. The problem is that perfect controls are nearly impossible to make. In such a case, there is usually some possibility that a correlation between the treatment and outcomes is due to group selection rather than a causal effect.

Of course, there are no hard-and-fast formulas for determining whether a regression analysis has properly addressed selection (and hence whether it answers the causal question). This depends on the context of the study, the quality of the data, and a host of other factors. It is a good reason why quasi-experimental and non-experimental research—but especially the latter—should be carefully reviewed before its conclusions are taken at face value. And carrying out such a review requires a deeper understanding of various approaches to quasi-experimental and non-experimental research. That is the purpose of the following section.

QUASI-EXPERIMENTAL APPROACHES

Matching

Of the many quasi-experimental designs, matching is probably the most common in education.[1] The goal is to pair students—or classrooms or schools—in a treatment group with "similar" units in the comparison group. But where matching is concerned, the devil is really in the details. A good match might approximate a randomized experiment and

> Where matching is concerned, the devil is in the details.

answer the causal question at hand. A poor match can result in treatment and comparison groups that are different in many unobserved ways and produce a heap of hard-to-interpret results.

So how can one tell the difference? There are some basic elements that should be present in every study. First, it should carefully describe the variables that were used to conduct the match. This sounds like a pretty basic requirement, but it is not uncommon to read assertions that schools were matched on a vaguely specified variables, such as "student poverty." What measure of poverty? Who collected it and when?

Second, it should describe the procedures used to conduct the match. Researchers would do well to follow the same advice that is given to students in elementary school mathematics: Show your work. Occasionally, authors purport to have matched schools or students but seem to have done little more than apply the "eyeball" method (not described in any textbook that we are aware of). Eyeballing involves little more than observing that a couple of schools are "close enough," by some poorly elucidated definition of the researcher. There are many sophisticated methods for matching (e.g., Shadish et al., 2002, p. 121), and it is suspicious if authors don't appear to describe or follow them.

Third, the study should provide some minimal data to support the assertion that treatment and comparison groups are similar. At the very least, this means that authors should compare each group's average on the variables used to conduct the match and any other relevant variables that are available (e.g., a pretest administered to treatment and comparison students).

Fourth, the study should provide some discussion of potential pitfalls in the matching process. The most obvious one is that "matched" units are different in unobserved ways, which hinders the causal interpretation of the quasi-experiment. This can vary depending on the context of the study, so it deserves a careful discussion. As an example, consider the Success for All (SFA) program of Robert Slavin and his colleagues, a school-based intervention designed to improve the reading abilities of disadvantaged children. Numerous quasi-experimental evaluations have been conducted—many by Slavin and his colleagues—that are summarized in Slavin and Madden (1999). The authors of these studies matched each SFA school with a comparison school, using variables such as the percentage of students receiving free and reduced lunch. However, SFA schools must all demonstrate staff "buy-in." That is, the majority of the staff in each treatment school must be committed and presumably motivated to address low levels of reading achievement. A natural question is whether the apparent success of the treatment in raising achievement is partially due to unobserved variables, such as the "energy" of teachers and principals.[2] Ultimately, this can't be easily determined. But when points like these are not discussed in quasi-experimental research, they undermine the credibility of the causal findings.

Fifth, the study should not oversell or misrepresent its quasi-experimental methods. To provide one example, many studies use the term "experiment," even when they are really using a quasi-experimental approach. In their review of evidence on SFA, for example, Slavin and Madden (1999, p. 13) refer to "experimental-control comparison" and a "multi-site replicated experiment." Although their quasi-experimental evidence is substantial, it does not rely on randomized assignment to treatment and control groups.

Interrupted Time Series

There are a variety of quasi-experimental approaches besides matching. They often occupy a great deal of space in research manuals, and deservedly so, because they can produce causal results that are more believable than matching (especially a study in which the "matching" is done haphazardly). Still, these approaches often make disproportionately few appearances in education journals, so you are less likely to encounter them.

One such design is the interrupted time series.[3] Imagine that we are trying to evaluate the causal effect of a whole-school reform. One option is to construct a long time series of data on an outcome variable such as student achievement. Ideally, the series should begin well before the implementation of the reform and continue for some years afterward. If the reform has some effect, we would expect to see achieve-

> If the reform has some effect, we would expect to see achievement rise in its wake.

ment rise in its wake. To make a causal interpretation, we need to rule out other explanations. In the case of the interrupted time series, one of the most plausible is history—the possibility that some other event occurring at the same time was responsible for the gains. This evaluation design was recently used to evaluate the impact of the Accelerated Schools model of whole-school reform on school achievement (Bloom et al., 2001).

Bad Quasi-Experiments

On occasion, quasi-experiments are so deficient that they hardly deserve the name. They may fulfill some minimal definition of a quasi-experiment in that the researcher controls when and how the treatment is applied. But they fall well short of establishing a causal relationship between that treatment and outcomes. Think back to Chapter 3. There, we discussed two common but often

> On occasion, quasi-experiments are so deficient that they hardly deserve the name.

flawed approaches to answering causal questions: the before-and-after approach and a simplistic version of the comparison group approach.

The before-and-after approach does not use a comparison group. Instead, it relies on two measurements of outcomes, applied before and after a treatment is applied. If outcomes rise, the treatment is presumed to have "worked." Although the treatment may have caused a change in outcomes, there are many other explanations, including history, maturation, and testing. A good quasi-experiment should be able to rule these out, but the simplest before-and-after design usually isn't up to the task.[4]

The second approach seems to be an improvement because it uses an important design element: a comparison group. But as we have repeatedly emphasized, it is very important how this comparison group is chosen. If it is obviously different from the treatment group—as it was in our original example—then it is difficult to extract any causal meaning from the quasi-experiment. Differences between the two groups could just as easily be due to selection.

NON-EXPERIMENTAL APPROACHES

Correlational Studies

In non-experimental studies, researchers have no control over when and how the treatment is applied. Even more important, they have no control over who participates in the treatment. The study is driven entirely by the selection decisions of students, parents, teachers, principals, and other stakeholders.

> In non-experimental studies, researchers have no control over when and how the treatment is applied.

Consider, for example, a large urban school district that was offering an intensive training course to teachers, designed to improve reading instruction. The district's new superintendent was interested in whether the training program is "working"—whether it is really having some effect on reading achievement. Unfortunately, she didn't begin her job until a few months after the program had started. By then, teachers had already been selected for the program. More to the point, they were allowed to choose for themselves whether they would attend the training course. Random assignment was never even considered because it was thought to be politically untenable.

After the fact, the district hired an outside researcher to conduct a non-experimental evaluation, using a correlational approach. He collected a large amount of data from district records on students and their teachers, including student reading scores, whether each student's teacher received the training course, whether the teacher was state certified, whether the teacher had a master's degree, and other variables. He immediately recognized that it made little sense to compare the average test scores of the treatment group (students with trained teachers) and the comparison group (students with untrained teachers). Because of selection, it appeared that trained teachers were more likely to be certified and more likely to hold master degrees. Naturally, this made it difficult to determine whether achievement was higher because of the training or because the trained teachers were more qualified in other ways.

So he conducted a regression analysis in which student achievement was the dependent variable. The independent variables included an indicator of whether the student's teacher received training, whether the teacher had an MA, and whether the teacher was certified. The analysis allowed a comparison of the achievement of treatment and comparison students, while holding constant the values of other variables. Ultimately, it suggested that training was positively associated with student achievement, even after controlling for education and certification.

Of course, the researcher was not entirely convinced that the study demonstrated that training *caused* test scores to rise. The trained teachers he had met seemed to be a rather energetic group, full of ideas and motivation. He was also concerned that a disproportionate number of these teachers came from just a few schools in the district—schools with dynamic principals who pushed their teachers to attend a variety of professional development activities. It was possible, he surmised, that the positive effects of training were really reflecting these unobserved differences between teachers and schools. At best, his correlational study provided evidence that was not inconsistent with a causal effect of training.

Correlational studies like the preceding one are very common in education—considerably more common than randomized experiments. One of the most famous and hotly debated studies was conducted by James Coleman et al. (1966). The authors of the "Coleman Report" collected an enormous sample of data from across the nation on the characteristics of students and their schools. They explored the correlations between school resources and student outcomes, controlling for other variables, such as the socioeconomic status of students. Since then, literally hundreds of other correlational studies have been conducted. They are referred to by many names, including school effectiveness studies, input-output studies, and production function studies (for reviews of this evidence, see Greenwald, Hedges, & Laine, 1996; Hanushek, 1986, 1997).[5]

A common feature of all these studies is that researchers do not have design elements such as randomized assignment at their disposal. To make treatment and comparison groups as similar as possible, the best they can do is use statistical methods,

A common feature of all these studies is that researchers do not have design elements such as randomized assignment at their disposal.

such as regression analysis, to control for a wide range of student and school variables. Unfortunately, this means that the studies are potentially subject to validity threats, such as selection, occasionally casting doubt on the causal interpretation of the results. There is no formula, however, for determining whether the causal findings of a correlational study are undermined by selection. This is best considered on a case-by-case basis, something that we do later on in the case studies.

"Natural" Experiments

In a very few cases, a non-experimental researcher may stumble on a "natural" experiment. Again, the researcher does not exercise direct control over who receives a treatment and who does not. Nonetheless, a peculiar set of circumstances can result in the treatment being allocated in a way that resembles random assignment— even if it was not intended.

For example, economists are often very interested in the relationship between education and earnings. We naturally expect that people with higher levels of education will earn more. However, does this really reflect the causal effect of more education? Or does it simply reflect the fact that smarter people—already prone to earn more— obtain higher levels of schooling? It is hard to determine whether a correlation between education and earnings has a causal interpretation.

> It is hard to determine whether a correlation between education and earnings has a causal interpretation.

To resolve this issue, we might think about conducting a randomized experiment. But that would involve a dubious and impractical task—randomly assigning some children to stay in school and others to leave. And yet, there are some cases where the amount of schooling that is received by a child appears "as if" it were due to chance or randomness.[6] For example, children who are born early in a calendar year tend to enter elementary school at a later age than other children because of laws governing the age of school entry (Angrist & Krueger, 1991). However, children can usually drop out of school when they reach the age of 16. The net result is that children born early in the year may receive fewer years of schooling just because they happened to be born in January instead of December. The key point is that the amount of schooling received in this case is, to some extent, affected by the luck of the draw rather than unobserved variables, such as each student's ability.

Unfortunately, one can never plan a "natural" experiment like this. So this type of research isn't always well suited to applied-education researchers who need to know whether a particular policy or program worked in a specific context. Nonetheless, natural experiments are a good reminder that quasi-experimental and non-experimental research should be judged by a simple criterion: How closely does it approximate a true experiment?

Bad Non-Experiments

Non-experimental studies are so common, especially correlational studies, that it would be surprising if a few weren't lacking in quality. By quality, of course, we mean a study's ability to answer a causal question. Asking a few simple questions can help you detect whether a correlational study falls short of the quality mark.

- How were students—or classrooms or schools—selected to participate in the treatment (was there a strong element of self-selection)? Is there anything that is obviously "special" about the units in the treatment group that might lead them to obtain better (or worse) outcomes, independently of the treatment? For example, do students or teachers in the treatment group appear especially motivated?

- Does a correlational study control for the most obvious determinants of student outcomes—and even some less obvious ones? For example, if a correlational study explores the effect of tutoring on student achievement, does it also control for important student characteristics, such as socioeconomic status, race and ethnicity, and gender?

- If some important variables are excluded from the analysis and not controlled for, does it seem plausible that they correlated with the treatment? For example, are excluded variables, such as student motivation, correlated with the likelihood that a student receives tutoring? Could the "causal" effect of tutoring really be explained by differences in student motivation?

Above all, your goal is to assess whether the causal interpretation of the results is clouded by threats to validity, such as selection. In some studies, it is hard to believe that selection does not play some role in explaining the results. Either the controls are so minimal or the amount of selection seems so strong that it's almost impossible to determine if "correlation implies causation." Some authors have an unfortunate tendency to overlook the deficiencies of their studies and focus on selling them to the reader in strongly

> Above all, your goal is to assess whether the causal interpretation of the results is clouded by threats to validity, such as selection.

worded terms. It is like walking onto a used-car lot and being immediately bombarded with a strong sales pitch, as if that could mask the deficiencies of a rusting lemon. Look past rhetoric and focus on the real merits of the study at hand.

To be fair, many correlational studies make detailed statistical controls for differences between treatment and comparison groups. They also provide detailed discussions of how and why the results could be biased by selection. These studies are almost always more useful. Even if their results are not definitive, they can provide one more useful ingredient in your overall assessment of whether a treatment "works."

CASE STUDY   Does Class Size Reduction Work?

Despite the attention given to Tennessee's STAR experiment, most of the evidence on class size reduction is non-experimental or quasi-experimental. Alex Molnar et al. (1999) conducted a quasi-experimental evaluation of Wisconsin's SAGE program.[7] Class sizes were typically reduced from 21 to 25 students per teacher to 12 to 15. To participate in the program, Wisconsin school districts were required to have at least one school in which 50% or more of the children were defined as "poor." The final treatment group consisted of 30 elementary schools in 21 districts. In the 1996-97 school year, class size reduction was implemented in kindergarten and first grade. Higher grades were added in subsequent years.

The SAGE program was not randomly assigned to students or schools. Instead, the researchers identified 17 comparison schools with regularly sized classes that were located in the same school districts as treatment schools. The baseline data suggested that students in the treatment and comparison schools were similar, on average. Both groups had a high percentage of minorities and poor students. Furthermore, students in both groups took a pretest in Fall 1996, before the program was implemented. There were no statistically significant differences between the average test scores of each group.

At the end of the 1996-97 school year (and in subsequent years), students took a posttest—the Comprehensive Test of Basic Skills. There were statistically significant differences in the average posttest scores of treatment and comparison students. These differences persisted even after regression analysis was used to control for student characteristics, including pretest scores, eligibility for free and reduced lunch (a measure of family income), and race. Expressed as an effect size, the magnitude of the difference is between 0.1 and 0.2, with somewhat larger effects for minority students.

Given the quasi-experimental design, a plausible threat to validity is selection. SAGE districts volunteered to participate in the program, but little is known about how individual schools were chosen within each district. A lurking possibility is that SAGE schools were "special" in some way—an exceptional principal, perhaps—and that this specialness was responsible for some of the test score gains. These suspicions are difficult to test, but they are partly allayed by the similar pretest scores between SAGE and comparison students.

In contrast to the limited experimental and quasi-experimental studies, there are hundreds of non-experimental studies that use a correlational approach. In these studies, the researchers had no control over which students actually attended large or small classes. Instead, they compared the achievement of students who were observed to attend large or small classes, while making statistical controls for the socioeconomic status of students. Hanushek (1997) reviewed these studies and concluded that they showed no consistent link of class size to student achievement.

However, it is plausible that these non-experimental results were afflicted by selection. For example, Boozer and Rouse (1995) show that the allocation of students to large and small classes is clearly *non*random. For example, lower-ability students are often assigned to smaller, remedial classes. If regression analysis does not control perfectly for student ability, then it is possible that correlational studies will find small classes to be associated with *lower* achievement. However, this might reflect unobserved differences between treatment and comparison groups—and not the negative effects of class size reduction. This is a good explanation as to why one randomized experiment in Tennessee has proven to be much more influential than hundreds of correlational studies.

CASE STUDY   Does Phonics Instruction Work?

The "Houston Study," as it has come to be known, was a quasi-experiment that investigated the effectiveness of various instructional methods in a sample of at-risk students (Foorman et al., 1998). The difference between the instructional approaches, all of which were implemented in the context of a literature-rich environment, was the degree of explicitness with which phonics instruction was delivered.

The initial sample was composed of 285 students, all identified as eligible for Title I services based on participation in the federal lunch program. They were evenly distributed across 65 regular education classrooms (Grades 1 and 2) in eight elementary schools. Non-Title-I students also attended these classes, but no data was collected on them.

Each of the 65 classrooms was assigned to one of four conditions: (a) a control group, in which the district's standard curriculum was taught; (b) direct code (DC), which consisted of direct instruction in letter-sound correspondences practiced in decodable text; (c) embedded code (EC), which consisted of less direct instruction in systematic spelling patterns (onset rimes) embedded in connected text; and (d) implicit code (IC), which consisted of indirect, incidental instruction in the alphabetic code embedded in connected text. Each treatment was implemented during a daily language arts period. The teachers who delivered the treatments received 1 week of summer in-service training, followed by retraining and demonstration lessons 1 month into the school year. The control group teachers were trained and supervised by district personnel.

However, the assignment of classrooms to the treatment and control groups was not random. It was instead governed by "the willingness of the principal and teachers to participate" (Foorman et al., 1998, p. 39). The study does not report whether the treatment and control groups were similar according to any baseline data, such as student background characteristics.

The results suggest that students who were directly instructed in the DC treatment improved in word-reading skill at a significantly faster rate than students in the other groups. Nearly half of the students in the IC (46%) and EC (44%) groups exhibited no demonstrable growth in word reading compared with only 15% of students in the DC group. Students in the DC group who had lower PA skills at the beginning of the study showed more growth in word-reading skills than children with low PA skills in the other instructional groups. The end-of-year achievement scores for students in the DC group approached the national average on decoding (43rd percentile) and passage comprehension (45th percentile) compared with the IC group (29th and 35th percentiles respectively) and the EC group (27th and 33rd percentiles, respectively; Foorman et al., 1998).

These results must be interpreted cautiously, however. The schools and teachers in this study volunteered to participate, raising the possibility of selection bias. There are a variety of scenarios one might imagine that would affect the outcome in either direction. Suppose that principals who volunteered for the treatment were located in particularly "bad" schools (and recognized a need for outside assistance). Or suppose that teachers who volunteered for the treatment were particularly enthusiastic and talented. In either case, the receipt of the treatment would be associated with unobserved characteristics of schools, teachers, and students that affect outcomes in both positive and negative ways. Overall, it is difficult to assess the net direction of the bias.

CASE STUDY   Do Private-School Vouchers Work?

The overwhelming majority of evidence that addresses this question is not drawn from randomized experiments. In fact, it is not even drawn from evaluations of specific instances in which private-school vouchers were offered to students. Rather, it is from correlational studies that compare the outcomes of students who are observed to attend private schools—usually because they pay tuition—and public schools.

These studies were kicked off with controversy in the early 1980s by Coleman, Hoffer, and Kilgore (1982). These authors used data from the High School and Beyond (HSB) survey, which is still freely available from the National Center for Education Statistics (2002a). HSB collected data on the school and family characteristics of a sample of high school sophomores in 1980. It has since collected additional data on these students, up until 1992.

When they wrote their book, Coleman et al. (1982) only had access to data from a limited time frame. They compared the achievement of students in private schools—mainly Catholic—and public schools. Because the study was correlational, they used regression analysis to control for student background characteristics, such as socioeconomic status. This is especially important in studies like this, because children who attend private schools usually have higher socioeconomic status. Without making statistical controls, we cannot determine whether private-school children have higher achievement because of their school or because they come from more privileged families. The authors argued that attending a private school rather than a public school had positive effects on student achievement. Many other authors reanalyzed the same data, also using regression analysis. These studies typically found effect sizes of no more than 0.1.[8]

Since then, dozens of additional studies have used subsequent data—particularly the National Education Longitudinal Study (NELS; National Center for Education Statistics, 2002b), which collected data from a sample of eighth-graders in 1988 and then tracked their progress in later years.[9] Regarding effects on academic achievement, these correlational studies seem to turn up similar patterns of evidence as previous research. There is only a small achievement effect of attending a private school, once student background is held constant with regression analysis.[10]

Because HSB and NELS followed students well into their college-age years, some studies have looked at a broader set of student outcomes—such as the likelihood of graduating from high school and attending college. On the whole, the correlational studies that examined these outcomes were much more favorable to private schools. Students who attended private schools, on average, were more likely to graduate from high school and attend college, holding constant to the family background of students.

A natural concern is whether the correlational studies have controlled for *every* important characteristic of students. Is it possible that students who attend private schools are more motivated or able in some unobserved way? Can these unobserved traits—instead of benefits produced by private schools—plausibly explain why private-school students do better than public-school students? This thorny issue has consumed the attention of researchers, but no clear conclusions have arisen from the debate.[11] Many have attempted to identify a reasonable "natural" experiment—some instance in which student attendance at private schools is determined by chance or some factor unrelated to achievement. Just like the debate over class size reduction, however, the evidence from randomized experiments has proven to be more easily understood and also more credible.

CASE STUDY   Does Whole-School Reform Work?

Randomized experiments are rarely used in evaluations of whole-school reform (Cook et al., 1999; Cook et al., 2000). Existing evaluations usually rely on a quasi-experimental approach. One of the best was conducted on the Comer School Development Program, already described in Chapter 3 (Millsap et al., 2000).[12] Early in 1994, Detroit schools submitted proposals to participate in the reform. To be selected, they had to demonstrate "how the program matched school objectives, how the schools were already engaged in reform efforts, and evidence of staff support for the initiative" (p. 5). Overall, at least 75% of the full-time staff and 55% of other staff had to demonstrate support. A district planning team selected six schools to participate in the first wave of the reform in 1994-95. After repeating the same application process, six more schools were selected to begin the following school year.

The 12 schools constituted the treatment group that would participate in the School Development Program. Each of these treatment schools was matched with two comparison schools located in the same geographic area of the city and identified as having similar enrollments, percentages of non-white students, percentages of students receiving free and reduced-price lunch, and percentages of students scoring at or above grade level on achievement tests. After the matching process was completed, there were no statistically significant differences in these characteristics between treatment and control schools.

Despite the careful matching process, eight schools were dropped from the study because of missing data or, in one case, implementation problems with the Comer model. This raises the possibility of bias from attrition. However, the observed characteristics of the remaining treatment and comparison schools were similar, diminishing these concerns.

On average, the researchers found that the School Development Program did not have any effects on student achievement in mathematics, reading, or science. They obtained this finding by comparing the average achievement of students across treatment and comparison schools, while making controls for student characteristics. They also did not find any differences in the academic and social climate of treatment and comparison schools.

Three of the treatment schools appeared to be implementing the Comer model more faithfully than other schools. Hence, the researchers compared these "good-implementers" with their matched comparison schools. In this case, the program did appear to have positive effects on student achievement. This seems to be a commonsense finding, but the quasi-experimental design suggests that is should be cautiously interpreted. Is it possible, for example, that there is something "special" about the good implementers that we do not observe? Did they have an exceptional principal, perhaps? Most important, can these factors explain the success of the good implementers rather than the School Development Program?

FURTHER READING

The definitive guide to quasi-experimental designs is the classic work of Cook and Campbell (1979) and its substantially revised edition (Shadish et al., 2002). They eschew many technical details, instead focusing on the essential intuition behind different quasi-experiments. They also provide a much more comprehensive catalog of various quasi-experimental designs. To fully appreciate the logic of non-experiments, it is helpful to explore the mechanics of regression analysis. Almost any textbook on educational statistics includes at least a chapter on regression analysis (it often ends up relegated to the very end of a statistics course). Even more helpful might be an intuitive introduction to the topic that relies more on visual illustrations than equations; one such book is Lewis-Beck (1980).

NOTES

1. Although it is one of the most common, this does not necessarily imply that it is the "best," as gauged by its ability to confidently address a causal question. In fact, less common approaches, such as regression-discontinuity analysis, often provide more credible results.

2. For further discussion of points like these, see Levin (2002).

3. For a thorough description of the interrupted time series approach, see Chapter 6 in Shadish et al. (2002). Another important quasi-experimental design is called regression-discontinuity, discussed in Chapter 7 of Shadish et al. (2002). It has a long history in evaluation research and is favorably reviewed in almost every textbook, but it is infrequently used in education research. This is beginning to change (e.g., Angrist & Levy, 1999; Guryan, 2001), but we do not emphasize the design here.

4. Nevertheless, it may be possible to improve this design by adding more design elements, such as additional pretests and posttests (to test for trends in outcomes that are not caused by the treatment) or an appropriate comparison group.

5. Hanushek's studies (1986, 1997) suggest that school resources, such as school spending, are not consistently linked to student achievement. Greenwald et al. (1996) use different methods to summarize these studies and generally find more optimistic conclusions. An important point to remember is that no matter how these studies are summarized and reviewed, they are still drawn from non-experimental data. Thus they are subject to all the critiques that we summarize in this chapter, particularly threats to internal validity like selection.

6. For a discussion of studies like this, see Ashenfelter and Rouse (2000).

7. Other quasi-experimental research has evaluated the effect of class size reduction in Bolivia and Israel, using a regression-discontinuity design (Angrist & Levy, 1999; Urquiola, 2000).

8. Levin (1998), Neal (1998) and Witte (1992) provide reviews of this evidence.

9. See http://nces.ed.gov/surveys/nels88/.

10. For a good example of one of these studies using NELS, see Gamoran (1996). For a review of many of these studies, see McEwan (2000).

11. See McEwan (2000) for a discussion.

12. For a discussion of other quasi-experimental evaluations, see Levin (2002).

5

The Process Question

How Does It Work?

There are many technologies that we trust to dazzle us whenever we turn them on—computers, cable TV, digital cameras, hand-held organizers, and cellular phones, to name just a few. Yet if called on to explain precisely how these wonders actually work, or heaven forbid, to troubleshoot problems, most of us are helpless. Knowing *that* something works is not the same as understanding *how* it works. How is it possible to receive messages from family members halfway around the world in seconds? How do images travel from a tiny camera through a cable into a computer and emerge as glossy prints from your printer? Thankfully, we don't have to understand how these technologies work to know that they do. However, having affirmative answers to causal questions is not enough for educators. If you plan to use research to inform practice and decision making in your classroom, school, or district, you will also need plausible answers to the how-does-it-work questions for the programs, methodologies, and policies you choose to implement.

Suppose you are a principal, department chair, or grade-level team leader who is intrigued by the potential of cognitive-strategy instruction (e.g., techniques and tools to summarize, question, monitor, and organize during reading) for helping upper-grade students to understand and remember the content of specific disciplines. Many students aren't able to "read to learn," and you suspect that most teachers don't understand how to remediate this situation. You read several studies and conclude that the evidence is solid.

Cognitive-strategy instruction works. But how does it work? During classroom observations, you hear teachers talking to their students about the need to read for meaning, and you see teachers testing recall and understanding of what has been read, but there is little systematic instruction designed to help the students who "read it, but don't get it." The burning question for practitioners is how to translate what researchers have shown works in an experimental setting into a successful staff development program and schoolwide implementation. Qualitative research holds promise for doing just that.

What Is Qualitative Research?

The term *qualitative research* first made its appearance in the 1960s when it was used to describe field studies in disciplines other than anthropology (Filstead, 1970). To some, qualitative research is simply a set of information-gathering techniques or methodologies (i.e., interviewing, observation, and document analysis). To others (e.g., Fleischer, 1995; McLaren, 1998), qualitative research is a philosophical or political perspective that drives a research agenda in the activist tradition of Freire (1970/1993). It is not our intent to fully explore all of the permutations and combinations included under the rubric of qualitative research; we will later recommend several books, if you are interested in pursuing this topic. We are primarily concerned with the role that qualitative data, whether combined with experimental data or presented on its own, can play in expanding your understanding of how educational interventions actually work.

> It is not our intent to fully explore all of the permutations and combinations included under the rubric of qualitative research.

To many, qualitative research is embodied in the term *ethnography*, which includes both observations made by an individual during an extended stay in a specific culture and the construction or interpretation of that culture in a written form. For some, the term evokes the well-known photo of famed anthropologist Margaret Mead on the island of Samoa (Bogdan & Biklen, 1998, p. 9). Mead's work is true ethnography because it describes a specific culture. Cultural anthropologists-in-training (those who are working toward a PhD) are expected to spend at least 1 year on location in an exotic or remote setting where a different language and culture provide the opportunity to "make the strange familiar . . . by translating . . . observations into logic and expressions" that will be understandable to those who would read the descriptions (Spindler, 1982, p. 23).

Ethnographies, although undeniably the most well-known type of qualitative research, do not comprise its totality. There are at least three other broad categories: (a) case studies, (b) naturalistic inquiries, and (c) life history methodologies. Brief definitions will give you a flavor of the variety of qualitative research. Case studies are common and often used by authors to focus on particular aspects of organizational or human behavior. Patton (2002) notes two well-known books that appear on most of our shelves—*In Search of Excellence* and *The 7 Habits of Highly Effective People.* Their authors used case studies of companies (Peters & Waterman, 1992) and highly effective people (Covey, 1990), respectively, as a way of sampling and then extracting attributes and habits from recurring themes in the cases.

The process of conducting a naturalistic inquiry, another type of qualitative research, is similar to the approach taken by the ethnographer—that of being a firsthand witness to what is happening in a specific setting. However, the emphasis in a naturalistic inquiry is not concerned with defining and explaining a culture so much as "studying human action in some setting that is not contrived, manipulated, or artificially fashioned by the inquirer" (Schwandt, 2001, p. 174) and reporting on it to the reader. The life history methodology, as its name suggests, is a biographical approach that focuses on telling the life story or history of an individual. Some biographers have the benefit of interviewing their subjects; others generate their data from letters, journals, diaries, newspaper accounts of events, and interviews with those who knew the subject personally.

Any attempt to place most contemporary qualitative studies into one of these four seemingly well-defined categories will only lead to frustration, however. Schwandt (2001), whose dictionary we recommend for the serious student of qualitative research, defines every variety of qualitative method, design, and philosophical perspective and then cautions, "Given this diversity in intellectual origins, strategies, methods, and practices, it becomes difficult to define in any precise way who the qualitative inquirer is and what it is that he or she does" (p. 20). Suffice it to say that in addition to the major types of qualitative research mentioned here, there are dozens of lesser-known and more theoretical types that are not germane to our discussion.

> Any attempt to place most contemporary qualitative studies into one of these four seemingly well-defined categories will only lead to frustration.

THE QUALITIES OF QUALITATIVE RESEARCH

Qualitative research that is specific to education has many characteristics in common with its anthropological ancestor. In fact, much of the early qualitative education research was done by trained anthropologists whose methodologies were easily translated from the fieldwork they had done in remote places to the elementary school down the street (Spindler, 1982; Wolcott, 1973). When done

> Qualitative research, when done well, is a rigorous and exhaustive undertaking.

well, qualitative research is a rigorous and exhaustive undertaking. That it differs from its quantitative cousin in substantial ways makes it no less valuable to educators. Qualitative research also seeks answers to important questions. It just looks for them in different places, with contrasting methods, and for different purposes than does its quantitative cousin. It has three principal characteristics: It is (a) naturalistic, (b) descriptive, and (c) focused on meaning.

Naturalistic

Qualitative research is naturalistic in that researchers (observers) go where the action is—a coffee shop where students hang out after school, to talk with them about the dropout problem; to a principals' meeting, to observe firsthand how decisions are made in a district; or to a math class, to track down how teachers make algebra intelligible (or unintelligible) to 9th graders. Whereas quantitative researchers structure their research environments to the greatest extent possible, qualitative researchers simply plunk themselves down where it's happening and try to figure out how and why.

Descriptive

Qualitative research is also descriptive. Words are the coinage of the qualitative researcher. Quantitative researchers try to control for every extraneous variable that might interfere with getting a definitive answer to the causal question; qualitative researchers take in as much detail and information as possible, recording the most insignificant and seemingly unimportant tidbits. Qualitative researchers write rich and multifaceted descriptions.

Focused on Meaning and Explanation

Qualitative researchers are constantly focused on explaining and interpreting what they observe, hear, and read. Whereas quantitative researchers ask one "big" question and test it with an experiment, qualitative researchers ask multiple and ongoing questions about how and why things work the way they do in particular settings. For example, why are teachers failing to follow the prescribed curriculum, even after intensive training, or why do certain types of students fail to succeed in certain types of instructional settings. Qualitative researchers are constantly considering a variety of possible interpretations and explanations about what they have observed, whereas quantitative researchers seek to rule out every possible answer except one.

Bogdan and Biklen (1998) put their fingers on the essence of qualitative research: "You are not putting together a puzzle whose picture you already know. You are constructing a picture that takes shape as you collect and examine the parts" (p. 7). The Sherlock Holmes analogy seems an apt one. Think of the qualitative researcher as an education detective looking for clues to the mystery of a school's unmotivated readers, searching for the missing piece to the reading puzzle, or combing the cumulative folders of special education students to find clues regarding their lack of academic progress.

> Think of the qualitative researcher as an educational detective looking for clues.

THE POWER OF QUALITATIVE RESEARCH

To fully appreciate the power that qualitative research can pack in terms of answering the how-does-it-work question, let's return to our earlier example in which you imagined yourself as an educator who wants to implement cognitive-strategy instruction in your school. Qualitative research cannot provide every answer you need to carry out a successful implementation, but it offers a variety of explanations for the how-does-it-work question. To that end, you might locate several practitioner-based qualitative studies (e.g., Gaskins & Elliot, 1991; Pressley et al., 1995; Santa, 1986; Schoenbach, Greenleaf, Cziko, & Hurwitz, 1999; Wood, Wolosyn, & Willoughby, 1995) that provide observations, anecdotes, conversations, and descriptions of how researchers, teachers, and administrators have wrestled with the day-to-day development, implementation, and evaluation of cognitive-strategy instruction programs. Here are just some of the questions you can find answers for in the studies:

> Qualitative research cannot provide every answer you need to carry out a successful implementation, but it offers a variety of explanations for the how-does-it-work question.

• How does the teacher's style and instructional methodology affect the effectiveness of cognitive-strategy instruction?

• How do the characteristics of the reader affect the degree and type of cognitive-strategy instruction that is needed?

• How is cognitive-strategy instruction best delivered in the classroom?

- How long does it take for the average teacher to become skilled at teaching cognitive strategies to students and with what kinds of training?

- How much time should be devoted to cognitive-strategy instruction?

- How do various cognitive strategies interact with each other during the act of reading?

Without answers to these and other critical "how" questions, implementation of cognitive-strategy instruction could well become an administrative nightmare or, at the very least, an exercise in futility.

QUALITATIVE RESEARCH METHODS

One of the most attractive aspects of qualitative research to many graduate students is that, at first glance, it looks easy to do. After all, what could be more relaxing than just sitting around watching and listening to people? But qualitative research only looks easy. Ask principals what the toughest part of their job is, and a sizable share of them will identify the supervision and evaluation of teachers as their biggest challenge—sitting around and watching teachers teach. There is, in fact, a great deal of similarity between the methods used to conduct qualitative research and those employed in the supervision and evaluation of teachers: *interviewing* teachers in preobservation and postobservation conferences, *observing* instruction and students in the classroom, and *analyzing documents* such as lesson plans, report cards, student work samples, teacher portfolios, and reflective journals.

> The use of multiple data collection methods is one way to lessen the likelihood that a researcher will jump to conclusions based on insubstantial evidence.

The use of multiple data collection methods (i.e., interviewing, observing, and analyzing documents) is known as *triangulation*. Whether used during qualitative research *or* to evaluate teachers, it lessens the likelihood that a researcher (or a principal) will jump to conclusions based on insubstantial evidence. In fact, a most instructive way to illustrate the critical attributes of qualitative research methods is to follow a typical principal during a cycle of observation and evaluation.

Interviewing

The evaluation cycle usually begins with a preobservation conference. Holding such a conference or interview enables the principal to find out from teachers exactly what they have planned for the observation period. The principal might ask questions like the following, before observing: (a) What outcomes do you expect your students as a result of the lesson or activity? (b) What lessons or activities have preceded today's lesson? (c) Are you trying anything for the first time today? (d) Are there any students you would like me to especially notice during the lesson? (e) Is there anything that you've been working on that you'd like me to notice (e.g., note the use of various types of questions, tally the number of positive and reinforcing comments versus negative comments to students with behavior difficulties, or track the use of transition time more effectively)? (f) What instructional methods are working especially well for you? (g) What's your biggest challenge at the moment? The best preobservation conferences are interactive and free flowing, with an open exchange of ideas and information. The data gathered in this interview sets the stage for a meaningful and more interpretable observation.

Interviews, however, are not foolproof. Administrators often misjudge, misinterpret, and misunderstand teachers during interviews, encountering the same difficulties that qualitative researchers do when conducting interviews in the "field." Possibilities include "distorted responses due to personal bias, anger, anxiety, politics, and simple lack of awareness since interviews can be greatly affected by the emotional state of the interviewee at the time of the interview. Interview data are also subject to recall error, reactivity of the interviewee to the interviewer, and self-serving responses" (Patton, 2002, p. 306). If the principal has a preconceived notion and regards a particular teacher as "poor" or "ineffective," this bias could function as a screen or filter to distort the quality of the exchange as well as the accuracy of the data. If the teacher has emotional problems or is highly anxious during the interview, again, the data will be less representative of what might occur under "normal" circumstances.

Observing

Having "interviewed" the teacher, the principal is now prepared to observe in the classroom. Observations, whether conducted for purposes of qualitative research or teacher evaluation, are also fraught with possibilities for misinterpretation and confusion. For example, the principal could well assume that a particular teacher has outstanding classroom management, when what is really being seen are the effects on the students of the principal's being in the classroom (or, conversely, poor student behavior may be a reaction to an outside presence). Another problem is that the principal cannot know what is happening in the teacher's mind. An energetic and talented novice can suddenly become so nervous that a wonderful lesson plan flies out the window, and the lesson goes downhill from there. The principal would know that the teacher's behavior is quite uncharacteristic only if multiple unannounced visits had been made over a period of months, during which highly effective instruction was observed or if the teacher was able to articulate in the postconference precisely what happened.

On the other hand, the principal who observes a reasonably well-prepared and organized teacher early on Monday may not realize that the teacher prepped the entire weekend for the observation and immediately after the principal left, returned to business as usual—"winging it." Multiple observations of different subjects or classes, or observations made at different times of the day, are as essential to a valid and reliable teacher evaluation as they are to a plausible and informative qualitative research study.

> Multiple observations are as essential to a valid and reliable teacher evaluation as they are to a plausible and informative qualitative research study.

Some of the questions that arose or confusion the principal felt during the observation might well be clarified in a postobservation interview. In that context, the principal can query the teacher about why certain things were done or said, how the lesson had gone, and what were areas of particular strength or instructional techniques that needed fine-tuning.

Analyzing Documents

To triangulate data gathering for evaluative purposes (in the best tradition of qualitative researchers), the principal also examines and analyzes documents, including student work samples, lesson plans, and perhaps even the teacher's portfolio, which could include a reflective journal compiled over the course of the school year. Document analysis can fill in some of the missing data pieces or it can raise a host of new questions regarding the accuracy of observations and interpretations, necessitating further conversations with the teacher or possibly even another observation.

> Document analysis can fill in some of the missing data pieces or it can raise a host of new questions regarding the accuracy of observations and interpretations.

For example, in reading the teacher's reflective journal, the principal might discover that that the teacher is confused about some important aspects of instruction that were not evident during the observation. Also, in looking at student work samples assembled over a period of months, evidence of the kind of improvement and growth that is generally seen may be lacking. The principal's original judgment regarding the teacher could well be called into question. Or in reviewing the report cards for the students in a particular class, the principal might pick up on a disturbing grading and comment pattern for a certain group of minority students. These aspects of the teacher's performance could have been missed, but for the documents that alerted the principal to the problems.

We hope you are gaining an appreciation for the intricacies and demands of qualitative data gathering (whether for research or teacher evaluation purposes) as well as some of its potential shortcomings in providing answers to how-does-it-work questions.

FROM WHENCE COMES THE QUALITY IN QUALITATIVE RESEARCH?

We know from our earlier discussion that the credibility of an experimental study rests largely on the presence of randomization in the research design. When randomization is present, the causal description, although not "proving" beyond a shadow of a doubt that something works, can substantially reduce the uncertainty. Unfortunately, there is no single characteristic or methodology of qualitative research that offers this same likelihood.

Cunningham (1993) suggests that qualitative researchers be held to a standard set forth in British common law. Qualitative research must be read and evaluated "not [to find] . . . a demonstration of absolute 'lawlike certainty' as is obtained in a laboratory experiment in the physical sciences, [but rather] a moral certainty, which is the degree of proof which produces a conviction in an unprejudiced mind" (p. 181). Of course, if your own values and beliefs strongly resonate with a qualitative study (i.e., you do not have an unprejudiced mind), you may find moral certainty in anything, regardless of its quality. However, there are a number of criteria that when met in a qualitative study can satisfy the common law burden of proof very nicely. As you make sense of qualitative data, whether in the context of an experiment or as the only evidence in a qualitative study, envision yourself as both judge and jury in a civil or criminal case.

> As you make sense of qualitative data, whether in the context of an experiment or as the only evidence in a qualitative study, envision yourself as both judge and jury in a civil or criminal case.

A qualitative "private eye" has assembled the case and it comes to you in the form of personal observations, quotations from interviews, and descriptions of documents. The investigator has undoubtedly put a "spin" on the case, as any prosecutor or defense attorney would do, but your evaluation of the data will ultimately decide the case. You won't have to render a "guilty" or "not guilty" verdict; you will simply need to determine if the data answers the how-does-it-work question to your satisfaction. Do the answers make sense to you in the light of your background and experience?

Sometimes, you may be tempted to find the defendant "not guilty" (or the research study plausible) without hearing all of the evidence. Qualitative studies that are conducted collaboratively by practitioners and academics are of inestimable value when used in conjunction with corroborating experimental evidence. Unfortunately, it is the one-shot case studies done by charismatic and highly persuasive practitioners that are more frequently advanced as a basis for revamping and overhauling classrooms and even entire schools. Qualitative research is somewhat like that proverbial "little girl with the curl in the middle of her forehead—when [the research] is good, [it] is very, very good, but when [it] is bad, [it] is horrid" (Bruce, 1969, p. 32). In the absence of solid experimental evidence, be wary of academics, gurus, consultants, and publishers whose glowing vignettes and rich descriptions of teaching techniques and methodologies promise results for your classroom and school. Be wary of anecdotalism—"findings . . . based on a subjectively selected, and probably biased, 'sample' of cases that happen to fit the analytic argument" (ten Have, 1998, p. 8).

Qualitative research can be rendered nearly worthless if researchers fail to disclose their biases, predispositions, and even connections to the subject of the study. Intellectually honest researchers are constantly on the lookout for data that supports alternate conclusions and are willing to present negative examples that do not support their findings. Don't pronounce your verdict based only on the persuasive manner of the researchers just yet. Determine how long they spent collecting the data. If the data was collected in just a few sessions and over a short period of time, the evidence is suspect, and the sweeping conclusions are merely the products of the researchers' wishful thinking and imagination. The quality in qualitative research comes from the depth and extent of its observations. It takes time to become adjusted to a setting and to gain the trust and respect of the informants. It is not uncommon for qualitative researchers to spend several years gathering data.

> Qualitative research can be rendered nearly worthless if researchers fail to disclose their biases, predispositions, and connections to the subject of the study.

In addition, a good qualitative research study should detail the role the researcher played in the research setting (e.g., participant, silent and uninvolved observer, or a combination of both), which doors were opened and closed as a result of the role chosen, and the impact that the role had on the data. Because a qualitative study has no "built-in" controls, such as those found in experiments, the burden of proof falls on the researcher to constantly present reasons and evidence why the reader should find the causal explanations believable. Qualitative researchers are obligated to share personal biases that might have affected either data collection or interpretation, suggest alternative hypotheses for consideration by the reader, and leave no "data" stone unturned to increase the plausibility of their causal explanations.

Qualitative researchers should provide precise and specific details that offer the reader a front-row seat for all of the action. The methods of the study should be described in enough detail so that the reader can imagine exactly how they occurred or even replicate them if desired. Validity can only be conferred on a qualitative study if the researcher specifies methods, how the informants were selected, how various populations or influential groups were sampled, and what kinds of analytic techniques were used.

> Qualitative researchers should provide precise and specific details that offer the reader a front-row seat for all of the action.

Our bottom line with regard to evaluating qualitative research is similar to Silverman's (2001): "If there is a 'gold standard' for qualitative research, it should only be the standard for any good research, qualitative or quantitative, social or natural science—and that requires affirmative answers to two questions. Have the researchers demonstrated successfully why we should believe them? And does the research problem tackled have theoretical and/or practical significance?" (p. 189).

Our vision of education research is one that cares deeply about the causal issue, and we would strongly discourage practitioners from the adoption and full-scale implementation of any methodology or program that is based solely on qualitative data. Focusing on the how-does-it-work question in advance of knowing that something actually does work is usually a poor use of everyone's time. Principals and teachers will recover from an error in judgment. The students may not.

CASE STUDY   How Does Class Size Reduction Work?

The Tennessee STAR experiment and the SAGE quasi-experiment showed that class size reduction "works" in raising student achievement. Many of the calls for class size reduction have focused exclusively on these findings. Nonetheless, these positive effects do not occur through some mystical alchemy. Rather, they occur because the size of the classroom has affected some important feature of the instructional environment. That is, teachers and students behave differently, on average, in smaller classes, which presumably leads to beneficial outcomes for student achievement. Despite the power of an experimental design, it is usually not well-suited to understanding what lies within the "black-box" of the effect—to unde standing how class size reduction works.

In the SAGE quasi-experiment (see Chapter 4), the researchers also included a qualitative research component (Zahorik, Molnar, Ehrle, & Halbach, 2000). They identified a small sample of 13 teachers, all teaching in a smaller class (9 were identified as "high-achieving" and 4 as "low-achieving"). The qualitative data, including classroom observations and interviews, were collected over a 6-month period. Each teacher in the sample was observed at least four times in their classroom, twice during reading lessons and twice during mathematics. The observers of classes took field notes that were used to prepare narrative descriptions of classroom events. The researchers also conducted three interviews with each teacher, mainly focusing on the instructional philosophy and self-perceptions of their instruction. These were tape-recorded and transcribed.

The researchers found, on average, that teachers in high-achieving classrooms shared a number of traits. First, they placed emphasis on basic skills and concepts that are illustrated with "explicit teaching, such as explaining, modeling, checking, and evaluating" (Zahorik et al., 2000, p. 67). Second, they had structured and organized classrooms. Third, they used individualized student instruction that was oriented toward teaching basic-skills, using teacher instruction.

In contrast, the teachers in lower-achieving classrooms had several other traits in common. First, they placed greater emphasis on the personal development of students, using less teacher-centered instruction and more experiential learning. Second, they had more tolerant styles of classroom management. Third, they used individualized instruction, but it was "less teacher-directed and basic-oriented" (Zahorik et al., 2000, p. 67).

Overall, they found that small classrooms did not uniformly lead to "better" instruction that was uniformly similar among teachers. Rather, the teachers of smaller classes were more likely to affect student achievement if they "employed particular kinds of instruction and management" (Zahorik et al., 2000, p. 72). In this sense, a small class can be viewed as a necessary but not sufficient condition for improving achievement; class size reduction "works," but only to the extent that it leads to improved instruction. This is a valuable lesson for a decision maker who is contemplating a class size reduction plan, particularly if there are also decisions to be made about teacher hiring and staff development.

CASE STUDY   How Does Phonics Instruction Work?

What do educators do when their students experience frustration in the typical phonics program? Many educators pronounce phonics a failure. Some, however, become qualitative researchers, investigating how the curriculum, instructional methodology, and characteristics of the learner interact to produce success or frustration in reading. At the private Benchmark School in Philadelphia, Director Irene Gaskins and her staff work with bright but underachieving learning disabled readers in Grades K-8 (Gaskins, 1998). These educators knew that a standard form of phonics instruction worked for many of their students, but they were puzzled by a hard-to-reach group of beginning readers for whom a different approach was needed if they were to learn to decode with ease. In the course of exploring the how-does-phonics-work question, they developed an alternative word identification program to meet the needs of these students.

Gaskins and her first grade teachers began with a thorough review of the existing research on beginning reading and discovered an approach in the literature that was not available in commercially prepared phonics programs—the analogy approach, also called analytic phonics. Three qualitative studies describe the development, implementation, evaluation, and fine-tuning of the Word Detectives Program (Gaskins et al., 1988; Gaskins, Ehri, Cress, O'Hara, & Donnelly, 1997a; Gaskins, Ehri, Cress, O'Hara, & Donnelly, 1997b). When read in concert, the studies cover nearly a 10-year span and answer the question, "If poor readers are made more aware of how their language works and taught to use a systematic decoding strategy, will they exhibit decoding strategies that are more successful than those they used previously?" (Gaskins et al., 1988, p. 37).

The studies not only provided information regarding how reading-disabled children fail to learn but also how the Word Detectives program was fine-tuned, day-by-day and year-by-year. For example, the reading supervisor observed daily in the first-grade classroom, and the principal either observed or watched videotapes of instruction. Lessons were tape-recorded to make sure that no details of instructional dialogues were omitted, and the principal and supervisor kept notes on their observations. The careful observations yielded some important information common to all of the severely disabled readers: "They were unable to segment spoken words into their smallest sounds. They could, however, divide words into onset (the initial consonant sound or sounds) and rime (the vowel and what follows)" (Gaskins et al., 1997b, p. 313).

The teachers-administrator researcher team continued to test their observations and thinking against current research and theory. A major insight emerged when the group discovered "the need to provide students with a model of how to analyze and talk about the words they were learning, as well as to provide teacher-mediated opportunities for them to stretch out and hear sounds in words and to talk about letter-sound matches" (Gaskins et al., 1997b, p. 318).

Although experiments are well-suited to providing causal descriptions, they are less suited to explaining how and why something works, or fails to work. Qualitative studies can help address this shortcoming, and make the findings more relevant to the needs of practitioners. As Gaskins et al. (1997a) point out, "We have discovered that, when students understand the rationale for processes such as fully analyzing words, or generating and applying knowledge about how our language works, they are more motivated to used the strategies when they are learning" (p. 175).

CASE STUDY   How Do Private-School Vouchers Work?

Chapters 3 and 4 described a few of the experimental and non-experimental studies that compared student achievement in private and public schools. Although an essential component of decisions about the merits of private-school vouchers, these studies can't tell us everything. For one, they are ill suited to explaining how private schools may or may not produce their beneficial effects. The answers to this question could have important implications for policy. Consider that most private-school students currently attend a Catholic private school. If these schools are observed to produce positive effects for students, one might ask whether it is because of a unique religious orientation or because they operate in the private sector. The answer might help us determine whether their effects would be duplicated by secular private schools, or whether "Catholic-ness" is an essential element of their success.[1]

In the early 1980s, Bryk, Lee, and Holland (1993) undertook an extensive qualitative study of seven Catholic high schools in order to explore the determinants of Catholic school success. They organized their qualitative fieldwork in two waves (fall 1982 and spring 1983). In each wave, a two-person team conducted fieldwork in each school for 10-12 days. The first wave, largely exploratory in nature, included interviews with staff, students, and parents; observations of the school and classrooms; and collection of documentation on the school. These data were used to elaborate 18 specific propositions about how Catholic schools worked. The second wave of fieldwork was designed to strengthen or refute these initial propositions. It included newly designed protocols for conducting interviews and observations. Overall,

they "interviewed approximately 280 participants, observed over 160 classes, and collected almost 2,000 questionnaires from students, teachers, and parents" (Bryk et al., 1993, p. 60).[2]

Bryk et al.'s (1993) qualitative data suggest a rich and complex portrait of Catholic schools, in which four broad factors account for their success. First, Catholic schools provide a common academic curriculum for all students, that is "predicated on a proactive view among faculty and administrators about what all students can and should learn" (p. 297). There is less room for picking and choosing among elective offerings, and more focus on ensuring that all students leave school with a common core of knowledge. Second, the organization of Catholic schools is "embedded within a larger communal organization" (p. 298). Schools function as communities in which students and teachers are encouraged to share experiences with one another. Teachers serve as more than subject-matter specialists, also involving themselves personally in their students' lives.

Third, Catholic schools operate with a decentralized governance structure. Schools have autonomy at the local level, in which "considerable deference is accorded to the principal" (Bryk et al., 1993, p. 299). Fourth, Catholic schools are organized around an "inspirational ideology" that "shapes the action of its members" by emphasizing values like caring and social justice (p. 303).

Taken together, the fieldwork suggests that the results of Catholic schools may not necessarily be duplicated by a diverse array of secular private schools. Although decentralized governance is important to their success, it also appears that the unique role of their "Catholic-ness" cannot be underestimated.

CASE STUDY   How Does Whole-School Reform Work?

In previous chapters we reviewed three experimental and quasi-experimental efforts to determine whether Comer's School Development Program "worked" in Maryland, Chicago, and Detroit. In each case, the researchers did not merely estimate the effects of the program on student outcomes. They also collected a variety of qualitative data in order to gain a deeper understanding of how the program worked or failed to work.

In the Maryland study, Cook et al. (1999) conducted interviews with the coordinator and facilitators of the School Development Project in Prince George's County. On one occasion, they also conducted telephone interviews with principals at the beginning and end of the evaluation and similar interviews with a sample of parents. The Chicago experiment (Cook et al., 2000) included an even more extensive ethnographic component by an outside team of evaluators. They conducted frequent visits to each study school in the first 4 years of the program, usually about twice a week.

The quasi-experimental evaluation in Detroit also collected an extensive amount of qualitative data (Millsap et al., 2000). The evaluation team conducted site visits to each Comer school twice a year, over the course of the study. During each school visit, the team conducted individual interviews with a range of participants in the Comer program, including principals and chairs of the various schoolwide planning teams (e.g., the School Improvement Team). Beyond interviews, the evaluators conducted observations of staff meetings in each school. Last, they interviewed and observed members of the district-level staff involved in the program.

The qualitative evidence of the Detroit researchers suggested that some schools were implementing the Comer program much more faithfully than others. (The qualitative observations were also borne out by quantitative measures of program implementation, collected from written surveys administered to staff members.) The schools that were implementing the program shared a number of characteristics. Most obviously, they had implemented the team structures that are mandated by the Comer model (e.g., the School Improvement Team and the Student Support Team). Furthermore, "there is a sense of integration across teams and a coherence in planning, staff, development, and self assessment that permeates the process" (Millsap et al., 2000, pp. 2-3). This is present when the various stakeholders in the school, including staff and parents, recognize and respond to the vital roles of teams. Based on these and other qualitative findings, the evaluators described a composite of the "good-implementers" in a short vignette, as well as a composite of the "bad-implementers." These results provide a vivid illustration of the implementation successes and difficulties that were encountered in each school.

Ultimately, the Detroit evaluation suggested that there was no program effect overall, except perhaps among "good-implementers" (see the case study in Chapter 4). This subtle finding would have been difficult, if not impossible, to uncover without the more detailed description of the Comer schools provided in the qualitative studies. Moreover, it would have made the experimental results much less useful to other districts and schools that are contemplating the Comer model. As it stands, the detailed evaluation results facilitate an understanding of how the program appeared to work (or not work) in some areas. This, in turn, provides some important clues about whether the model will work in a diverse array of other contexts (a topic more fully explored in the next chapter).

FURTHER READING

If you are intrigued by the world of qualitative research and want to explore its vast and confusing terrain on your own, we recommend four volumes. For an overview that is not only comprehensive and readable but highly entertaining, see Patton (2002). If you are thinking about doing your own qualitative research, Silverman (2001) provides clear and understandable guidelines for analyzing your interviews, observations, and documents. King et al. (1994) offer a coherent and very helpful discussion regarding how to design qualitative research that qualifies as "scientific." Last, if you want to speak the language of qualitative research, Schwandt's (2001) dictionary provides nearly 300 pages of definitions.

NOTES

1. As Evans and Schwab (1995, p. 972) observe, "it is not clear that they succeed because of the importance of religious or the discipline of [private] competition."

2. In addition to their qualitative fieldwork, the authors conducted extensive analyses of quantitative data on student achievement in public and private schools, drawn from the HSB database.

6

The Cost
Question

Is It Worthwhile?

To many of you, cost analysis probably sounds as appealing as a
root canal. And that can lead to some very predictable consequences. Most education practitioners and even researchers think
that costs are something for somebody else to consider—the business
manager, an outside consultant, or perhaps a faceless bureaucrat in
the state department of education. In contrast, this chapter will
attempt to convince you that precisely the opposite is true—that a
thoughtful consideration of costs is *essential* to making good,
research-based decisions in districts and schools.

The logic of cost analysis is closer to your heart than it might
appear. Think for a moment about how most of us buy a car. Very few
educators, save for those who have won the lottery, rush out to buy the
first piece of shiny metal that catches their attention. Educated consumers engage in a bit of research, consult automotive authorities for
opinions on the style and performance of various models, kick some
tires, and go for a few test drives. We love the gleaming Porsches and
Jaguars, but we wouldn't think of making a decision until we considered the cost implications of our decision. How much does each model
cost up front? Will gas cost an arm and a leg? Will repairs break the
bank? In short, we would ask two important questions: (a) Can we
afford the cost of a particular model? and (b) Is there another car that
delivers the same performance (and even some style) at a more reasonable cost, giving us more bang for our buck? Later, we will call
these the cost-feasibility and cost-effectiveness questions, respectively.

And yet, the basic logic of cost analysis is often estranged from
important education decisions. Entire states have run willy-nilly towards

class size reduction without giving adequate consideration to how much it would cost, and whether the money could be spent more profitably on another intervention. Districts are prone to lurch madly from one faddish reform to another—changing the school day, changing the school year, or even changing the type of school—often without enough information about how much these reforms will cost (much less their effects on student outcomes). School and classroom leaders, even when they don't control a large budget, must decide how to allocate their scarce time—which can have costly implications for student learning.

The purpose of this chapter is not to turn you into an accountant. It does aim to convince you that education research—or researchers—that ignore the cost implications of their recommendations can produce unfortunate consequences that extend far beyond the district's business office. We hope to give you some conceptual tools for thinking more carefully about the cost implications of education research—about whether something is "worthwhile." To begin answering the question posed in the title of this chapter, however, it is first necessary for us to obtain broader agreement on what exactly we mean by "cost."

> Education research—or researchers—that ignore the cost implications of their recommendations can produce unfortunate consequences that extend far beyond the district's business office.

THE CONCEPT OF COSTS

In the most rudimentary sense, the cost of something is what we pay for it. A textbook costs $40, a notebook costs $5, and so on. That is the common-sense definition of costs, the one used by accountants who monitor cash flow and construct balance sheets. It also has a great deal of relevance to how this chapter approaches the notion of costs. But our definition is broader still, extending beyond the simple equating of cost with the price of goods or services.

When we implement a program, policy, or intervention in schools, it uses resources. These resources include the time and energy of personnel like teachers, as well as more tangible resources such as facilities, equipment, and instructional materials. Using those resources for a particular end—such as a new program—entails a sacrifice. We are sacrificing what we might have gained from using those resources for another useful purpose.

In our definition, the cost of an intervention is the value of those sacrifices. More specifically, it is the value of all the resources that were used, had they been assigned to their most valuable alternative use. Economists refer to this as the opportunity cost of an intervention. A slightly more poetic turn of phrase might be the "cost of opportunities lost." Both terms are intended to capture the idea that costs should measure the value of opportunities that have been forgone. By using resources in one way, we are giving up our ability to use them in another, so a cost is incurred.[1]

In some respects, that squares nicely with our initial definition of costs. If we spend $40 on a textbook, then we are forgoing similarly valued opportunities that might have been obtained with the same money. The market price of textbooks provides a good measure of its opportunity cost. But there are opportunity costs even when a resource isn't purchased in a store. We're all familiar with the maxim that "time is money." Think of the time that you may have spent in college classrooms. By spending time in classrooms, you weren't spending that time in other valuable pursuits—you were forgoing the opportunity to work, for example. For some of us, that time did not represent a substantial opportunity cost, nothing more than the value of forgone earnings from a job at McDonald's. For a star basketball player, however, the opportunity cost of spending a senior year in college might be substantially higher, upwards of a million dollars! It provides a compelling reason why so many college players are tempted to leave (or actually do) before graduation: the opportunity costs are simply not compensated by the economic benefits of a college diploma.

The opportunity costs of time do not appear in any budget, but they are no less relevant to decisions made by individuals. And so it is with education. Even when opportunity costs appear difficult, even impossible, to compute in monetary terms, the concept still provides a useful framework for organizing our decision making about education. To illustrate this point, let's consider a case where resources are simply reallocated within a school, rather than purchased. Suppose that a principal uses existing Title I funds, currently employed in a traditional remediation program, for a new reading program (in fact, this is exactly what the developer of the Success for All program, Robert Slavin, has advocated that schools do).[2] In this example, you can assume that no new resources are expended; the existing ones are simply moved to a new use. The program is "cost-free," right?

> The opportunity costs of time do not appear in any budget, but they are no less relevant to decisions made by individuals.

Superficially, that is the case. However, there may be opportunity costs to the decision. You need to ask the question, What is sacrificed by the reallocation? Is something given up? If the resources were *entirely* ineffective in their previous use, then the opportunity cost is effectively zero. But what if mathematics instruction is reduced in the wake of the shift, and mathematics achievement declines? That decline is certainly difficult to put in money terms. But it does represent a real opportunity cost to schools.[3]

THE INGREDIENTS METHOD OF COST ANALYSIS

"That is all well and good," you may be saying of the previous section. "But surely, you don't expect *me* to actually *do* a cost analysis. I was a liberal arts major."

"But surely, you don't expect me to actually do a cost analysis."

It is no wonder that cost analysis is perceived as mystifyingly complex, the exclusive domain of the number crunchers. In fact, doing a cost analysis is less complex and more intuitive than it might appear.

A simple approach to doing so that matches nicely with our common sense is called the *ingredients method* (Levin, 1975; Levin & McEwan, 2001). It relies on the straightforward concept that every intervention uses up "ingredients" that have a cost—an opportunity cost to be more exact. If we can systematically identify those ingredients and attach a cost value to each of them, then we can identify the overall cost of the intervention. This information is quite useful when making decisions about the cost-feasibility and cost-effectiveness of interventions. A later section will describe these two concepts in greater detail. First, however, we will discuss the ingredients approach.

Identifying Ingredients

The ingredients method involves two general steps. First, the researcher identifies all of the ingredients that comprise an intervention, program, or policy. These ingredients will naturally vary with the type of intervention that is being contemplated, but they usually fall into one of the following categories: (a) personnel, (b) facilities, (c) equipment and materials, and (d) client-provided ingredients. A final "miscellaneous" category can encompass any remaining ingredients.

Personnel ingredients include any individuals who play a role in delivering the intervention, even if they are seemingly indirect or insubstantial. This obviously includes teachers, who are on the front lines of delivering instructional services. But it almost always includes other personnel—instructional aides, administrative support, janitorial services, and so on. It is important to specify in detail the exact roles, qualifications, and time commitments of each individual, for this information will be necessary to place a value on the ingredient. With respect to time commitments, for example, it is quite possible that teachers or aides will spend only a portion of their workdays on an intervention, with the rest devoted to other duties.

A frequent issue that arises in the analysis of school costs is the issue of volunteers. Many interventions rely to some extent on volunteers who receive only minimal reimbursement for their time, if any. This seems to be an example of a "cost-free" ingredient. In reality, however, there *is* a cost to this ingredient, but its burden is simply shifted away from the school. The volunteer's time has an opportunity cost. This is particularly evident, for example, when a corporation volunteers the services of its employee in a local school. The corporation is sacrificing a certain amount of gain. But it is even true of individuals who sacrifice their leisure time to work in a school.

It is important to cast the net as widely as possible when identifying the ingredients—personnel and otherwise—that comprise an intervention, even if they don't seem to be directly assumed by the school. There are some practical reasons for this. One is that it facilitates an analysis of how the cost burden is distributed across different groups, ranging from parents to the local community. We return to this point in a later section. A related reason is that it allows consumers of cost research to make informed decisions about whether a cost analysis is germane to their own circumstances. Suppose you are a principal who is deciding to implement a tutoring program. In previous incarnations, the program has relied heavily on volunteers, but a cost analysis that you read treated the volunteers as "free." However, your district is located in a lower-income area where adults have less time to give to school activities. As a result, you must hire tutors, and the cost burden is shifted to the school. In this case, a cost analysis that completely ignores volunteers provides a very poor indicator of the costs of implementing the intervention in your circumstances.

Beyond personnel, the researcher must identify the facilities used in the intervention, such as classroom and office space. As with personnel, the exact specifications must be described. If only a portion is used for the intervention, this must be established. The same goes for equipment and materials, including furnishings, instructional equipment, computers, office supplies, and so on. In both cases, it is important to identify all the ingredients that comprise an intervention—even if they are donated.

Client-provided inputs provide another special case, like volunteers, that often escapes the attention of the cost analyst. Public schools are nominally "free" but parents are sometimes formally or informally obligated to provide inputs such as classroom volunteerism, transportation, uniforms, instructional supplies, and so on. If these form an integral part of the contemplated intervention, then they should be identified.

When identifying ingredients, it is important to limit one's attention to the *additional* ingredients that are required to implement a new intervention. Perhaps only a percentage of a teacher's time is spent on implementation, for example, or only a portion of a new computer's availability will be reserved for the intervention. In these cases, it would be misleading to attribute the full cost of the ingredient to the intervention. This can occasionally be quite challenging, as in cases where interventions are not simply "add-ons" that are grafted onto existing school operations. For example, whole-school reforms often dramatically shift the allocation of existing ingredients, as well as add new ingredients to the mix (Levin, 2002). This instance is addressed further in the case studies.

Valuing Ingredients

The next step in an ingredients-based cost analysis is to place a value on each ingredient. In the case of personnel, this includes the salary and fringe benefits that are due to each employee (or a fraction thereof, if only a portion of time is devoted to the intervention). The valuation of some personnel ingredients, particularly volunteers, is trickier. One rule of thumb is to imagine what type of employee would be needed to provide services comparable to those of the volunteer. The prevailing salary of that employee can be used as a rough gauge of the opportunity cost of the volunteer's time.

> The valuation of some personnel ingredients, particularly volunteers, is tricky.

The valuing of facilities and equipment ingredients often requires a little more thought. The reason is apparent to anyone who has examined the annual budget of a school district. In some years, an entire building might be purchased, or a large investment made in durable equipment, such as computers. Yet one's goal is often to estimate the annual cost of the intervention, because we usually wish to compare costs with an effect derived from a year-long experiment. It hardly makes sense in this case to include a $5 million building purchase in an "annual" cost. In fact, the building will be around for many more years, still providing its services to students. Only a portion of the building is "used up" in a given year, a process of wear and tear referred to as depreciation. Economists and accountants attempt to quantify the annual cost of a building (or computer or other durable ingredient) by making assumptions about how long the ingredient will last.[4] One alternative way of deriving the annual value of facilities is to consider the annual rental value of a building. A real estate agent can often provide a very accurate estimate of the local cost of renting facilities of a specified quality.

The valuing of client inputs often runs into the same challenges as valuing volunteers. For one, there is no space in a school or district budget for such inputs. They are considered to be "free" in a sense, and are typically ignored. Nonetheless, they should be included if they are an integral part of the intervention. As with other inputs, it is helpful to use a little creativity. The value of a student uniform (assumed by the parents) might be directly obtained from parent interviews or by calling a store. The value of parent-supplied instructional materials might be obtained through similar means. The methods of valuing cost ingredients are described in more detail in Levin and McEwan (2002, Chap. 4).

Analyzing the Distribution of Costs

By summing the values of all the ingredients, the researcher can obtain the total cost of implementing an intervention. It is often helpful to divide this by the number of students who are served, in order to arrive at the per-student cost. Both figures provide a great deal of information; exactly how this information can be applied to decision making is addressed in a later section.

> By summing the values of all the ingredients, the researcher can obtain the total cost of implementing an intervention.

However, there is more involved in analyzing costs. At several points we have alluded to the importance of considering how costs are distributed across different constituencies or stakeholders. Naturally, these constituencies vary with the context of the intervention that is being analyzed, but they can typically be grouped into four areas: (a) the school or district; (b) other government agencies, such as a branch of local or state government; (c) private organizations, such as a foundation or community group; and (d) parents and students.

The cost of a particular intervention is rarely borne exclusively by one group. A simple example will suffice to illustrate this point. Imagine that an after-school science program is provided for students (for a similar example with detailed data on costs, see Levin & McEwan, 2002, pp. 84-87). The ingredients include the time of teachers and local university professors, lab facilities, various materials to support instruction, and parent volunteers. A careful application of the ingredients method yields a total cost for implementing the program. These costs are borne by several parties: the local school that pays for teachers, labs, and materials; the local university that funds professors; and parents. In addition, the state government provides a cash grant to the school district, shifting part of the burden to the state's taxpayers.

Understanding the distribution of costs in interventions like the previous one is important for at least two reasons. First, the decision about whether an intervention is "worthwhile" may vary depending on the perspective. What is "worthwhile" from the perspective of one group may be less so from the perspective of another. Of course, for any particular constituency to make reasoned assessments about this, it has to have appropriate information on how the cost burden will be spread around.

Second, a knowledge of how costs are distributed can aid in understanding the support, or lack thereof, that different groups may evince for an intervention. More than one reform has run aground because it placed—perhaps unwittingly—an excessive burden of costs on a particular group.

Aren't Budgets Good Enough?

At this point, you may be wondering whether it is really necessary to jump through all these hoops. Isn't it possible to simply scan a state or district budget and obtain all the relevant information about costs? The answer is that although budgets are a helpful, even essential part of conducting a cost analysis, they do not provide all the relevant information (Levin & McEwan, 2001, pp. 45-46). Quite often, the analysis requires a bit more legwork on the part of researchers.

> You may be wondering whether it is really necessary to jump through all these hoops.

First and most obviously, the official budget does not contain any cost ingredients that were not paid for by the district (or another unit whose budget is being examined). For example, any resources that were donated or volunteered are not included. Second, many resources that are paid for by other levels of government or private organizations do not appear in a particular budget, but still comprise a portion of the overall cost. Third, it is often difficult to discern the cost of individual ingredients because they are lumped into broad "line-items" in the budgets. Say that you want to estimate the additional cost incurred by a reading program. The reading program required several new teachers aides to be hired, but the budget did not distinguish between the cost of "new" aides and existing aides. It is even more complicated when only a percentage of each aide's time is spent on the program. Similar examples could be cited for other common ingredients. The best solution is to construct a cost analysis "from the ground up" using the ingredients approach. It is the best means of ensuring that some ingredients are not ignored, or that costs are over-stated by erroneously including ingredients that were used for other purposes.

A Cost Analysis Caveat

Thus far, we have described the ingredients method in very general terms. There are, of course, many additional levels of complication (just as in the conduct of a randomized experiment or a qualitative study). These tools and techniques are described further in Levin and McEwan (2001). But even without delving into these details, it is easy to appreciate the fundamental logic of identifying and valuing the ingredients that go into a new policy, program, or intervention. You wouldn't repair your car without getting an estimate for parts and labor—and you shouldn't reform your school without conducting a similar analysis.

Despite the relevance of studying costs, education researchers rarely broach the topic. Indeed, educational cost analysis is a rare breed in the pages of education journals and other scholarly publications, especially when compared to the copious number of correlational studies.[5] This is true even for high-profile issues, such as class size reduction, private-school vouchers, phonics instruction, and whole-school reform (a shortcoming that is further noted in the case studies of this chapter). To put it charitably, this seems unwarranted when millions of dollars are being allocated to new initiatives like these every year.

> Despite the relevance of studying costs, education researchers rarely broach the topic.

If you do happen to stumble on a cost study, be on the look-out for common errors like omitting a key category of cost ingredients, or failing to consider how the cost burden is distributed across groups (McEwan, P. J., 2002). In the worst of cases, terms like "low-cost," "cost-effective," "cost-efficient," and others are used in a purely rhetorical fashion, with no data whatsoever. Clune (2002) reviewed 541 studies listed in the ERIC database of education research that used the term "cost-effectiveness." He found that 83% used the term as rhetoric or presented almost no research-based data. This isn't encouraging for the poor practitioner looking for some minimal guidance on costs.

Neither is it realistic to expect that practitioners conduct their own cost analysis. Of course, we do not believe that they are incapable of doing so. Quite the contrary, a simple version of an ingredients-based cost analysis can be conducted by a district or school team, with only a bit more training and guidance. They are often well poised to conduct these studies because they are intimately familiar with how ingredients are combined to deliver an intervention. Rather, the most pressing constraint is likely to be time. Being a reasoned consumer of research is difficult enough to schedule, without venturing into the production of new research.

Instead, we encourage the reader to at least incorporate cost considerations into their "way of thinking" about making research-based decisions. A decision that is based on the best experimental and qualitative evidence is good. A decision that further relies upon the best available cost data and the reasoned cost judgments of experienced administrators and teachers is even better. To better illustrate this point, however, we need to further investigate and describe the two questions that educational cost analysis is best suited to answer.

Two Important Cost Questions

Cost analysis is not just an exercise in bureaucratic number crunching. It can and should be used to improve research-based decisions. This chapter posed a very broad question that good information on costs can help address: Is it worthwhile? We use this broad question to encompass two more specific ones: (a) Is it cost-feasible? and (b) Is it cost-effective?

Is It Cost-Feasible?

The question of cost-feasibility is really one of affordability: Is a specified intervention feasible or affordable, given the resources available to a state, district, or school? It sounds like a simple enough question, and many of you probably already pose it before making a decision. Usually, however, it is framed as a budgetary issue. Will the additional money expenditures on an intervention fit within our budget?

This chapter has asked you to broaden your perspective to include the concept of opportunity cost. In doing so, you may decide that a particular intervention is less cost-feasible than it first appears. Consider the example of a new program that is designed to provide extra homework assistance to low-achieving students after school. It relies in equal part on the assistance of instructional aides and existing teachers to spend additional time in their classrooms after school, helping students. The instructional aides will be hired with funds from the district budget. However, the contribution of teachers is apparently "free" because their existing salaries and fringe benefits are already paid within the existing budget.

The program is clearly feasible in a budgetary sense. Yet, one must further inquire about the opportunity costs of the teachers' time. Is it also cost-feasible in that sense? In fact, a further inquiry suggests that teachers are likely to evince one of three responses to the program: (a) spend less time planning lessons after school; (b) assign less homework to students, thus reducing the time spent grading after school; or (c) work later hours and grumble behind the principal's back about the excessive workload. In each case, there may be an opportunity cost to the program. Something is sacrificed, whether it is the benefits produced by good lesson plans, homework, or a motivated staff.

None of these is easy to express in monetary terms, thus escaping our attention as "costs" in the traditional sense of the word. However, they represent clear opportunity costs to implementing the program. A principal may decide that they diminish the cost-feasibility of a program.

Is It Cost-Effective?

The question of cost-effectiveness is nearer to your heart than you might think. When you visit an electronics store, you may happen upon two brands of television. Both produce a crisp picture on a 25-inch screen; both are highly rated by independent consumer research organizations. And yet, one brand is deeply discounted, costing 20% less than the other brand. Which do you purchase? In this context, the answer is obvious. The discounted television is the more cost-effective of the two: It provides the same amount and quality of television viewing at a lower cost. The cost-effectiveness decision could also be turned on its head. There might be two televisions that cost exactly the same amount, yet one receives exceptional ratings and the other is roundly criticized. Again, the decision is obvious. The more cost-effective television provides a higher level of effectiveness for the same cost.

> The question of cost-effectiveness is nearer to your heart than you might think.

The same logic can be applied to educational decisions. Every school or district has made a decision to adopt a new reading series, as one example. There are innumerable publishers touting the effectiveness of their wares—presumably their ability to improve reading achievement. Even if districts did not conduct a formal analysis of cost-effectiveness, they may have loosely employed a cost-effectiveness criterion in their decision making. If both textbook series seem to be equally effective, then the district (hopefully) opted for the less costly one. Or if both series cost about the same, the district (hopefully) opted for the more effective of the two. In short, the district sought to choose the most cost-effective series—the one that provided the most reading "bang" for the district's "bucks."

This is the general logic that governs a decision about cost-effectiveness. To fully implement a cost-effectiveness analysis, however, one must possess more than a hunch about whether an intervention is more effective or less costly than another. We first require good data about whether two or more interventions "work." More specifically, we must have an estimate of how effective each intervention is in fulfilling its stated objectives. This can only be obtained through experimental, quasi-experimental, or non-experimental studies of the sort described in Chapters 3 and 4. Furthermore, we require some knowledge of the additional costs of each intervention, best obtained by applying the ingredients method. In the previous example, there are some fairly obvious ingredients, not least of which is the textbooks. However, there may be other costs as well, such as the training workshops that teachers receive and the added time that teachers spend in preparing new lessons and classroom assessments.

> To fully implement a cost-effectiveness analysis, however, one must possess more than a hunch about whether an intervention is more effective or less costly than another.

Once the effects and costs are obtained, the two textbook series can be compared to assess which provides a given amount of achievement at the least cost (or the most achievement for a given cost). Three important points about cost-effectiveness analysis need be emphasized. First, a decision about cost-effectiveness is fundamentally *comparative*. That is, we can ascertain whether a particular intervention is more cost-effective than another. But we cannot state that a single intervention, viewed in isolation, is uniquely "cost-effective" (nevertheless, this is an assertion that we have all heard many times). Suppose that we discover that an intervention produces three additional percentile points of achievement, on average, for an additional cost of $200 per student. Is it "cost-effective"? There is nothing, short of an arbitrary standard, that can help in answering that question. We can assert, however, that the intervention is *relatively* more cost-effective than another—if, for example, another intervention only succeeds in producing a 1-percentile gain, on average, for the same cost of $200 per student.

> We cannot state that a single intervention, viewed in isolation, is uniquely "cost-effective" (nevertheless, this is an assertion that we have all heard many times).

Second, and related to the first point, is that cost-effectiveness analysis can only be used to compare interventions with similar objectives and outcome measures. If one intervention is designed to improve students' self-esteem, and another focuses on mathematics achievement, then it hardly makes sense to state that one is more cost-effective than another. By the same token, you wouldn't assert that it is more cost-effective to buy a car than a tractor-trailer. One is less costly than another, to be sure, but they were designed with very different objectives in mind. This can create some interesting problems for the decision maker, however. It is a common dilemma that districts and schools are obligated to choose among very different alternatives for whole-school reform. However, these reforms often have vastly different objectives; some are explicitly aimed at achievement in a single domain, and others attempt to improve a broad range of outcomes (Levin, 2002). We return to this example in the case studies.

Third, it is frequently the case that the term "cost-effective" is confused with "low-cost" or "cheap" in everyday language. To some extent, that may explain why an intervention that is described as cost-effective is viewed with some suspicion by educators, who interpret it as code-word for cost-cutting. Given how often the term is misused and abused, we can't help but feel that their suspicions are occasionally justified. Nonetheless, when the terms are used properly, they are referring to completely different concepts. It is quite possible that the less costly intervention is *not* the more cost-effective option. For example, an intervention that yields an effect of 2 percentile points on a standardized achievement test for a cost of \$100 (\$50 per point) is not more cost-effective than another that yields four points for a cost of \$120 (\$30 per point). The latter is able to produce each unit of effect at a lower cost.

Why Does This Matter?

It would be easy to lose hope at this point (and we have seen more than a few despairing practitioners do just that). After all, the education research profession tends to ignore or downplay the importance of costs in its research. The number of studies is not overwhelming. It is tempting to ask whether one can simply "get by" without delving into the messy business of costs. In fact, that is the usual approach. Many debates about education research revolve around the issue of whether a particular intervention is effective or whether it is more or less effective than another intervention du jour. These debates face their own challenges, especially in regards to the quality of their evidence on effectiveness (see Chapters 3 and 4). However, they often suppress the issue of costs.

> It is tempting to ask whether one can "get by" without delving into the messy business of costs.

We want to re-emphasize that the implications of this neglect extend beyond the district business office or budget. They could have significant implications for student outcomes. As Levin and McEwan (2001) observe, the size of the education "industry" in the United States is enormous—over $700 billion. What if new educational approaches were uncovered that produced roughly similar outcomes but at a savings of just 2%? That implies that $14 billion would be available to spend on other interventions to improve student learning. At the level of a school district, such an improvement would provide an additional $120 per student or about $3000 per classroom. These are not insignificant sums of money. And yet, these savings can only be achieved if we think carefully about the cost implications of our decisions. Is an intervention cost-feasible? Is it the most cost-effective option, or are there less costly means of accomplishing the same goals?

CASE STUDY   Is Class Size Reduction Worthwhile?

The debate on class size reduction is obsessed with effectiveness—that is, whether reducing class size "works" in raising student outcomes. And yet, there is good reason to suspect that reducing class sizes will not come cheaply. It requires more teachers and—if space is limited—new classrooms. It is essential to ask whether schools and districts can afford these costs. More importantly, it must be asked whether there is another means of obtaining the same effects more cheaply—a more cost-effective alternative for raising student outcomes.

There are a few attempts to measure the costs of class size reduction with an ingredients approach. In the wake of President Clinton's call for national class size reduction, a group of researchers at RAND estimated the cost-feasibility of such a plan (Brewer, Krop, Gill, & Reichardt, 1999). The ingredients necessary to reduce class size include new teachers, support staff, and supplies. They further include new buildings, facilities, and equipment to furnish those classrooms. The RAND researchers, lacking information on facilities, concentrated on estimating the ingredients costs of new personnel and supplies. They assumed each new teacher would receive a salary and benefits worth about $34,000 (1998 dollars). Overall, they estimated that reducing class size to 20 in Grades 1-3 would cost about $2.1 billion in 1998-1999, or $189 per student. Of course, similar costs would be incurred in subsequent years to maintain small classes.

These estimates are naturally subject to some caveats. The most important is that they exclude building and facilities costs. Also important is that they assume that an unlimited quantity of new teachers can be hired at the same salary. In fact, this seems to be a common assumption among policy makers who support class size reduction. But this is probably unrealistic given teacher shortages in many states. California's experience with class size reduction, described further in Chapter 7, suggests that many schools were unable to locate well-trained and certified teachers (Stecher & Bornstedt, 2002). In lieu of raising salaries to attract such teachers, schools simply hired less qualified teachers. Unless teacher quality was unimportant, it seems likely that lower class sizes created an unexpected opportunity cost—the cost of less-qualified teachers. Although difficult to value, this should factor into decisions about cost-feasibility.

The issue of cost-feasibility is also affected by how the burden of costs is distributed across different stakeholders. With so many states and the federal government providing assistance, it is rare that districts are asked to bear the full burden of costs (the state of California, as one example, provided a cash grant for each student in a small class). This may improve cost-feasibility from the district's perspective, although it could be viewed differently from other perspectives, such as the state's.

None of this has touched on the issue of whether class size reduction is really the most cost-effective means of raising student outcomes. In the late 1980s, Levin, Glass, and Meister (1987) compared the cost-effectiveness of four educational inventions and found that class size reduction was not the most consistently cost-effective intervention. More recent evidence, though scarce, is consistent with these early findings. Grissmer (2002) finds that investing in teacher resources is more cost-effective than class size reduction, at least among "average" students. It is a more cost-effective option for disadvantaged students. Harris (2002) finds that raising teacher salaries, thereby attracting more qualified teachers is a more cost-effective option.

CASE STUDY   Is Phonics Instruction Worthwhile?

Reading Recovery©, developed by New Zealand educator Marie Clay (1985) in the early 1970s, is one of the most well-known and popular remediation programs in the United States. Phonics instruction in this program is implicit, provided in the context of reading and writing connected text. Since 1984, over 850,000 students have been "served," although less than 500,000 actually completed the program sequence and met the criteria for "performing within average range of classmates" (Reading Recovery Council, 2002a).

Treatment consists of 20 weeks of a daily 30 minute one-to-one tutorial for first-graders identified at-risk for reading failure, delivered by a certified, experienced, and highly trained teacher. All certified RR teachers receive one year of graduate-level, on-the-job instruction, tutor eight students in one half of the day, and typically conduct small reading groups during the other half of the day.

If the program's Web site is to be believed, "Reading Recovery is a cost-effective prevention and early intervention for lowest-performing first graders" (Reading Recovery Council, 2002b). Is this an evidence-based assertion, or is it mere rhetoric of the kind that we criticized in this chapter? Even if we put aside the issue of effectiveness—of whether it "works"—it is clear that good evidence on the additional costs of implementing the program is needed.

In one study, Dyer (1992) argued that the cost-per-student is $2,063. It was arrived at by dividing an average teacher salary ($33,000 in 1990-1991) by 16, the number of students served by a full-time teacher in some applications of the program. By now, however, you should be asking some hard questions of an assertion like this. Did the cost study identify all of the relevant ingredients needed to implement the program? On the face of it, several important categories have been ignored: the fringe benefits, and not just salary, received by the teacher; the resources needed to provide intensive training to teachers; and the facilities and equipment needed to conduct the tutoring (Hiebert, 1994). Furthermore, one must place a value on these ingredients. If such a cost study has been judiciously conducted, then we are unaware of it. Yet it would be necessary for a district to establish whether Reading Recovery is cost-feasible.

Cost-effectiveness is another matter entirely. To make judgments about cost-effectiveness, we need to assess whether RR provides each unit of outcome at a lower cost than other models. It is, as we have emphasized, a *comparative* assessment that requires information on the costs and effects of other approaches to preventing reading failure. An outright assertion that RR is "cost-effective" begs an important question—cost effective relative to *what*?

There is, however, some suggestive evidence that the "standard" version of RR might be less cost-effective than other variations of the program. For example, Greaney, Tunmer, and Chapman (1997), have shown that when an explicit sound-spelling component is added to the standard Reading Recovery lesson, the time needed for students to complete the program successfully is reduced by 30%. Other studies have compared the effectiveness of the "standard" RR—with only one student per teacher—to a modified version with a larger number of students. There was no apparent difference between the outcomes produced in each study.[6] Both of these examples suggest instances in which the costs of RR can be reduced—either by reducing instruction time or raising group sizes—without sacrificing effectiveness. Each alternative, if borne out by the research, would be an improvement in cost-effectiveness.

CASE STUDY   Are Private-School Vouchers Worthwhile?

The debate over private-school vouchers hinges vitally on issues of costs. Indeed, proponents argue vociferously that providing vouchers to students will make the education system more efficient and cost-effective. Certainly a necessary condition for making this argument is some concrete evidence on costs. But contrary to expectations, the evidence is mostly rhetorical.

Hoxby (1998) and others have argued that private schools are about half as costly as public schools. These assertions are based on the observation that private-school tuition is generally much lower than the average per-pupil expenditure in public schools (Boaz & Barrett, 1996). But is this a fair comparison of costs? Many private schools, especially religious ones, obtain resources from sources other than tuition, including subsidies from local parishes and donated materials (Levin, 1998). A more reasonable approach would be to conscientiously apply the ingredients method to a sample of public and private schools, carefully identifying and valuing each resource that is used. The difference in per-pupil costs between the two schools would provide a more reasonable indicator of whether private schools are really less costly. Unfortunately, this approach has rarely been followed.[7]

And yet, this would still tell only part of the story. Implementing a voucher system on a large scale might bring about other costs. Levin and Driver (1997) conducted an ingredients-based analysis of the costs of a voucher system. They were hampered by the lack of an agreed-upon definition of what a voucher plan should resemble, for no such plan has yet to be implemented on a large scale in the United States (there are relatively smaller voucher systems in Milwaukee and Cleveland, and a nascent one in Florida).

Nonetheless, they identified and valued five plausible categories of cost ingredients. First, there are costs of accommodating students who currently attend private schools. These students have already opted out of public schooling, but they may be eligible to receive publicly funded vouchers. To some extent, this isn't a new cost. It merely shifts part of the cost-burden—currently assumed by individuals in private schools—back to the taxpayers. Second, there are costs of record-keeping and monitoring. To determine student eligibility and disburse funds, states or local governments would need to design and implement an information system. Third, a voucher plan may have effects on transportation costs. Currently, most families send their children to a local public school in their neighborhood. Under a voucher plan, families could maintain their residence but enroll their children in more distant private schools. Whether assumed by individuals or taxpayers, these represent additional costs to the system. Fourth, the voucher plan may require the collection and dissemination of additional data about student and school performance. These data collection efforts would not be without cost. Fifth, a voucher plan may require some mechanism for resolving disputes among the parents, schools, and the government (if, for example, parents feel their children are eligible for vouchers, but the government does not). These mechanisms for adjudication—already employed in other areas like special education—are costly.

Based on a variety of assumptions about the quantity and value of these ingredients, Levin and Driver (1997) constructed a range of cost estimates of implementing a voucher plan. To some extent, these costs might be compensated by cost-savings at the school level—if private schools are less costly than public schools—but this cannot be determined without a careful study. Overall, the scarcity of cost information suggests that we are far from being able to make reasoned judgments about the cost-feasibility and cost-effectiveness of voucher plans.

CASE STUDY   Is Whole-School Reform Worthwhile?

Despite the vast resources devoted to whole-school reform, there are relatively few attempts to assess its cost-feasibility or cost-effectiveness. Researchers have, in a few instances, tried to estimate the costs of implementing a reform model such as Comer's School Development Program. However, these studies are based on rough assumptions about the quantity and value of cost ingredients. Barnett (1996) mainly relied upon program documents to estimate the cost of the Comer model.[8] He identified several categories of ingredients necessary to implement the model. The personnel included a program facilitator who devotes at least 25% of her time to a reform school; a mental health specialist (at least 25% time); and a staff member to work with children outside classrooms (at least 50% time). Other significant categories are the training workshops for participants—although this is not broken down into its constituent ingredients—and the time commitments of parents. Recall from the previous descriptions of the Comer model that parents, in the guise of a Parent Team, are expected to be active and integral participants in the reform process.

Ideally, each ingredient should be carefully assigned a cost value. Barnett (1996) did not have access to a great deal of data, however, and made rough assumptions about the personnel salaries and training costs. Despite the acknowledged importance of parents to the model, he was unable to estimate the cost of parents' time. Given these limitations, he estimated that the annual cost of the program is no lower than $57,000 (expressed in 1994 dollars), or about $115 per student if we assume that a school enrolls 500 students.

So is the Comer model cost-feasible? That will depend on issues that districts and schools need to assess for themselves. The first factor is the size of the budget constraint. Cost-feasibility is, in part, a function of what the district is able to spend. Second, it depends on how the district or school plans to implement the model. It may choose, for example, to use more or less of a particular ingredient. Third, it depends on the value of the cost ingredients in different contexts, such as salaries of personnel. Fourth, it depends on whether resources are newly acquired or merely reallocated from their existing uses. In some applications of the Comer model, it is assumed that existing school personnel can be shifted over from other duties. Despite the appearance of being a "cost-free" reallocation, one must ask if there is an opportunity cost to this decision. What is sacrificed by eliminating one set of duties and creating another? Fifth, it depends on *who* is assuming the burden of costs, and the perspective of the decision maker. The Comer model places a substantial burden on parents, although prior studies have not placed a value on their time. In both Maryland and Chicago, local foundations bore many program costs like the salaries of facilitators (Cook et al., 1999; Cook et al., 2000). These factors obviously improve the program's cost-feasibility from the perspective of a school or district. Of course, it also highlights that what is feasible for one of the stakeholders may be less so for another.

The issue of the Comer model's cost-effectiveness is a more difficult issue to resolve. In part, this is because cost-effectiveness judgments are fundamentally comparative. They require good evidence on the effects and costs of at least one other model. Although there is a mounting evidence base in this respect there is still a long way to go. The Comer model is still the only one, for example, with good experimental evidence on effects, and none of the models has been subjected to an exhaustive cost study (Levin, 2002).

FURTHER READING

Cost analysis is beginning to come of age in education, but the progress has been slow. Levin and McEwan (2001) provide a book-length discussion of the issues raised in this chapter, including much more detail on the nuts-and-bolts of conducting a cost analysis. They also provide many references to the applied research on cost analysis. A more recent volume (Levin & McEwan, 2002) is an edited collection of literature reviews and new cost studies.

NOTES

1. See Levin and McEwan (2001, Chapter 3) for a more complete discussion.

2. See, for example, Slavin and Madden (1999).

3. Levin (2002) provides more discussion of a similar point.

4. In addition to the annual cost of depreciation, one should also consider the cost of income that is forgone by having funds tied up in a large investment such as a building. Think of a building that is valued at $1 million. The value of that building cannot be invested in a bank account, for example, to earn interest. That lost interest represents an opportunity cost that should be accounted for in the annual cost of the building. For further details, see Levin and McEwan (2002, pp. 66-70).

5. For further evidence on this point, see Levin and McEwan (2001, 2002).

6. See Elbaum, Vaughn, Hughes, & Moody (2000) and Evans (1996) in *Evidence-Based Research on Reading Recovery,* a letter signed by an international group of researchers (Baker et al., 2002). This letter is available at http://www.educationnews.org/Reading Recoveryisnotsuccessful.htm.

7. For one exception, now quite old, see Bartell (1968).

8. King (1994) conducted a similar cost analysis. Levin (2002) provides a critique of both of these pioneering cost studies.

7

The Usability Question

Will It Work for Me?

Good education research can tell you *whether* an intervention works (the causal question), *how* it works (the process question), and even *whether it is worthwhile* (the cost question). In the ivory towers of academia, this is usually good enough. And yet, from the perspective of teachers and principals, something more is needed for research to be truly useful in informing day-to-day practice. Good research should also provide clues to assist you in assessing whether an intervention will work *in your setting*.

Making these judgments can be a daunting task. How many times have you read an article touting the latest "best practice" in reading instruction? By now, you know enough to take such claims with a grain of salt, at least until you have asked a few important questions. If you are fortunate, the claims are founded on systematic research, perhaps using a randomized experiment. If you're even more fortunate, they are based on research showing how the program works and what it may cost. But this research, however compelling, does not automatically tell you whether the intervention is the "best practice" for *your* classroom, school, or district. Perhaps the research was conducted in a suburban school district enrolling students from wealthy families. Your district, on the other hand, is urban and poor. Will the intervention still work, despite the different context? Will it work *in your setting*?

Unfortunately, there are no hard-and-fast rules for answering this question—no scientific algorithm for determining whether research findings can be generalized beyond the context in which a study was conducted. In fact, answering the will-it-work-for-me question relies at least as much on the common sense and good judgment of the practitioner as it does on evidence provided in research studies. Quite frankly, this tends to unnerve some of our more technical colleagues, who like straightforward questions with rigorous answers (such as those provided by a randomized experiment).

And yet, the goal of most education research is—or should be—to inform real decisions in real educational environments. Making decisions in the real world is often equal parts art and science. This chapter will arm you with some simple concepts and rules of thumb for making your own decisions about whether research can be generalized to your classroom, school, or district.

WILL IT WORK IN MY SETTING?

You may have heard snippets of the following conversation in the teachers' lounge: Did you hear that Professor Bigego will be at our all-day inservice on Friday? Apparently he's done some new research—a randomized experiment no less—that showed his school reform model raises achievement by leaps and bounds. He's recommending it for any school with low reading scores—his Web site practically guarantees an increase of 20 percentiles! This sounds like just what we need to raise test scores. Plus he's providing free training grants for the first 10 school districts that jump on the bandwagon. What do you think? What have we got to lose?

Both the professor and his admirer are to be commended for their taste in research design (by now, of course, you are well acquainted with the merits of experiments in assessing whether an intervention works). But they are falling prey to a logical trap that ensnares all of us at one time or another—whether evangelizing researcher or enthusiastic practitioner. It happens when we assume that a successful intervention in a particular instance implies, *ipso facto,* that it will be successful in *every* instance. Many well-meaning practitioners have made that leap of faith, only to be disappointed with the results.

To better define our predicament, it is helpful to review some old terms and introduce some new ones. An internally valid research study is able to identify—with a high degree of certainty—that a causal relationship exists between an intervention and an outcome. Such a study provides a believable answer to the does-it-work question. Much of the researchers' task, at least as described in Chapters 3 and 4, is devoted to improving the internal validity of their research.

It is quite another matter to assess whether that causal relationship will hold in other instances, outside the immediate context of the research study. If it does, then the study is said to possess *external* validity.[1] There are many reasons why a causal relationship that exists in one instance may not in another, and these reasons are collectively referred to as threats to external validity. These threats can be roughly classified into four groups. In each case, a threat to external validity exists because a causal relationship does not hold (a) across students; (b) across settings, including schools or communities; (c) across variations of the treatment; or (d) across outcome measures (Shadish et al., 2002, p. 83).

Students

The students who participate in a given research study may bear only a passing resemblance to those in your school or district. This doesn't necessarily pose a threat to external validity, unless we have reason to believe that the effects of an intervention will vary among students. Unfortunately, these suspicions are often justified.

Think about one of the studies that we discussed in Chapter 3. The Tennessee STAR experiment evaluated the effects of class size reduction among elementary students in—no surprise here—Tennessee (Krueger, 1999). About 50% of the students received free lunch (an indicator of family income) and about 30% belonged to a minority group (mainly African American). To read news accounts of the study, one might surmise that it makes a very broad statement about whether class size reduction "works." Indeed, California implemented a statewide plan to reduce class size, largely based on the positive findings from Tennessee (more on this later in the case studies).

To make a logical leap like this, we need to assure ourselves that the causal findings can be generalized from a group of disadvantaged students in Tennessee to other groups of students. Will the Tennessee results still hold among Inuit children in Canada? What about economically advantaged children in suburban Utah? Sometimes, the studies themselves can aid us in answering these questions. The Tennessee experiment, for example, found that lower-inc,ome and minority children reaped larger gains from class size reduction than others. Still, of course, a research study can rarely provide all the information we need to make well-informed decisions. Thus we often need to rely on our good judgment and experience if we want to generalize results beyond the immediate sample of students.

> A research study can rarely provide all the information we need to make well-informed decisions.

Settings

We must also think about whether causal relationships can be generalized across different settings, including diverse schools and communities. It is commonly presumed that what "works" in one setting will necessarily work in another. But this may not always be the case.

Again, a few examples will help clarify the issues. In an evaluation of Comer's School Development Program in Chicago, the initial sample included "volunteer" schools in which the principal had requested to be included in the program (Cook et al., 2000). If our only concern is internal validity—answering the does-it-work question—then the use of volunteer schools doesn't matter, as long as they are randomly assigned to treatment and control groups. But we are also concerned about external validity and answering the will-it-work-for-me question. To do so, we must be able to confidently generalize the findings of the Chicago experiment to other schools. A logical question is whether the positive results obtained in the experiment would still hold if the program were implemented in other Chicago schools, even those that did not volunteer to participate. Naturally, we might be concerned that the unique experimental setting—including motivated principals—facilitated the success of the program. The corollary is that the program might not be as successful in other school settings.

The experimental research on private-school vouchers has typically been conducted in urban areas, such as New York City (e.g., Mayer et al., 2002). Nonetheless, we may wish to use this evidence to draw general lessons about the potential impact of vouchers in suburban or rural settings. Indeed, the New York voucher study has been publicized—at least by voucher proponents—as a clear-cut lesson on the beneficial effects of vouchers almost *anywhere* in the United States. But will the results necessarily generalize across different settings? What if, for example, urban families are particularly dissatisfied with their public school options, and more inclined to use vouchers? What if urban areas provide a more abundant and varied supply of private-school options? In either case, the causal effects of a voucher program may not be easily duplicated in a different setting.

Treatments

Discussions of school reform frequently use verbal shorthand to refer to novel "treatments." We have even indulged in this ourselves, making frequent reference to treatments like phonics-based instruction, class size reduction, whole-school reform, and private-school vouchers. However, each of these broad categories conceals wide variation in how treatments might be applied.

Phonics-based instruction may last for 20 minutes or 2 hours, relying on a range of curricula and instructional techniques. Class size reduction could mean that classes are reduced from 30 to 25 students, or it could refer to a reduction from 20 students to 10.

Or it might be understood that it will be accompanied by teacher training in how to increase achievement by manipulating the most powerful benefits of small classes—or it might not. Whole-school reform is perhaps the least instructive category of them all. There are a hundred models to choose from, with vastly different instructional goals. Even within a particular model of whole-school reform, the developers may tinker with new approaches to create a "second-generation" reform that bears slight resemblance to the original model. Private-school vouchers could be implemented in myriad ways. In some variants, religious schools would not be eligible to accept vouchers; in others, only poor students would receive vouchers. Either feature—and a thousand others—could drastically alter the face of the voucher plan.

Most research studies examine a single kind of treatment. In the Tennessee STAR experiment, class size was reduced from 22-25 students per teacher to 13-17 (Krueger, 1999). In the Chicago evaluation of the Comer School Development Program, the treatment was molded to the Chicago context in ways that distinguished it from SDP in other cities (Cook et al., 2000). The implementation relied heavily, for example, on a local organization of social workers called Youth Guidance.

When you read a research study, particularly with an eye toward implementing your own version of it, you need to ask some important questions: How similar or different is the treatment that I will be implementing? Can I assume that it will produce the same causal effect as other versions?

Outcomes

If a treatment is shown to "work" in improving one outcome measure, then it is tempting to assume that it will work for *all* outcomes. However, this needs to be assessed on a case-by-case basis. Imagine that you come across an experimental study of a novel reading program. It appears to improve reading achievement, but a closer examination reveals that the researchers used a special reading assessment. The assessment was closely aligned with the "drill-and-practice" methodology of the program, so it placed great emphasis on basic phonological awareness and word identification. Your school district also uses a similar assessment, but only as one element of a larger testing battery. In fact, your students will also be expected not only to answer comprehension questions after reading a story but also to demonstrate proficiency in a written performance assessment, in which short paragraphs must be crafted by each student. You wonder how the program will affect this wider set of outcome measures.

In many cases, researchers will collect data on a wide range of outcome measures, even if some of them are only of tangential interest. This can greatly aid the reader who is attempting to determine whether gains in one outcome also imply gains in another. In other cases, however, there is a limited range of outcome data and, once again, readers must fall back on their good judgment and make informed guesses.

SOME RULES OF THUMB
FOR MAKING GENERALIZATIONS

The previous discussion might leave you feeling a bit frustrated (we confess to similar feelings, on occasion). There are thousands of practitioners scattered across the country, all of them searching for coherent guidance on the best course of action. They are confronted with a relatively small body of research. The "body," such as it is, may occasionally consist of just a single study! From this, practitioners are supposed to make reasonable judgments about whether research findings can be generalized to *their* classrooms, schools, or districts.

It is easy to understand why many educators turn their backs on research altogether or at least regard it with jaded suspicion. We think this view is misguided, however. It is partly borne of the sense—often encouraged by the researchers themselves—that a single experiment should be capable of providing universal solutions to a given problem. This view mistakenly assumes that the answers to the "does-it-work" and the "will-it-work-for-me" questions are always the same.

> It is easy to understand why many educators turn their backs on research altogether or at least regard it with jaded suspicion.

In fact, they are not. Something that works in one context may not work in another. This is true not just of education but also fields like health and public policy. The fact still remains, however, that we need some systematic means of answering the will-it-work-for-me question. Shadish et al. (2002) convincingly argue that social scientists in almost every field of endeavor use simple rules of thumb to evaluate the generalizability of a research study.[2] If applied judiciously, these simple rules of thumb can provide helpful guidance to practitioners who are puzzling over questions of generalizability.

Employing the terms of Shadish et al. (2002), these rules of thumb include (a) surface similarity, (b) ruling out irrelevancies, (c) making discriminations, (d) interpolation and extrapolation, and (e) causal explanation.[3] To apply each rule, we presume that a research study has already been identified, and that you wish to apply its findings to another context—most likely your own classroom, school, or district.

Surface Similarity

This first principle has a great deal of intuitive appeal. It involves comparing the students, settings, treatments, and outcomes of a research study to one's own context. Presumably, it is more likely that research results can be generalized to a context with similar students, settings, treatments, and outcomes.

For example, are students similarly distributed according to gender, socioeconomic status, ability level, and language background? Are the settings similar (e.g., urban/rural location, school and classroom environments)? Will the treatment in the research study be exactly replicated in the new context, or will it undergo substantial modifications? Are the outcome measures the same in each case or at least similar enough to presume that the effects won't be vastly different?

Of course, making judgments about surface similarity is trickier than it might appear. There are an infinite variety of characteristics by which "similarity" might be judged. We have enumerated some of the most obvious, but you are left to rely on your good judgment to identify and compare the most salient features of a research study with your particular environment.

Ruling Out Irrelevancies

As we just pointed out, you will almost always note some *differences* between the students, setting, treatment, and outcomes in a research study, and those of your classroom, school, or district. In a few instances, there may be many differences. However, it is likely that some of the differences will have little bearing on the causal effect; they will be irrelevant to the generalizability of the research findings. To the extent that those differences can be identified and ruled out as threats to external validity, the results of the research can be generalized to your setting with more confidence.

In the best of cases, a research study can provide specific guidance on these issues. For example, you may be the principal of a school that enrolls only girls. You are interested in applying a novel mathematics curriculum, but the only available research was conducted in a mixed-gender school. Naturally, you are concerned that the math program affected boys and girls differently, thus limiting its generalizability to your school. However, the authors of the research estimated the effects of the program separately for boys and girls and found little difference. Although this is hardly iron-clad evidence that the same effects will be obtained in your school, it does suggest that gender is not a relevant determinant of the program's impact.

Making Discriminations

And yet, it is possible that some differences *do* matter. Some aspects of the students, setting, treatment, or outcomes could differ, and these could be important determinants of whether an intervention is successful. When feasible, you should try to discriminate between instances in which a causal effect will hold and those in which it will not.

Returning to the example of the New York City voucher program, it was found that attending a private school yielded some achievement gains for African American students but not for Latino students (Mayer et al., 2002). Knowing this, we might be less inclined to implement a voucher program that is significantly targeted toward Latino students (of course, that needn't satiate our curiosity about *how* the program works—or doesn't—for Latinos).

In other cases, the research study may not directly address these issues, for lack of time, money, or planning. Nonetheless, think carefully about whether unique features of the research study may limit its generalizability. Let's say you find a randomized experiment that assessed the effects of homogeneous ability grouping on the reading achievement of first-graders. A careful reading reveals that the study was conducted in the tightly controlled environment of a university lab

> Think carefully about whether unique features of the research study may limit its generalizability.

school. Moreover, the treatment was applied by highly trained graduate students—all former teachers—who were closely supervised by the faculty. You are somewhat doubtful as to whether the positive experimental results will generalize to your own setting, which has fewer resources to support a faithful application of the treatment. At the very least, you think that smaller effects might be obtained.

Interpolation and Extrapolation

At one time or another, we have all used interpolation or extrapolation to make generalizations, even if those terms are unfamiliar. Consider the following scenario: A school district wants to reduce the average class size from 25 to 20, based on the results of a recent experiment that found achievement gains of about 2 percentiles. Several principals suggest going even further, reducing class size from 25 to 15, under the assumption that effects will be twice as large. Unfortunately, the original research did not explore the effects of the larger reduction. To assume that it would produce double the effects is an example of extrapolating the results of a research study.

In another instance, a study might find strong effects of an intervention among the poorest students—those with family incomes in the lowest decile. Much larger effects are found among students in the highest decile. To generalize the conclusions to students in the middle deciles, our natural inclination is to assuming that the effect will fall somewhere within the effects for the lowest and highest deciles. This is an example of interpolation.

Of course, we are often on a slippery slope when extrapolating or interpolating results, because it requires us to make untested assumptions about effects. This is especially so with extrapolation. In the previous example, research found that lowering the class size from 25 to 20 students yielded an effect of 2 percentiles. Let's say that further research found that a reduction from 25 to 15 could yield an effect of 3 percentiles. In this hypothetical example, the principal's "extrapolated" effect of 4 percentile points would be incorrect. However, this can only be verified through a more complex research design that tested multiple versions of the treatment.

> We are often on a slippery slope when extrapolating or interpolating results, because it requires us to make untested assumptions about effects.

Causal Explanation

Experiments can tell us whether an intervention works, but they are less suited to explaining *how* the causal effect is obtained. In the typical class size reduction experiments, for example, we are told that they work in raising achievement, but we are unsure of the exact mechanisms that mediate the causal effect. They may work because of increased teacher motivation, because of better classroom discipline, or because of increased time spent with low-achieving students.

Nonetheless, obtaining a deeper knowledge of these causal mechanisms can make it easier to replicate the effect elsewhere.[4] Imagine that further research shows that class size reduction yields positive effects because it encourages teachers to reallocate their time toward low-achieving students. Armed with this knowledge, a principal who lowers class sizes may work closely with teachers to assist them in developing appropriate instructional strategies. The key point is that detailed knowledge about the "technology" of an intervention can help to ensure that causal effects observed in one context can be replicated in others. This is less likely to occur if an intervention is simply treated as a mysterious "black box" that produces its benefits through some obscure process. Not all research provides this needed information, although Chapter 5 described a range of qualitative methods that are suited to this task (also see Shadish et al., 2002, pp. 391-392).

RESEARCH REVIEWS AND META-ANALYSIS

You will often have only a single study on which to base your judgments about generalizability. In the best of cases, it may help you ascertain whether causal effects are uniform across certain kinds of students, or for certain variations in the treatment. Or it may tell you whether causal effects that exist in an urban area disappear in others, perhaps in rural schools. This knowledge, along with the rules of thumb just described, can greatly assist you in thinking critically about whether causal effects will persist in your own context.

The ability of a single study to answer the will-it-work-for-me question is inevitably limited. You will surely be confronted by uncertainties that cannot unambiguously be resolved by a single study. Can one experimental study of 100 sixth-graders in Tempe, Arizona, really tell me anything about *my* school? Can I duplicate the glowing results of a small-scale tutoring intervention even if I implement a different version of the treatment?

> The ability of a single study to answer the will-it-work-for-me question is inevitably limited.

These judgments are often made easier by appealing to wide range of studies on a similar topic, summarized in a research review.[5] It is increasingly common to find reviews of important topics in education research, especially as the amount of research grows by leaps and bounds in some areas (look particularly to specialized journals, such as the *Review of Educational Research*, published by the American Educational Research Association). These reviews are a necessary tool to draw general conclusions from what can often be a maddeningly complex array of research, scattered across a wide variety of journals and books.

Reviews generally fall into two general categories, with some degree of overlap. The first is referred to as a *narrative review*. It uses verbal descriptions to summarize, critique, and interpret a body of research. Although quite helpful, especially to obtain detailed descriptions of research studies, it is often difficult for narrative reviews to arrive at convincing "bottom lines."

The second category is referred to as *meta-analysis*, and it often relies on quantitative methods to summarize the results from a large number of experiments, quasi-experiments, or non-experimental studies. For example, there may be 30 quasi-experiments that assess the causal link between a particular whole-school reform and academic achievement. In a meta-analysis, the researcher extracts a measure of the causal effect—usually expressed as an effect size—from each study. The effect sizes can be summarized and

> In a meta-analysis, the researcher extracts a measure of the causal effect—usually expressed as an effect size—from each study.

analyzed in a number of ways. Most obviously, one can calculate the average effect size across the 30 different studies.

Even more interesting, one can assess whether effect sizes tend to be larger or smaller—or even zero—when the students, setting, treatment, or outcomes are varied from study to study. When analyzed with the rules of thumb described earlier, one can use these meta-analytic findings to assess the generalizability of causal effects. For example, does it appear that effect sizes are quite similar, even when characteristics of the setting are modified (e.g., urban vs. rural schools)? This would help in ruling out irrelevancies that do not hold any implications for generalizability. Or does it appear that effect sizes are much larger when an intervention is applied to a certain group of students (e.g., girls instead of boys)? This would aid in making discriminations that would allow for a more thoughtful consideration of whether an intervention can reasonably be applied to all students or whether it is best limited to a subset of students.

We have only provided a thumbnail sketch of meta-analysis (for a thorough summary, see the articles in Cooper & Hedges, 1994). However, the techniques have developed rapidly in the past few years, accompanied by an increasing number of thorough reviews. If a review article can be located on a topic of interest, it often provides an excellent resource for the practitioner who is beginning to delve into the research. Besides containing a lengthy bibliography of individual research studies, reviews often contain trenchant critiques of methodological issues that can assist in answering many of the questions posed throughout this book.

SPECIAL CONSIDERATIONS FOR QUALITATIVE AND COST STUDIES

Our discussion thus far has focused on the generalizability of causal results produced by experiments, quasi-experiments, and non-experiments—the question of whether we can assume that an intervention that works in one context will necessarily work in another. However, there are special issues that need to be considered in generalizing other types of research—including qualitative and cost studies—that are used to address the how-does-it-work and is-it-worthwhile questions.

Qualitative Studies

We have suggested that meta-analysis is a powerful way to synthesize or aggregate experimental research studies to determine the generalizability of a body of research to one's own unique setting. A similar technique (without the statistical analyses) has been suggested for synthesizing qualitative studies—"meta-ethnography" (Noblit & Hare, 1988). Rather than focusing on effect sizes across large numbers of studies, a qualitative synthesis identifies and extrapolates lessons that have been learned from a set of case studies or ethnographies. Patton (2002) offers an example of this kind of qualitative synthesis (p. 501). He was hired by a foundation to synthesize three evaluative case studies, unrelated to each other (and regrettably, to the field of education) except for the fact that they were each funded by the same philanthropic foundation. The case studies determined that each of the programs "worked." But the foundation wanted to know *how* and *why* these particular programs worked. What characteristics did the programs have in common, even though they dealt with such diverse projects as family housing, downtown development, and graduate programs for minorities? How could their successes be generalized or extrapolated to other projects? Patton carefully reviewed the written evaluations and also made site visits to conduct interviews.

> A qualitative synthesis identifies and extrapolates lessons that have been learned from a set of case studies or ethnographies.

Irrespective of the programs' dissimilarities, Patton (2002) found 12 success factors that were common to all three: high-quality people, substantial financial resources, creative partnerships, leverage, vision, a clear values orientation, self-sustaining institutions, long time frames, flexibility, cutting-edge foresight, risk taking, and leadership (p. 501). Although some would question whether we can generalize regarding constructs as vague and context bound as flexibility, risk taking, and leadership (Cronbach, 1975), we concur with Patton (2002) who suggests that extrapolations—"modest speculations on the likely applicability of findings to other situations under similar, but not identical, conditions" (p. 584)—can be very useful to practitioners who want to "transfer" what they see working in one setting to their own particular context.

Cost Studies

As Chapter 6 described, cost studies attempt to calculate the additional costs of a new intervention. This is best accomplished in a two-stage process: (a) identifying a comprehensive list of all the "ingredients" used in implementing the intervention and (b) attaching a cost value to each ingredient. With the additional cost of the intervention in hand, one can assess whether it is cost-feasible. Or if there is information on the costs and effects of another intervention, one can assess whether a particular intervention is relatively more cost-effective.

It cannot automatically be assumed that the results of a particular cost study will generalize to all contexts. One of the most important issues to consider is how the cost value of ingredients may vary from one context to another (Levin & McEwan, 2001; Rice, 1997). This is a lesson already familiar to us from other spheres of our lives. The same two-bedroom apartment may rent for vastly different sums in downtown Manhattan as compared to a small Midwestern town. Or the price of gasoline may be substantially higher in Hawaii than Texas.

> One of the most important issues to consider is how the cost value of ingredients may vary from one context to another.

The same logic can apply to educational ingredients, such as personnel and facilities. Imagine that a cost study of class size reduction was conducted in Nebraska. At the time of the study, it was relatively inexpensive to build new classrooms, given the low cost of both land and school buildings (at least relative to other states). California policymakers examine the Nebraska study to assess its relevance to their planning. They immediately notice that the cost of facilities is different in their state. Land is exceptionally scarce (and expensive) in urban areas of California, and construction costs have skyrocketed in recent years. Even the option of using portable classroom space is not viable because of the rising costs. The only other option is to house new classrooms in converted spaces, such as closets and cafeterias. But this obviously has its own set of opportunity costs, because these spaces are not well-suited to instructional needs. Ultimately, the California decision makers decide that class size reduction is not cost-feasible, a conclusion that would not necessarily follow from a naïve reading of the Nebraska study.

MAKING TRADE-OFFS

You will rarely be able to find a research study that perfectly answers *all* of the questions raised in this book. More often than not, a study that answers one question extremely well will fall short of answering another. Trade-offs of this sort are most commonly observed with the does-it-work and the will-it-work-for-me questions (Shadish et al., 2002, p. 96).

> You will rarely be able to find a research study that perfectly answers all of the questions raised in this book.

Randomized experiments provide a very good means of answering causal questions. However, it is often difficult to convince a large number of individuals or schools to submit to a process of randomized assignment between treatment and control groups. As a result, researchers often use convenience samples in which the units have volunteered to participate. Naturally, randomization ensures that any conclusions will have internal validity, adequately answering the does-it-work question. But the fact that the units are "special" in some unobserved way, owing to their volunteer status, may make it difficult to generalize the findings to a broader group of students or schools. It is more difficult for research consumers to answer the will-it-work-for-me question.

The trade-off may also work in the opposite direction. Non-experimental research, for example, often uses large samples of students or schools that are widely representative of larger populations. The treatments in these studies are never randomly assigned. Rather, individuals or schools choose treatments for themselves (or others choose for them, nonrandomly). For all the reasons described in Chapter 4, these studies often face a difficult task in ascertaining with certitude whether an intervention "works." Even so, the fact that the sample is more broadly representative of the population means the results may be more generalizable and more suited to answering the will-it-work-for-me question.

None of this is meant to discourage you. But it should help you to recognize that few research studies can definitively answer all of the questions raised in this book (and authors who claim otherwise may be a bit overenthusiastic in their sales pitches). Good evidence frequently needs to be combined with educated guesses, something that is particularly true when answering the will-it-work-for-me question.

CASE STUDY   Will Class Size Reduction Work for Me?

Although it often seems that education policy is dictated by the whims of politicians, there are instances in which research plays a clear role in guiding decisions. The California legislature passed a reform in 1996 to reduce class sizes on a large scale in grades K-3. In doing so, they were directly inspired by the results of Tennessee's STAR experiment. Legislators were attracted to the Tennessee results for the same reasons that they have been praised at many points in this book. In Tennessee, students were randomly assigned to small and regular classes. Thus the results provide a very convincing answer to the does-it-work question.

It appears that California legislators—and many others—were expecting the California plan to largely duplicate the positive findings of Tennessee. They presumed that answering the does-it-work question would also provide a reasonable answer to the ill-it-work-for-me question. However, there are a number of reasons why this logical leap may not have been justified. Many of these were lucidly revealed—with the benefits of additional data and hindsight—by a large-scale evaluation of California's class size reduction effort (Stecher & Bornstedt, 2002).[6]

The students in Tennessee were quite disadvantaged, on the whole (more than half received free lunch). That much is similar to California. However, the ethnic composition of the schools is vastly different. About 30% of the Tennessee STAR students belonged to a minority (mainly African American). In the 1996-1997 school year, more than half of California students were nonwhite; 40% alone were Latino.[7] Overall, about one third of the students in the early primary grades were classified as limited English proficient.

The settings were also different. Perhaps the most salient aspect is that the Tennessee schools participating in the experiment had access to sufficient teachers and adequate classroom space. In

California, those two elements were widely variable across the state. There were shortages of teachers, especially in poor communities and in special instructional areas, such as bilingual education, and there was limited classroom space in many areas.

Last, the treatment applied in Tennessee turned out to be quite different from California's version. First, the Tennessee plan reduced class size from 22-25 students to 13-15. In California, the average class size in primary grades had been 29 students—with a maximum of 33—and the legislation reduced this to 20. In other words, the "small" class in California was just slightly below the "regular" class in Tennessee!

Second, the treatment applied in California often relied on less-experienced teachers and lower-quality facilities. Many California districts, especially those serving poor students, had a difficult time locating sufficient numbers of qualified teachers and sufficient classroom space. The result was that many districts staffed the new classrooms with uncredentialed teachers and occasionally placed them in substandard classroom space. So the "treatment" that was delivered included smaller class sizes but also some negative—though inadvertent—side effects.

It is clear that California legislators were making some strong assumptions about the generalizability of the Tennessee experiment. They assumed that its causal findings would remain unchanged across variations in students, settings, and treatments. And these variations were quite substantial. This hardly invalidates the usefulness of the Tennessee findings, but it does suggest that some careful thought should precede their application. Will the results still hold among an ethnically diverse population where English is frequently a second language? Will they still hold when small classes may be staffed by less-qualified teachers?

CASE STUDY   Will Phonics Instruction Work for Me?

Phonics instruction in its many permutations is one of the most researched areas of reading instruction. The critical question facing practitioners is whether this research has anything to say about the likelihood of phonics instruction working in their settings. When a substantial body of experimental and quasi-experimental research is available, a meta-analytic approach is the ideal way to answer many of the questions regarding the generalizability of a particular method to your setting. One such study summarized 38 experimental and quasi-experimental studies that compared the effects of systematic phonics instruction to unsystematic or no-phonics instruction on learning to read (Ehri et al., 2001). The strength of this meta-analysis lies not only in the variety of students, settings, treatments and outcomes considered but also in the fact that all of the studies appeared in peer-reviewed journals.

The studies took place in regular school settings (as opposed to lab or university clinic settings) that enrolled students from a range of socioeconomic levels. The students came from various achievement and grade levels: normal achieving, at-risk, reading disabled, and low-achieving, from grades K-6. Instructional settings included whole class, small group, and tutorial. The treatments included both synthetic phonics (systematic sound-spelling instruction) and analytic phonics (larger phonetic units of instruction similar to those used in the Benchmark Word Identification program described in the Chapter 5 case study). The control groups included basal readers, a regular district curriculum, whole language, whole word, and a miscellaneous

category. The outcome measures included the decoding of both real and pseudowords, spelling words, reading text orally, and comprehending text.

The overall effect of phonics instruction on reading when *all* ages and types of readers taught with *different* phonics programs was moderate, with an effect size of .41. You, however, are interested in exactly when and for whom phonics instruction is most helpful. The meta-analysis provides an excellent discussion of the effect sizes for various settings, programs, and grouping plans so that one could determine what will work best in a specific classroom, school, or district. For example, effects are larger when phonics instruction begins early (.55) as compared to after first grade (.27). Small group instruction produced larger effect sizes than tutoring or whole-classroom settings. The meta-analysis found that there are many curricula that provide effective systematic phonics instruction, and no one program was superior to another. Most critical to positive student outcomes in word reading ability was the systematic and explicit nature of instruction.

Many of the studies found positive effects for phonics instruction when combined with whole-language approaches as compared to programs emphasizing only a whole-language philosophy. These findings suggest the need for a skillful combination of phonics instruction with activities that immediately require students to apply their decoding skills (the goal of phonics instruction as measured in the studies) to the reading of real text to build fluency, increase comprehension skills, and acquire knowledge.

CASE STUDY   Will Private-School Vouchers Work for Me?

There is tremendous debate about the potential impact of offering private-school vouchers to students, and much of it has turned on the perceived effectiveness of private schools. Does attending a private rather than a public school raise student outcomes? Most evidence is non-experimental, but several randomized experiments have fueled the debate. One experiment in New York City was briefly discussed in Chapter 3 (Mayer et al., 2002). It compared the outcomes of disadvantaged students who were randomly awarded tuition vouchers to the outcomes of students who were denied vouchers.

The results have frequently been portrayed as offering general lessons about the desirability of implementing vouchers on a larger scale in New York City or elsewhere in the United States. However, the authors themselves are quite circumspect about making such generalizations. They feel that "the results of the . . . program cannot be generalized to a large-scale voucher program that would involve all children in New York City or other central cities . . . Nevertheless, the results . . . may say something about the likely impact of a small-scale, publicly funded voucher program serving low-income families" (Mayer et al., 2002, pp. 12-13).

What might explain their caution in using the results to justify a significant expansion of vouchers? The context of the New York program was unique in several respects—the students it served, its setting, and the treatment it applied. First, the students in New York were from poor families, and around 90% of the experimental participants were either African American or Latino. The experiment found some positive effects for African Americans, on average, but none for Latinos. This immediately raises the question of whether a voucher program would have its intended effects if targeted toward a state or city with a strong Latino population. But even this generalization is not straightforward, since New York's Latinos are frequently Puerto Rican or Dominican. Without further evidence, it seems unwise to assume that a heavily Chicano or Mexican population, as in Arizona or California, would be affected (or not affected) in a similar manner.

Second, the setting in New York City is unique. There are many reasons why the causal effects observed in a very urban area might not generalize to other settings. Rural areas usually have very few private schools, and families must typically travel greater distances to reach them. Even in suburban areas, the supply of private schools—and the choices available to families—may be constrained. And opinion polls suggest that suburban families are more satisfied with their schools and less inclined to accept the offer of a private-school voucher.

Third, the voucher treatment in New York was unique. Most obviously, it was quite small in size, with around 1,300 students receiving vouchers. All of them could be accommodated in existing private schools (and most of these were Catholic). If the New York program were expanded, or if vouchers were implemented in a city with less space in private schools, then secular private schools might receive students. But very little is known about whether these schools would produce similar effects. Some qualitative evidence, described in Chapter 5, suggests that the "Catholic-ness" of private schools is a key determinant of their success.

For all these reasons, it seems that caution is warranted in assuming that the voucher research is generalizable. The New York research suggests that vouchers may be effective on a small scale, in large urban areas, and if targeted to disadvantaged African American students.

CASE STUDY   Will Whole-School Reform Work for Me?

With the increasing popularity of models for whole-school reform, it is inevitable that attention is devoted to results of evaluations. Did a particular model work? And just as important, can the results of a model be replicated in a wide range of contexts? Chapter 3 briefly summarized the results of two important randomized experiments on the Comer School Development Project (SDP; Cook et al., 1999; Cook et al., 2000). Each was notable for using a sophisticated and well-designed methodology to assess whether the reform succeeded in altering the school climate or improving achievement. Even so, the evaluations turned up different results. In Chicago, the reform contributed to increased test scores among participating schools. The same effects were not evident in another program site in Prince George's County, Maryland.

Stated this simply, it is hard to draw constructive lessons about the proper course of action for other schools. Which set of results is the most generalizable to the particular circumstances of other schools? To make judgments like these, it is important to take a closer look at the details of the students, settings, treatments, and outcomes in each case.

In Chicago, the students were elementary-aged, poor, and predominantly African American. In Maryland, the students were also mainly African American, but poverty rates were less intense. They were also attending middle schools rather than elementary schools.

The settings were also considerably different. The Chicago schools were located in quite urban areas, among the poorest neighborhoods in the city, whereas the Maryland schools were in a suburban area of Washington, DC. Although poor, the area is still more upwardly mobile than the typical Chicago communities. Another distinguishing feature of the Chicago setting was the city-wide emphasis on reform—particularly directed toward improving academic achievement—that influenced attitudes of key stakeholders. As Cook et al. (2000) note, "Staff did not have to be persuaded of the political necessity to change, of the consequences of not changing, and of the importance of working collaboratively in order to effect change. In addition the central district office left no ambiguity about the direction of desired change, emphasizing academic achievement." (p. 592).

The schools in Chicago and Maryland also received different versions of the Comer treatment.[8] One of the defining features of the Chicago version of the SDP was the involvement of a local organization of social workers (Youth Guidance) with a long history of community involvement. They served as program facilitators and liaisons with the community, and their involvement was highly regarded. Also important was that students were exposed to the treatment for more years in Chicago than in Maryland, principally because it was implemented in middle schools in Maryland.

And last, the outcomes measures were different. The Maryland evaluation was forced to rely on a state minimal competency test in mathematics. The Chicago evaluation was able to use the more comprehensive Iowa Test of Basic Skills.

Any of the differences mentioned could contribute to different results in Maryland and Chicago. Together, they suggest that positive results are most likely to hold when the program is targeted at the poorest students, when the program is targeted to elementary schools, when there is a strong desire for change and an emphasis on achievement, when there is well-respected and effective support, and when students are exposed to the program for more than just a few years.

FURTHER READING

In comparison to the vast literature on experimental and qualitative methods, there is a relatively small amount written on generalizing the results of research. Shadish et al. (2002) provide one of the few comprehensive explorations of this topic (albeit not focusing exclusively on education research). They clearly explain the ideas presented in this chapter, many of which they developed. For readers specifically interested in research reviews and meta-analysis, the collection of papers in Cooper and Hedges (1994) is useful.

NOTES

1. Shadish et al. (2002, pp. 83-87) describe the concept of external validity in much greater depth. Our discussion is largely inspired by theirs.

2. They refer to them as "principles of generalized causal inference" (Shadish et al., 2002, p. 353).

3. See Shadish et al. (2002, pp. 353-354).

4. As Shadish et al. (2002, p. 369) observe, "knowledge of the complete causal system . . . makes it easier to reproduce a given causal connection in a wide variety of forms and settings, including previously unexamined ones."

5. See the detailed discussion in Shadish et al. (2002, Chapter 13).

6. To be fair, some authors did raise questions about generalizing the Tennessee results before the California plan was implemented (e.g., Illig, 1996).

7. See http://www.cde.ca.gov/demographics/REPORTS/statewide/sums96.htm

8. To some extent, it is *expected* that the reform will mold itself to individual contexts since the SDP "is no cookie cutter whole school program" (Cook et al., 2000, p. 596).

8

The Evaluation Question

Is It Working for Me?

Those of us who have been involved in school improvement initiatives, whether "down-in-the-trenches" as a teacher or principal, or from across town in central office, can identify with Alice in Wonderland:

"Would you tell me, please, which way I ought to walk from here?"

"That depends a good deal on where you want to get to," said the Cat.

"I don't much care where—" said Alice.

"Then it doesn't matter which way you walk," said the Cat.

"—so long as I get somewhere," Alice added as an explanation.

"Oh, you're sure to do that," said the Cat, "if you only walk long enough."

(Carroll, 1946, p. 70)

Educators are desperate to get "somewhere" and are looking for anyone, even if it's a dubious character like the Cheshire Cat to provide direction. Once we set off on an implementation journey, we are frequently much less concerned with where we will eventually end up than that we are moving in some new direction. To many, implementation *is* the destination as opposed to a journey toward what matters most—the attainment of meaningful and measurable goals that are linked to student achievement.

It would be wonderful indeed if we could install a new program or whole-school reform in the same way that technicians install more memory into outdated computers. Unfortunately, as Cunningham (1993) points out, "a social change cannot be introduced in the same way as one would install a part in a machine; a social change involves acceptance and learning, with various degrees of understanding and resistance by different individuals" (p. 155). The implementation of a social change requires user-driven research to investigate, monitor, and evaluate.

> It would be wonderful if we could install a new program or whole-school reform in the same way that technicians install more memory into outdated computers.

Beset by the problems of "buses, budgets, and boilers," administrators often launch an implementation and immediately move on to the next project, failing to ask whether anything was achieved. Or more to the point, is this program, method, model, or policy working for me in my classroom, school, or district? To answer this question, *you* must become a user-driven researcher. Whenever educators implement new programs, methodologies, or policies, they have an obligation to evaluate them. The point of user-driven research is to determine, by gathering evidence, whether something is working or not. If it's working, tweak it and keep on doing it. If it's not working, modify it or drop it.

What Is User-Driven Research?

Undoubtedly, the term user-driven research is a new one to you. We have mentioned it in passing at various points in the book but have waited until this final chapter to define it in more detail. It is conducted by educators themselves, onsite in their classrooms and schools—not in response to the needs of professorial types (academic-driven research) or individual educators who may be taking a course or working on a dissertation (degree-driven research)—but in response to the immediate needs of the school community. The word *driven* implies a sense of motivation and forward movement but also communicates an edge of insistence and persistence.

You are no doubt familiar with its close cousin, action research. As it was originally conceived and conducted by John Dewey in education (1929, 1933) and Kurt Lewin (1946) in business and management settings, action research exhibited most of the critical attributes that we are ascribing to user-driven research. In its more recent incarnations, however, action research has come to refer to short-term projects done in graduate-level education courses. As it is currently practiced in many colleges of education, action research is a distant cousin, if related at all, to what we believe are the essentials of user-driven research. Our definition incorporates understandings and practices not only from Dewey's and Lewin's original conceptions of action research but also from various other approaches found in this seemingly ever-expanding category of onsite, practitioner-based research.[1]

One aspect of some models of action research that we do not include in our definition is the political dimension. User-driven research, by our definition, is undertaken to improve the effectiveness of a classroom, school, or district—not as a means of promoting liberation and justice among teachers, students, or parents. Although one by-product of user-driven research could very well be the "disruption of existing power relationships" (Brooks & Watkins, 1994, p. 12), user-driven research is not conducted with this goal in mind.

Productive and effective schools habitually operate in a user-driven research mode. As Kurt Lewin (as quoted in Sanford, 1981) originally conceived of action research, it consisted of "analysis, fact-finding, conceptualization, planning, execution, more fact-finding or evaluation—and then a repetition of this whole circle of activities; indeed a spiral of such circles" (p. 174). If you are thinking, "this is just plain common sense," then you are right. If you are an educator who routinely operates in a user-driven research mode, then give yourself a pat on the back. However, it was Voltaire who said that

> Productive and effective schools habitually operate in a user-driven research mode.

"common sense is not so common," and we suspect that all but the most disciplined among us periodically succumb to the seductive notions of serendipity and creativity in the conduct of schooling, failing to engage in continuing cycles and spirals of user-driven research.

Educators who are committed to evidence-based decision making and results-based goal setting continually identify problems, collaboratively discuss and debate possible solutions, determine what solution is most likely to succeed (based on available theory and research combined with past experience), develop an implementation plan, determine how results will be measured, monitor implementation, collect data (both quantitative and qualitative) to determine the outcomes of implementation, and then return to the drawing board to make necessary changes. Educators are generally more adept at identifying problems and generating innovative solutions than they are at evaluating implementation to determine if a solution actually works, and if it doesn't, to do something about it.

User-driven research is motivated by school-based needs and problems that are impeding the school's progress toward specific goals and ultimately the achievement of its mission and vision. It is conducted by the multiple "insiders" in school communities who continually and collaboratively ask three of the five questions presented throughout this book. Earlier, we asked these questions in the context of making sense of research conducted by others— preferably, *before* adoption and implementation. Now, we are advocating that you, the reader, ask these same questions regarding *any* implementation you undertake in your classroom, school, or district:

- The causal question: Is it working for me?
- The process question: How is it working for me?
- The cost question: Is it worthwhile for me?

The Causal Question: Is It Working for Me?

As we discovered in earlier chapters, the causal question is a difficult one to answer, except under the most favorable experimental conditions. That dilemma does not excuse us from asking it, however. Did the program lead to the desired outcomes? That is, did the activities and treatments of the program have any causal effect on the achievement, attitudes, behaviors, skills, or knowledge levels of the students (teachers in the case of a staff development program or parents in the case of a parent intervention program) who have been exposed to them?

To determine what kind of data to gather, one must know the desired outcome. For example, if you want to see improved student attitudes regarding school, then the data will likely come from questionnaires or surveys. If the desired outcome is increased mathematics or reading achievement, then standardized tests in reading or math are the measurements of choice. If you are looking for improved behavior, develop a description of what would constitute that behavior and the kind of data that would demonstrate the existence of that behavior (e.g., fewer behavior referrals, suspensions, expulsion, and police reports). The difficulty with many implementations is that educators cannot agree or do not specify the desired outcomes of a program. They are implementing on "hope and good intentions" (Patton, 1986, p. 151), wanting credit for hard work and sincerity (activity) instead of results (achievement). In the absence of well-defined outcomes, the likelihood of even approaching an answer to the does-it-work question is nil.

The Process Question: How Is It Working for Me?

The process question is much easier to ask and answer in the user-driven research mode than is its causal cousin. Who better to observe and explain the intricacies and interactions of implementation than insiders—trained teachers who understand how students, curricula, and teaching methodologies interact; administrators who know the culture of the school and can tease out the subtleties of classroom observations; and parents who know their children and have a huge stake in the outcomes. Answering the process question requires the collection of multiple kinds of qualitative data. To use this data, however, practitioners (especially administrators) must lay aside their reluctance to hear the "down side" of an implementation and open their minds to "detailed descriptions of situations, events, people, interactions, and observed behaviors; direct quotations from people about their experiences, attitudes, beliefs, and thoughts; and excerpts of entire passages from documents, correspondence, records, and case histories" (Patton, 1986, p. 187).

> Answering the process question requires the collection of multiple kinds of qualitative data.

Unfortunately, and we speak from personal experience, educators are far too prone to regard silence as golden and ignorance as bliss. We would sometimes rather not know that the program on which we spent tens of thousands of dollars isn't working or that the fabulous staff development we provided didn't transform every teacher into Jaime Escalante overnight. If we send out signals like the emperor in Andersen's favorite fairy tale, we too will hear only praise for our proverbial new clothes. The truth will be told only in parking lot meetings and whispered discussions in the teacher lounge if we do not ask the is-it-working-for-me question.

The Cost Question: Is It Worthwhile for Me?

The final question relates to whether an implementation is cost-feasible and cost-effective. To answer this question, look for the hidden costs of implementation that were not evident beforehand— the mounting costs for substitutes as you send staff members for additional training, the unexpected costs for new textbooks that are more adaptable to whole-group instruction, or the implementation costs being subsidized by other programs that will eventually suffer if not reimbursed. Has the innovation imposed some unexpected and almost unseen costs? For example, have your efforts to increase comprehension instruction schoolwide reduced the amount of time available for writing instruction? Although there are no monetary costs involved, "robbing Peter to pay Paul," is not always cost-feasible or cost-effective.

> Although there are no monetary costs involved, "robbing Peter to pay Paul" is not always cost-feasible or cost-effective.

User-driven research cannot provide definitive answers to the causal, process, and cost questions, but we cannot allow that lack of certainty to blind us to what it can do: help us improve programs and make more informed decisions that can enhance educational opportunities for all students.

User-Driven Research
At Lincoln Middle School

To fully appreciate the value of user-driven research, a site visitation is in order. Our visit takes us to Lincoln Middle School in Midtown, USA, an economically diverse community, and offers the opportunity to see user-driven research in action. Lincoln enrolls a melting pot of races and ethnicities, but its staff is largely white.

Although Lincoln is an imaginary composite of the schools in which we have worked or consulted during our professional careers, its experiences mirror those of many schools that have confused implementation with results; or as legendary UCLA basketball coach, John Wooden (1997), puts it, "mistake[n] activity for achievement" (p. viii). Fortunately, the principal, building leadership team, and staff of Lincoln are beginning to ask the right questions.

Middle School: Panacea or Pandora's Box?

A task force of administrators, board members, teachers, and community members touted the adoption of the middle school model as a panacea for Lincoln's problems. The group was mesmerized by the middle school movement that swept the country in the 1980s and used reports such as *Successful Schools for Young Adolescents* (Lipsitz, 1984); *This We Believe* (National Middle School Association, 1982); *Turning Points* (Carnegie Corporation, 1989), and *Caught in the Middle* (California Department of Education, 1987) as the basis for their decision. Filled with optimism and the abiding belief that the experts couldn't be wrong, the task force believed that the "middle school model" would be the miracle that would raise achievement, turn sullen adolescents into motivated students, and give teachers more planning time. Like many of us who have leaped into implementation with unbounded faith and optimism, they did not anticipate the need for conducting both formative and summative evaluations. They also overlooked the fact that the research on which their implementation was based provided few solid answers to the causal, process, and cost questions.

> Surely, the "middle school model" would be the miracle that would raise achievement, turn every sullen adolescent into a model student, and give teachers more planning time.

There was a period of euphoria during the first year, as veteran teachers enjoyed the additional planning periods, newly hired staff members infused fresh ideas and methodologies into a veteran faculty, and the entire school community engaged in team-building activities. Now, almost 3 years into implementation, many of the same "ills" that flew out when Pandora opened her mythical box are proving to be divisive and debilitating. Despite an extensive and expensive staff development effort, there is a deep philosophical divide among the staff regarding just what the goals of middle school should be. The initial burst of energy that accompanied the implementation has waned, and many are beginning to question if Lincoln is doing the right thing wrong *or* just the wrong thing. Discussions regarding the problems are conducted quietly—no one wants to be the bearer of bad news.

> Despite an extensive and expensive staff development effort, there is a deep philosophical divide among the staff regarding just what the goals of middle school should be.

One group of teachers is focused on the affective aspects of middle school; their top priority is providing a safe, caring, and supportive environment for students. Prior to implementation, they believed that achievement would follow. Once their students felt better about coming to school, they would just naturally learn more would obtain higher test. The group would rather ignore the achievement issue altogether. Another faction is depressed about declining achievement and frustrated about their inability to meet the needs of so many ability levels in their heterogeneous classes. These "instructionally relentless" pedagogues believe that middle school should not be an extension or an enhancement of elementary school but rather a transition to the academic demands of high school. They went along with those who promoted the idea of a middle school, but they secretly yearn for the "good old days" when teachers were in charge and students sat in rows. There is a growing sense of distrust between the groups. The district is too small to have an in-house research guru and too poor to hire an outside evaluator, but there *is* one possible solution to this perplexing problem: user-driven research. Like Pandora, the faculty and administration of Lincoln are hoping to discover there's still hope left in the box.

> Like Pandora, the faculty and administration of Lincoln are hoping to discover there's still hope left in the box.

Adopting the User-Driven Research Mind-Set

Let's consider how the administrators and staff at Lincoln might avoid further pitfalls, put their implementation back on track, and ensure that future implementations encounter fewer speed bumps. Our story begins when the chairperson of the Building Leadership Team (BLT), Steve Johnson, meets with Duane Dobbs, the principal.

Duane is an experienced educator, liked by most of his teachers and appreciated by the students for his keen sense of humor. He calls himself a laid-back leader. Steve is a senior faculty member and can be counted on for an honest appraisal of any situation. Although he can't always prod his principal into action, his message today is on target: "There's something I think you should know about."

Steve explained the growing dissatisfaction of the staff with many aspects of the middle school implementation and suggested that something should be done. Duane, although not overjoyed at the news, wasn't surprised. He knew that trouble was brewing and had been thinking about his options—retirement being one of them. He has read about an approach called user-driven research in which a school-based research team is formed not only to evaluate research in advance of adopting a new program or to solve specific site-based problems but also to monitor, evaluate, and fine-tune large-scale implementations. Perhaps such a team might have kept Lincoln's implementation on course. But it's never too late.

The user-driven research approach poses three questions to evaluate the implementation of a model, reform, or program. Principal Dobbs is attracted to its practicality. Steve expected some waffling from Duane and was somewhat taken aback by his apparent enthusiasm for what Steve thought was "bad news." "What are these questions?" Steve asked.

Duane explained and asked these questions: "Is the middle school model working at Lincoln School? What's the evidence that it's working? *How* is the middle school model working at Lincoln? Do we know what variables or forces are interacting to either move implementation forward or to impede it? Is the model worthwhile? How much is the implementation costing in terms of money, human resources, and unseen costs? Is it feasible to bear these costs? Is there a more cost-effective way of accomplishing the same goals?"

"Is the middle school model working at Lincoln School? How is it working at Lincoln? Is the model worthwhile?"

Steve, amazed at his principal's reaction and intrigued by the questions, suggested a meeting date to talk with the BLT about forming a user-driven research team.

For the first time in 2 years, Duane Dobbs looked forward to meeting with the BLT—usually *they* were telling *him* what needed to be done. He trusts this group of bright and committed teachers, but they usually move too fast for him. Once the meeting was called to order, he explained the user-driven approach and requested their help to form a research team. The team wisely advised that another group of teachers be recruited to research the implementation—a standing team that would be responsible for conducting research not only on the middle school implementation but on any future investigations and implementations as well. The leadership team already had a full plate, and the original middle school task force (another possible option for the research team) is not only "touchy" about the current problems with their "baby," but also "tired" from preimplementation planning.

"The research team needs people with energy and a fresh perspective," Steve explained to Duane. "We'll make a to-do list for them, but that's it for us."

Principal Dobbs called a faculty meeting to explain the BLT's recommendation, which after some discussion was supported by the faculty. The volunteers for the research team are perfect for the job—two math teachers (Mike and Matt), the media specialist, Connie, and an instructional aide with a degree in anthropology, Sally. Duane assigned an assistant administrator, Maria, to work with the team, gave their marching orders, and requested weekly updates.

ASKING THE RIGHT QUESTIONS

The user-driven research mind-set is all about asking the right questions. In the case of Lincoln Middle School, the questions are these:

- Is the middle school model working for us?
- How is it working (or not working) for us?
- Is it worthwhile for us?

Question Number One: Is the Middle School Model Working for Us?

The newly constituted user-driven research team exchanged greetings, rolled up their sleeves, and decided their first job was to backtrack and revisit the middle school research.

What Does the Research Say?

Although the original task force consulted the "research" in their investigation of the middle school model, the task force was dissolved once implementation began. Without a user-driven research team in place, there was no one monitoring the middle school research scene. The newly formed team searched for later studies and found one describing how middle schools similar in size and student composition to Lincoln were dealing with the challenges of implementation. They found that Lincoln was not alone in experiencing growing pains and that assessment data for middle schools overall revealed little change in student performance over a 10-year period (Haycock & Ames, 2000, p. 49).

They also located a study describing a core of successful and high-performing middle schools located in the area. The high-performing schools had four characteristics in common: academic excellence, developmental responsiveness, social equity, and a schoolwide learning community (National Forum to Accelerate Middle Grades Reform [National Forum], 2002).

"I wonder how Lincoln would measure up to these benchmarks?" asked Maria. "They seem like qualities any good school should have."

"We'll need some data," Connie said. "I'd like to know how our school compares achievementwise to other schools in the county that are demographically similar to ours."

> "I'd like to know how our school measures up to other students that are similar to ours."

"What's our average daily attendance rate?" asked Mike. "I never seem to have my whole class there on any given day."

"I wonder what the grade point averages are for the various teams and how they compare to the kids' standardized test scores," added Matt. "Are the students able to demonstrate what their grades say they've learned in class on a standardized test?

"I know test scores are important, but what does the faculty think? Isn't there some kind of survey we could use to find out?" asked Sally.

Analyzing Achievement Test Data

The research team gave their data requests to Principal Dobbs and asked him to attend the next meeting. After almost 3 years of implementation, the results were not encouraging. Only about one third of the school's graduates reached the proficient level in reading. This was slightly higher than scores on the same test prior to middle school implementation and seemed like a small cause for celebration until Mark asked how this improvement was distributed across ethnic groups. They quickly calculated that the white and Asian students made up the largest part of the proficient group, whereas the percentage of proficient African American and Latino students actually declined after middle school implementation. The same disturbing achievement gap was evident in math and science.

The team listed some questions to guide their analysis of the data: (a) Is there any relationship between attendance and test scores? Attendance and grade point averages? (b) Is there any relationship between test scores and students' grade-point averages? (c) When the data is disaggregated by socioeconomic status, what are the trends?

By ethnic group? (d) How does Lincoln compare with the highest-achieving schools in the state? (e) How does it compare with the lowest-achieving schools in the state? (f) What do the data trends over the past 10 years show? (g) What are the achievement trends since we began the middle school implementation? (h) In what curricular area is our achievement the lowest? Highest?

"We need better data displays," said Mike. "If you give me a day of release time," he told Duane, "I'll set up some spread sheets and graphs to make sense of all of these numbers." Duane looked a little guilty and nodded. He knew when to say yes.

Question Number Two: How Is the Middle School Model Working (or Not Working) for Us?

"We know that it's not working," said Maria, at the beginning of the next meeting, "but there's a lot I'd like to know about *how* and *why* it's not working."

"Let's survey the staff," said Sally. "They're the ones who are down in the trenches. I've got an idea about using those four indicators from the high-performing middle schools to create an instrument."

Surveying the Faculty

The team developed a closed-ended questionnaire based on the four indicators of high-achieving middle schools that they downloaded from the Middle Grades Reform Web page (National Forum, 2002). They asked the faculty to rate the presence of each indicator in the school on a scale of 1-5 (*Never, Seldom, Sometimes, Usually, Always*) and planned to follow up with in-depth interviews and observations after identifying the major problems.

Three academic problems jumped out immediately. The team was astounded at the low average scores for the following survey items:

- All students are expected to meet high academic standards. Teachers supply students with exemplars of high-quality work that meets the performance standard. Students revise their work based on feedback until they meet or exceed the performance standard. (Average Score of 1.9)
- Curriculum, instruction, and assessment are aligned with high standards. They provide a coherent vision for what students should know and be able to do. The curriculum is rigorous and nonrepetitive; it moves forward substantially as students progress through the middle grades. (Average Score of 2.6)

- The curriculum emphasizes deep understanding of important concepts, development of essential skills, and the ability to apply what one has learned to real-world problems. By making connections across the disciplines, the curriculum helps reinforce important concepts. (Average Score of 2.9)

Developmental responsiveness, the second of the four characteristics of high-performing middle schools seemed to describe the ability of the faculty to meet the "unique developmental challenges of early adolescence" (National Forum, 2002). In addition to the earlier academic concerns, three descriptors of developmental responsiveness were given low ratings by faculty members:

- Teachers use a wide variety of instructional strategies to foster curiosity, exploration, creativity, and the development of social skills. (Average Score of 2.6)
- The school develops alliances with families to enhance and support the well-being of their children. It involves families as partners in their children's education, keeping them informed, involving them in their children's learning, and ensuring participation in decision making. (Average Score of 2.9)
- Faculty and administrators expect high-quality work from all students and are committed to helping each student produce it. Evidence of this commitment includes tutoring, mentoring, special adaptations, and other supports. (Average Score of 2.1)

The third indicator, social equity, was defined as "socially equitable, democratic and fair . . . providing every student with high-quality teachers, resources, learning opportunities, and supports" (National Forum, 2002). Three social equity descriptors received overall low scores from the Lincoln staff:

- The school continually adapts curriculum, instruction, assessment, and scheduling to meet its students' diverse and changing needs. (Average Score of 2.3)
- All students have equal access to valued knowledge in all school classes and activities. (Average Score of 2.5)
- The faculty is culturally and linguistically diverse. (Average Score 1.5)

The final descriptor encompassed the overall culture and climate of the school as a learning community. Four descriptors received overall low ratings:

- A shared vision of what a high-performing school is and does drives every facet of school change. Shared and sustained leadership propels the school forward and preserves its institutional memory and purpose. (Average Score of 2.1)
- Someone in the school has the responsibility and authority to hold the school improvement enterprise together, including day-to-day know-how, coordination, strategic planning, and communication. (Average Score of 1.9)
- The school is a community of practice in which learning, experimentation, and reflection are the norm. Expectations of continuous improvement permeate the school. (Average Score of 2.8)
- The school devotes resources to ensure that teachers have time and opportunity to reflect on their classroom practice and learn from one another. At school, everyone's job is to learn. (Average Score of 2.3)

The research team received a day of release time to talk about the survey. They took their materials to a conference room at central office where they wouldn't be disturbed and shared their interpretations. There was overwhelming consensus regarding the "big" problems: a fuzzy mission, lack of measurable goals, lack of strong administrative leadership, overall low expectations for students, lack of appropriate staff development, and a need to do a better job with minority students—both academically and socially.

"We changed the sign on the front of the building, put some teams together, and hired a bunch of new people, but we forgot to work on the innards of the school," said Mike. "The outside looks great, but the important stuff isn't working."

> "We changed the sign on the front of the building, put some teams together, and hired a bunch of new people, but we forgot to work on the innards of the school."

Interviewing the Faculty

"We need to talk to the teachers one-on-one," said Sally. "I'll put a list of questions together. We'll guarantee their anonymity." Sally's anthropology background proved invaluable in gathering qualitative data. She had done field work for a professor while in college and understood the value of open-ended questions to get at the *how* and *why* answers that would explain the abysmally low ratings for some of the descriptors. Duane authorized some release time and extra-duty pay, and she did her "field-work" in the teachers' lounge and at team meetings. Wherever there were teachers, Sally was there asking questions and listening.

Once the research team heard the problem described in the words of their colleagues, it became real.

"I'm not sure exactly what I'm supposed to be doing."

"Most of the teachers on my team are using the middle school philosophy as a way of letting kids off the hook. Rather than notching up the standards and raising the expectations, we've dumbed everything down."

"The staff development has been terrible, and it's hindering rather than helping us. Stop bringing in 'experts' from outside, and let the teachers who are really good show us how they're doing it. There must be some bright spots in this school somewhere. Let's find them and build on them."

"I'm sick and tired of the quick-fix mentality where you bring in some expert from someplace else and they tell us what to do. Why can't we solve our own problems for a change? I'd be glad to take all that money we paid those fancy consultants and come up with a better plan than they did."

> "The principal really pushed for this middle school idea, and now we never see him. We need some support around here from him, and fast."

"The principal really pushed for this middle school idea, and now we never see him. We need some support around here from him, and fast."

"I thought there was supposed to be a lot of research on this middle school thing, but I haven't read anything yet that really proves this thing works or that tells us how to do it."

"I know we have a team planning period, but that's hardly enough time to talk about the kids and their problems. When do we get to talk about the teachers and their problems?"

"We've got a lot of problems with all the different kinds of kids in our school and as the only teacher of color, I feel like most of my colleagues just don't get it. They're stuck 20 years ago when this school was like Lake Woebegone and all the kids were above average. I'm tired of hearing their excuses for why kids of color or poor kids can't learn. Whatever happened to high expectations?"

Interviewing Students and Parents

"I think we're getting closer to the big picture," said Maria, "but I'd also like to hear from the students and their parents. Do you think you can do one more round of interviews, Sally?"

The results of Sally's conversations with parents and students were definitely more positive than the research team had expected, but there were some disturbing problems between certain teachers and certain groups of kids. "This is a problem for Duane to address," said Maria. "We need to be careful how we use this data."

Question Number Three: Is the Middle School Model Worthwhile for Us?

The final question concerned costs, and once again, the team turned to the principal for data. They peppered him with questions:

"How are we paying for this implementation?"

"We hired additional teachers, added instructional aides, increased the number of exploratory periods to the day, built a technology center, and hired another counselor. I've heard rumors that the board is going for another referendum. Did we think about money before we started implementing?"

"How much did all of that fancy staff development cost? I'd like to be one of those consultants."

> "How much did all of that fancy staff development cost? I'd like to be one of those consultants."

Counting the Costs

The team added up all the costs of implementation and calculated the additional cost per student for each of the 3 years of implementation. They were stunned to discover that not only were they spending an average of $250 more per year for each enrolled student over the 3-year implementation period than they had previously spent under the "junior high school model," but that costs were going up each year. "At this rate, we'll be broke before our achievement goes up," moaned Connie.

"Where has all of this money come from?" said Maria.

Duane looked a little sheepish. "Well, I've been moving my budgets around to make things come out even, but sooner or later, Peter won't have any money left to pay Paul."

Cost-Effective?

"I think you need to have a meeting with the superintendent and the business manager as soon as possible," said Mark. "Unless we change the way we're doing business, we're going to go out of business."

"We're spending more money and our achievement is going down. Good thing I'm a quiet guy," said Mike. "The newspaper would love to get its hands on this information."

REFOCUSING ON OUTCOMES

The last item on the agenda was to articulate and then operationally define the specific and desired outcomes of middle school implementation for Lincoln School. The research team carefully examined all of the documents produced by the original task force and could find no such description.

"This could be a big part of the problem," Maria said. "Everyone has been doing their own version of the middle school." There were no goals for increasing achievement or decreasing the number of students who were not proficient in reading or mathematics. The goal was implementation (activity)—not achievement.

"The staff should join the discussion now," said Maria. "We need goals that everyone will support. We also need to let them talk about these problems as a group. But first, let's tell the BLT what we've found."

DEFINING THE PROBLEMS

Mark had emerged as the leader of the user-driven research team during their 6 months of meetings, and he was the unanimous choice of the BLT to make a PowerPoint presentation to the faculty.

"What we have to say will come as no surprise to you," explained Mark, as he showed the first slide to the faculty. "We believe there are solutions to the problems we're going to describe. But our job wasn't to come up with solutions. That's your job. Our assignment was to ask three questions and determine the answers."

Mark continued. "The first question we asked was, Is the middle school model working at Lincoln? The answer is no. It's not working at all. We adopted this model to address some specific issues, and they are still there. Some of the problems have even gotten worse."

> "Is the middle school model working at Lincoln? The answer is no. It's not working at all."

He went on. "The second question was, How is the middle school model 'not working' at Lincoln? The answer is that a bunch of things are going on inside 'the black box' of our middle school making some pretty messy situations that aren't going to change unless we do something. Here are the problems you identified in the survey and interviews: (a) an ill-defined mission, (b) lack of strong administrative leadership, (c) overall low expectations for students, (d) lack of appropriate staff development, (e) and a need to diversify the faculty and make it more responsive to students."

Mark took a deep breath and kept going. "The third question was, Is the middle school implementation worthwhile? We've never asked that question around here about anything. But we did ask it this time. And the answer is—not at the moment. We're spending a lot more money per student (more than $250 a year) than we did in the past, and we're getting worse results now than before implementation started. We're not delivering any bang for all of these bucks we're spending. If we're going to be accountable to the community and honest with ourselves, things need to change, and fast."[2]

Lincoln Middle School's story, although imaginary, is all too common in the "real world." Fortunately, their story has a happy ending. The administration and faculty came to understand that merely adopting a new model was not the answer to the challenges they faced. Their site-specific problems needed solutions that could only be derived from their own version of user-driven research—a version that combined many of the characteristics of the following exemplars.

EXEMPLARS OF USER-DRIVEN RESEARCH

There are many contemporary exemplars of user-driven research. We have chosen four—two school-based projects and two whole-school models to illustrate some of the dynamics of this methodology. Knowing what a "good one" looks like is valuable when one commits to a user-driven research approach. There are many ways to use site-based, practitioner-driven research, and these exemplars should inspire you to form your own school-based research team. User-driven research can be used at multiple and varying points in the ongoing cycle of fact finding, problem solving, decision making, implementation, and evaluation in a school or district: (a) evaluating a specific program or method after a defined period of implementation (e.g., the summative evaluation of block scheduling), (b) evaluating a program during implementation to fine-tune and tweak it (e.g., formative evaluation of the staff development program that supports the implementation of a new reading curriculum), (c) solving a specific school-based problem (e.g., how to improve an excessive drop-out rate or narrow the achievement gap in mathematics and science), or (d) as the basis for schoolwide systemic reform to turn around a low-achieving school.

CASE EXEMPLAR
Inquiry for School Improvement:
The Accelerated-School Model

The Accelerated School Model was developed in 1986 by then Stanford University economist Henry M. Levin. As of September, 2001, there were 1,300 Accelerated Schools serving students in grades K-8 (Northwest Regional Educational Laboratory, 2002, p. 1). Differing from many other whole-school reform approaches (e.g., Success for All), the Accelerated Schools Model does not prescribe curricular materials or instructional methodologies but, rather, trains teachers, administrators, and parents in the use of a collaborative inquiry process, through which they are able to explore their unique problems, hypothesize possible reasons for these problems, brainstorm solutions, develop an action plan, pilot the plan, and then evaluate and reassess their progress (National Center for Accelerated Schools, 2002b). The genius of this model lies in its ability to sidestep the one-size-fits-all type of reform that inevitably falters because it can never quite be made to fit the specifics of a unique school. As teachers, parents, and administrators become a part of the inquiry process, their values, goals, and vision for what their school can become are changed. The solution is a process rather than a prescription.

Although the inquiry process is not unlike the steps most of us go through when we encounter a problem, when the process is done collaboratively with colleagues and after a period of training by Accelerated Schools' personnel, it enables teachers and administrators to view problems as opportunities rather than obstacles. Recall the earlier instance of our imaginary middle school. Without preparation, training, and consultation, faculties are frequently forced to rely on trial and error during implementation. Accelerated Schools receive training and a template for solving problems. The answers and solutions, however, come from each individual faculty as they work together. There are no recipes.

Although the inquiry process that lies at the heart of the Accelerated Schools model is what is most germane to the topic of this chapter, a brief explanation of how the term *accelerated* is used to drive the inquiry process is helpful. Typically, the term is associated with gifted instruction and fast-paced classes that move students quickly through easier material and on to more challenging content. In contrast, low-achieving students are usually labeled as *remedial* and given instructional methods and materials well below their age-grade levels. Accelerated Schools turn this traditional way of thinking about learning upside down and strive to bring all students to age-appropriate academic levels. Their goals are achieved by raising expectations and providing extended and enriched learning opportunities. Equity, participation, communication, collaboration, reflection, experimentation, discovery, trust, and risk taking are key principles for the parents, students, teachers, and administrators of Accelerated Schools, but collaborative inquiry is the engine that drives improvement, finds solutions, and evaluates outcomes (National Center for Accelerated Schools, 2002b).

CASE EXEMPLAR
Closing the Literacy Gap:
The Reading Apprenticeship

The Strategic Literacy Initiative (SLI) was conceived and implemented by classroom teachers at the Thurgood Marshall Academic High School in San Francisco and two senior staff members of a research and professional development project at WestEd, a nonprofit education research, development, and service agency headquartered in San Francisco (Schoenbach et al., 1999). Teachers identified a highly problematic, school-based issue that frustrated them and their students alike: the low reading levels of entering high school freshman. This problem led teachers to dramatically lower expectations for the quality and quantity of textbook and outside reading that students would do, which in turn further exacerbated low literacy levels. The teachers and researchers gave this problem a name: *the literacy ceiling.* They gathered data (both qualitative and quantitative) to determine the nature and extent of the problem. Their research activities were extensive and are described in *Reading for Understanding: A Guide to Improving Reading in Middle and High School Classrooms* (Schoenbach et al., 1999). They included, among other activities, (a) investigating the existing research on reading comprehension, (b) detailed video- and text-based case studies of a group of 30 ninth-grade students identified by their teachers as representative of the range of students who had difficulty reading and understanding assigned texts, (c) in-depth reading history interviews with selected students, (d) videotaped episodes of students reading and discussing texts, and (e) teachers' reflections on and analysis of student performance (pp. 11-12).

As the teachers and researchers jointly examined the quantitative and qualitative data, a possible approach to solving this pervasive problem began to emerge. They decided to call their fledgling approach a *reading apprenticeship* and described it thus: "a method in which the classroom teacher serves as *master reader* to his or her *student apprentices*" (Schoenbach et al., 1999, p. 12) and in which "teachers invite students to become partners in a collaborative inquiry into their reading processes" (p. 14). A critical attribute of the reading apprenticeship model is the ongoing modeling and thinking aloud by teachers in order to make their use of cognitive strategies visible to students. Students are able to observe the teacher, try out the strategies for themselves in a safe environment, and then gain the confidence to apply the strategies on their own, much like apprentice plumbers or electricians would learn their trades.

Quantitative data was collected in the form of pretests and posttests. In addition, students' reading attitudes and habits were assessed. In the pilot year of the program, 200 students improved from an average late-seventh grade level to an average ninth-grade level as measured by a norm-referenced reading test (Greenleaf, 1999). Follow-up tests in subsequent years showed that the reading gains were not just holding, but they were growing at an accelerated rate, as measured by the standardized reading test.

SLI more than meets our qualifications for user-driven research. It combines inquiry, reflection (both personal and collective), collaboration, problem solving, qualitative and quantitative data collection, and knowledge generation in an ongoing cycle of action to ameliorate important and pressing problems related to teaching and learning in classrooms, schools, or districts. User-driven research projects don't necessarily have to culminate in the publication of a book, as this first exemplar has, but they do have to result in the generation and dissemination of some type of "useable" knowledge.

CASE EXEMPLAR
Teachers as Staff Developers:
East Side Community High School

East Side Community High School (ESCHS) in Manhattan is a small Grades 7-12 school affiliated with the New York Networks for School Renewal. As a condition of their affiliation with the network, teachers at the school are expected to "formulate a question that [is] both deep and broad enough to sustain rigorous inquiry over time, with the potential to improve practice throughout their school" and "involve a significant group of teachers . . . to ensure truly 'school-based' research, not simply the work of a few individuals" (Barnes, 2001, p. 40). The teachers at ESCHS framed this question: "How [can] teachers . . . support and encourage each other through staff development?" (p. 40). Cultural anthropologist Nancy Barnes was part of the project's evaluation team and describes both the research project and her qualitative evaluation of the project in an *Education Week* essay.

Barnes (2001) drew three conclusions from her research at ESCHS: "(a) Teachers engaged in inquiry projects that they have designed get to think about things that matter in their schools; (b) Participatory school-based research, like other forms of action research, can actually make changes and fix things, as well as document and evaluate . . . [producing] concrete results and [building] a democratic community; and (c) Teachers making decisions and exercising power in the course of an inquiry project (not just having their voices included) [creates] a meaningful new form of accountability and leadership development" (p. 42).

CASE EXEMPLAR
Sustaining School Improvement:
The Professional Learning Community

During the late 1980s, principals in the state of Illinois were invited to participate in an instructional leadership project sponsored by the Illinois Principals Association (IPA). The state legislature had recently mandated that principals spend at least 51% of their time in activities that were loosely defined as "instructional leadership." The association engaged Richard Andrews (1989) to consult with IPA's directors and staff regarding instructional leadership and then made his professional assistance available to principals in the state who wished to have their instructional leadership capabilities evaluated and developed. Those who volunteered were expected to give teachers a questionnaire to determine their perceptions of their principals' instructional leadership profiles, submit those questionnaires to Andrews for evaluation, and then receive an overall rating—strong, average, or weak. Each principal then had the privilege of meeting with Andrews one-on-one to discuss and evaluate the results. The association also selected a group of strong instructional leaders from various geographic areas of the state to provide staff development to their fellow principals. The group included two dozen elementary and middle school principals. Only one high school principal, Richard DuFour, then principal of Adlai Stevenson High School in Lincolnshire, Illinois, made the list.

DuFour served as the principal of Stevenson for a number of years and during that time garnered numerous awards, both personally and for his school. He moved from the principalship to the superintendency of High School District 125 and continued to refine his model for sustaining school improvement. He and academic Robert Eaker call their model a *professional learning community* (DuFour & Eaker, 1998). The label one affixes to the process of sustained inquiry to the end of school improvement is not really that important. What matters most is a relentless commitment to evidence-based decision making in a culture of collaborative inquiry. DuFour and Eaker describe six characteristics of professional learning communities: (a) shared mission, vision, and values, (b) collective inquiry, (c) collaborative teams, (d) action orientation and experimentation, (e) continuous improvement, and (f) results orientation (pp. 25-29).

It is one thing to think and write about creating a professional learning community. It is quite another to *do* it. During DuFour's tenure in the Stevenson district as both principal and superintendent, the school has been named as one of America's best schools six times and has received commendations from the U.S. Department of Education and the College Board (DuFour & Eaker, 1998, p. ix).

Our imaginary middle school implementation recounted earlier in the chapter could have used DuFour's leadership. In a column in the *Journal of Staff Development,* he described what drives improvement at Stevenson. "Developing a collective sense of what the school might become is an essential step on the journey to becoming a learning community, but it is not sufficient. Schools also must be willing to assess their current reality with total candor and honesty, and then describe the specific measurable results they expect to see as a result of achieving their vision. Using data is the most effective strategy for translating the good intentions described in a vision statement into meaningful improvement" (DuFour, 2000, p. 71).[3]

Further Reading

The articles and books that describe each of the exemplars are worth reading in their entirety (Barnes, 2001; DuFour & Eaker, 1998; Schoenbach et al., 1999). For a complete description of Accelerated Schools, visit their Web site: www.acceleratedschools.net.

Notes

1. Following are the terms and types of action research we encountered in our literature search: action inquiry (Torbert, 1981, 1987, 1991); action learning (Revans, 1982); action science (Argyris, Putnam, & Smith, 1985); action technologies (Brooks & Watkins, 1994); appreciative inquiry (Harman, 1990; Srivastva, Fry, & Cooperrider, 1990); collaborative activist research (Hale, 2000); collaborative inquiry (Bray, Lee, Smith, & Yorks, 2000); critical action research (Zeichner & Gore, 1995); emancipatory action research (Carr & Kemmis, 1986; Grundy, 1982); experiential research (Heron, 1981); practitioner research (Anderson, Herr, & Nihlen, 1994); praxis (Freire, 1970/1993); school-based inquiry (Barnes, 2001); useable knowledge research (Lindblom & Cohen, 1979); use-inspired research, (Stokes 1997); and implementation research (Shavelson & Towne, 2002).

2. This case study has been inspired and informed by the *Proceedings of the National Conference on Curriculum, Instruction, and Assessment in the Middle Grades: Linking Research and Practice.* This conference was convened by the National Educational Research Policy and Priorities Board (2000b), which gathered a group of researchers, policymakers, and practitioners to share the latest research regarding middle schools. Practitioners can only hope that this type of conference will be convened to study other pressing issues for practitioners.

3. Schmoker (2001) provides a comprehensive description of the practical aspects of DuFour's work at Stevenson.

Resource

Bibliographies for Case Studies

CLASS SIZE REDUCTION

Angrist, J., & Levy, V. (1999). Using Maimonides' rule to estimate the effect of class size on scholastic achievement. *Quarterly Journal of Economics, 114*(2), 533-576.

Boozer, M., & Rouse, C. (1995). Intraschool variation in class size: Patterns and implications (Working Paper No. 5144). Cambridge, MA: National Bureau of Economic Research.

Brewer, D. J., Krop, C., Gill, B. P., & Reichardt, R. (1999). Estimating the cost of national class size reductions under different policy alternatives. *Educational Evaluation and Policy Analysis, 21*(2), 179-192.

Grissmer, D. (1999). Class size effects: Assessing the evidence, its policy implications, and future research agenda. *Educational Evaluation and Policy Analysis, 21*(2), 231-248.

Grissmer, D. (2002). Cost-effectiveness and cost-benefit analysis: The effect of targeting interventions. In H. M. Levin & P. J. McEwan (Eds.), *Cost-effectiveness and educational policy: 2002, yearbook of the American Education Finance Association* (pp. 97-110). Larchmont, NY: Eye on Education.

Hanushek, E. A. (1997). Assessing the effect of school resources on student performance: An update. *Educational Evaluation and Policy Analysis, 19*(2), 141-164.

Hanushek, E. A. (1999). Some findings from an independent investigation of the Tennessee STAR experiment and from other investigations of class size effects. *Educational Evaluation and Policy Analysis, 21*(2), 143-163.

Harris, D. (2002). Identifying optimal class sizes and teacher salaries. In H. M. Levin & P. J. McEwan (Eds.), *Cost-effectiveness and educational policy: 2002, yearbook of the American Education Finance Association* (pp. 177-191). Larchmont, NY: Eye on Education.

Illig, D. C. (1996). *Reducing class size: A review of the literature and options for consideration.* Retrieved June 11, 2002, from http://www.library.ca.gov/CRB/clssz/clssiz.html#RTFToC13

Jacobson, L. (2001, Feb. 28). Research: Sizing up small classes. *Education Week.* Retrieved April 23, 2002, from http://www.edweek.org/ew/ewstory.cfm?slug=24classize.h20

Krueger, A. B. (2000, October). *Understanding the magnitude and effect of class size on student achievement* (Working Paper No. 121). Economic Policy Institute. Retrieved May 27, 2002, from http://www.epinet.org/Workingpapers/class_size.html

Krueger, A. B., & Whitmore, D. M. (2001). The effect of attending a small class in the early grades on college-test taking and middle school test results: Evidence from Project STAR. *Economic Journal, 111*(468), 1-28.

Levin, H. M., Glass, G. V., & Meister, G. R. (1987). Cost-effectiveness of computer assisted instruction. *Evaluation Review, 11*(1), 50-72.

Molnar, A., Smith, P., Zahorik, J., Palmer, A., Halbach, A., & Ehrle, K. (1999). Evaluating the SAGE Program: A pilot program in targeted pupil-teacher reduction. *Educational Evaluation and Policy Analysis, 21*(2), 165-177.

Mosteller, F. (1995). The Tennessee study of class size in the early school grades. *The Future of Children, 5*(2), 113-127.

National Center for Education Statistics. (2002). *High school and beyond.* Retrieved May 28, 2002, from http://nces.ed.gov/surveys/hsb/

Nye, B., Hedges, L. V., & Konstantopoulos, S. (1999). The long-term effects of small classes: A five-year follow-up of the Tennessee class size experiment. *Educational Evaluation and Policy Analysis, 21*(2), 127-142.

Stecher, B. M., & Bornstedt, G. W. (2002). *Class size reduction in California: Summary findings from 1999-00 and 2000-01* (Technical Report). CSR Research Consortium. Retrieved May 28, 2002, from http://www.classize.org/techreport/index-01.htm

Urquiola, M. (2000). *Identifying class size effects in developing countries: Evidence from rural schools in Bolivia.* Unpublished manuscript, Cornell University.

PHONICS INSTRUCTION

Baker, S., Berninger, V. W., Bruck, M., Chapman, J., Eden, G., Elbaum, B., et al., (2002, May 21). *Evidence-based research on Reading Recovery.* [A letter sent to educational policymakers regarding the effectiveness of Reading Recovery] Retrieved May 28, 2002, from http://www.educationnews.org/ReadingRecoveryisnot successful.htm

Carbo, M. (1988). Debunking the great phonics myth. *Phi Delta Kappan, 70,* 226-240.

Carbo, M. (1996). Whole language or phonics? Use both. *Education Digest, 61,* 60-64.

Chall, J. S. (1967). *Learning to read: The great debate.* New York: McGraw-Hill.

Chall, J. S. (1989). Learning to read: The great debate 20 years later— A response to "Debunking the Great Phonics Myth." *Phi Delta Kappan, 70,* 521-537.

Clay, M. M. (1985). *The early detection of reading difficulties* (3rd ed.). Auckland: Heinemann.

Coles, G. S. (1997, April 2). Phonics findings discounted as part of flawed research [Letter to the editor]. *Education Week,* 45.

Dyer, P. (1992). Reading Recovery: A cost-effectiveness and educational outcomes analysis. *ERS Spectrum, 10,* 10-19.

Ehri, L. C., Nunes, S. R., Stahl, S. A., & Willows, D. (2001). Systematic phonics instruction helps students learn to read: Evidence from the National Reading Panel's meta-analysis. *Review of Educational Research, 71*(3), 393-447.

Elbaum, B., Vaughn, S., Hughes, M. T., & Moody, S. W. (2000). How effective are one-to-one tutoring programs in reading for elementary students at-risk for reading failure? A meta-analysis of the intervention research. *Journal of Educational Psychology, 92*, 605-619.

Evans, T. L. P. (1996). *I can read deze books: A quantitative comparison of the Reading Recovery program and a small-group intervention.* Unpublished doctoral dissertation, Auburn University, Auburn, Alabama.

Foorman, B. R., Fletcher, J. M., Francis, D. J., Schatschneider, C., & Mehta, P. (1998). The role of instruction in learning to read: Preventing reading failure in at-risk children. *Journal of Educational Psychology, 90*(1), 37-55.

Foorman, B. R., Fletcher, J. M., Francis, D. J., & Schatschneider, C. (2000). Response: Misrepresentation of research by other researchers. *Educational Research, 29*(6), 27-37.

Gaskins, I. W. (1998). There's more to teaching at-risk and delayed readers than good reading instruction. *Reading Teacher, 51*(7), 534-547.

Gaskins, I. W., Downer, M. A., Anderson, R. C., Cunningham, P. M., Gaskins, R. W., & Schommer, M. (1988). A metacognitive approach to phonics: Using what you know to decode what you don't know. *Remedial and Special Education, 9*(1), 36-41.

Gaskins, I. W., Ehri, L. C., Cress, C., O'Hara, C., & Donnelly, K. (1997a). Analyzing words and making discoveries about the alphabetic system: Activities for beginning readers. *Language Arts, 74*, 172-184.

Gaskins, I. W., Ehri, L. C., Cress, C., O'Hara, C., & Donnelly, K. (1997b). Procedures for word learning: Making discoveries about words. *The Reading Teacher, 50*(4), 312-327.

Greaney, K. T., Tunmer, W. E., & Chapman, J. W. (1997). Effects of rime-based orthographic analogy training on the word recognition skills of children with reading disability. *Journal of Educational Psychology, 89*, 645-651.

Hiebert, E. H. (1994). Reading Recovery in the United States: What difference does it make to an age cohort? *Educational Researcher, 23*(9), 15-25.

Lindamood, C., & Lindamood, P. (1984). *Auditory discrimination in depth.* San Luis Obispo, CA: Gander.

Mathes, P. G., & Torgesen, J. K. (1997). A call for equity in reading instruction for all students: A response to Allington and Woodside-Jiron. *Educational Researcher, 29*(6), 4-14.

McEwan, E. K. (2002). *Teach them all to read: Catching the kids who fall through the cracks.* Thousand Oaks, CA: Corwin.

National Reading Panel. (2000). *Report of the National Reading Panel: Teaching children to read: An evidence-based assessment of the scientific research literature on reading and its implications for reading instruction. Reports of the Subgroups.* Rockville, MD: National Institute of Child Health and Human Development.

Reading Recovery Council of North America. (2002a). *Reading Recovery Facts and Figures (U.S. 1984-1999).* Retrieved May 28, 2002, from http://www.readingrecovery.org/sections/reading/facts.asp

Reading Recovery Council of North America (2002b). *The cost-benefits of Reading Recovery.* Retrieved May 28, 2002, from http://www.readingrecovery.org/sections/reding/cost.asp

Taylor, B. M., Anderson, R. C., Au, K. H., Raphael, T. E. (2000). Discretion in the translation of research to policy: A case from beginning reading. *Educational Researcher, 29*(6), 16-26.

Torgesen, J. K., Wagner, R. K., Rashotte, C. A., Rose, E., Lindamood, P., & Conway, T. (1999). Preventing reading failure in young children with phonological processing difficulties: Group and individual responses to instruction. *Journal of Educational Psychology, 91*(4), 579-593.

PRIVATE-SCHOOL VOUCHERS

Bartell, E. (1968). *Costs and benefits of Catholic elementary and secondary schools.* Notre Dame, IN: Notre Dame Press.

Boaz, D., & Barrett, R. M. (1996). *What would a school voucher buy? The real cost of private schools* (Cato Briefing Paper No. 25). Washington, DC: Cato Institute.

Bryk, A. S., Lee, V. E., & Holland, P. B. (1993). *Catholic schools and the common good.* Cambridge, MA: Harvard University Press.

Chubb, J. E., & Moe, T. M. (1990). *Politics, markets, and America's schools.* Washington, DC: Brookings Institution.

Coleman, J. S., Campbell, E. Q., Hobson, C. J., McPartland, J., Mood, A. M., Weinfeld, F. D., & York, R. L. (1966). *Equality of educational opportunity* (Office of Education Publication No. OE-38001). Washington, DC: Government Printing Office.

Coleman, J. S., Hoffer, T., & Kilgore, S. (1982). *High school achievement: Public, Catholic, and private schools compared.* New York: Basic Books.

Evans, W. N., & Schwab, R. M. (1995). Finishing high school and starting college: Do Catholic schools makes a difference? *Quarterly Journal of Economics, 110*(4), 941-974.

Fetterman, D. M. (1982). Ibsen's baths: Reactivity and insensitivity. *Educational Evaluation and Policy Analysis, 4,* 261-279.

Friedman, M. (1955). The role of government in education. In R. A. Solo (Ed.), *Economics and the public interest* (pp. 123-144). New Brunswick, NJ: Rutgers University Press.

Gamoran, A. (1996). Student achievement in public magnet, public comprehensive, and private city high schools. *Educational Evaluation and Policy Analysis, 18*(1), 1-18.

Greene, J. P., Peterson, P. E., & Du, J. (1998). School choice in Milwaukee: A randomized experiment. In P. E. Peterson & B. C. Hassel (Eds.), *Learning from school choice* (pp. 335-356). Washington, DC: Brookings Institution.

Howell, W. G., Wolf, P. J., Campbell, D. E., & Peterson, P. E. (2002). School vouchers and academic performance: Results from three randomized field trials. *Journal of Policy Analysis and Management, 21*(2), 191-217.

Hoxby, C. M. (1998). What do America's "traditional" forms of school choice teach us about school choice reforms? *Federal Reserve Bank of New York Economic Policy Review, 4*(1), 47-59.

King, J. A. (1994). Meeting the needs of at-risk students: A cost analysis of three models. *Educational Evaluation and Policy Analysis, 16,* 1-19.

Levin, H. M. (1991). The economics of educational choice. *Economics of Education Review, 10*(2), 137-158.

Levin, H. M. (1998). Educational vouchers: Effectiveness, choice, and costs. *Journal of Policy Analysis and Management, 17*(3), 373-391.

Levin, H. M. (2002). Issues in designing cost-effectiveness comparisons of whole-school reform. In H. M. Levin & P. J. McEwan (Eds.), *Cost-effectiveness and educational policy: 2002, yearbook of the American Education Finance Association* (pp. 71-96). Larchmont, NY: Eye on Education.

Levin, H. M., & Driver, C. E. (1997). Costs of an educational voucher system. *Education Economics, 5*(3), 265-283.

McEwan, P. J. (2000). The potential impact of large-scale voucher programs. *Review of Educational Research, 70*(2), 103-149.

Mayer, D. P., Peterson, P. E., Myers, D. E., Tuttle, C. C., & Howell, W. G. (2002). *School choice in New York City after three years: An evaluation of the School Choice Scholarships Program* (Report 8404-045, Mathematica Policy Research). Retrieved May 25, 2002, from http://www.mathematica-mpr.com/PDFs/nycfull.pdf

Millsap, M. A., Chase, A., Obeidallah, D., Perez-Smith, A., Brigham, N., & Johnson, K. (2000). *Evaluation of Detroit's Comer Schools and Families Initiative: Final report.* Cambridge, MA: Abt.

Moe, T. M. (Ed.). (1995). *Private vouchers.* Stanford, CA: Hoover Institution.

Molnar, A., Smith, P., Zahorik, J., Palmer, A., Halbach, A., & Ehrle, K. (1999). Evaluating the SAGE Program: A pilot program in targeted pupil-teacher reduction. *Educational Evaluation and Policy Analysis, 21*(2), 165-177.

Neal, D. (1998). What have we learned about the benefits of private schooling? *Federal Reserve Bank of New York Economic Policy Review, 4*(1), 79-86.

Olson, L. (1996, Sept. 4). New studies on private choice contradict each other. *Education Week.* Retrieved May 28, 2002, from http://www.edweek.org/ew/vol-16/01choice.h16

Rouse, C. E. (1998). Private school vouchers and student achievement: An evaluation of the Milwaukee parental choice program. *Quarterly Journal of Economics, 113*(2), 553-602.

West, E. G. (1967). Tom Paine's voucher scheme for public education. *Southern Economic Journal, 33,* 378-382.

Witte, J. F. (1998). The Milwaukee voucher experiment. *Educational Evaluation and Policy Analysis, 20*(4), 229-251.

WHOLE-SCHOOL REFORM

Barnett, W. S. (1996). Economics of school reform: Three promising models. In H. F. Ladd (Ed.), *Holding schools accountable: Performance-based reform in education* (pp. 299-326). Washington, DC: Brookings Institution.

Bloom, H., Ham, S., Kagehiro, S., Melton, L., O'Brien, J., Rock, J., & Doolittle, F. (2001). *Evaluating the Accelerated Schools Program: A look at its early implementation and impact on student achievement in eight schools.* New York: Manpower Development Research Corporation.

Cook, T. D. Habib, F. N. Phillips, M., Settersten, R. A., Shagle, S. C., & Degirmencioglu, S. M. (1999). Comer's School Development Program in Prince George's County, Maryland: A theory-based evaluation. *American Educational Research Journal, 36*(3), 543-597.

Comer School Development Program. (2002, February 14). Retrieved May 29, 2002, from Yale University, Yale Child Study Center Web Site http://www.med.yale.edu/comer

Cook, T. D., Murphy, R. F., & Hunt, H. D. (2000). Comer's School Development Program in Chicago: A theory-based evaluation. *American Educational Research Journal, 37*(2), 535-597.

Levin, H. M. (2002). Issues in designing cost-effectiveness comparisons of whole-school reform. In H. M. Levin & P. J. McEwan (Eds.), *Cost-effectiveness and educational policy: 2002, yearbook of the American Education Finance Association* (pp. 71-96). Larchmont, NY: Eye on Education.

National Center for Accelerated Schools. (2002). Retrieved April 23, 2002, from http://www.acceleratedschools.net/

Northwest Regional Educational Laboratory. (2001). *The catalog of school reform models.* Retrieved April 23, 2001, from http://www.nwrel.org/scpd/catalog/modellist.asp

Slavin, R. E, & Madden, N. A. (2001). *One million children: Success for All.* Thousand Oaks, CA: Corwin.

References

Advantage Learning Systems. (n.d.). *Accelerated Reader.* Wisconsin Rapids, WI: Author.

Anderson, G. L., Herr, K., & Nihlen, A. S. (1994). *Studying your own school: An educator's guide to qualitative practitioner research.* Thousand Oaks, CA: Corwin.

Andrews, Richard. (1989). The Illinois principal as instructional leader: A concept and definition paper. *Illinois Principal,* pp. 4-12.

Angrist, J. D., & Krueger, A. B. (1991). Does compulsory schooling affect schooling and earnings? *Quarterly Journal of Economics, 106,* 979-1014.

Angrist, J., & Levy, V. (1999). Using Maimonides' rule to estimate the effect of class size on scholastic achievement. *Quarterly Journal of Economics, 114(2),* 533-576.

Argyris, C., Putnam, R., & Smith, D. M. (1985). *Action science: Concepts, methods, and skills for research and intervention.* San Francisco: Jossey-Bass.

Ashenfelter, O., & Rouse, C. (2000). Schooling, intelligence, and income in America. In K. Arrow, S. Bowles, & S. Durlauf (Eds.), *Meritocracy and economic inequality* (pp. 89-117). Princeton, NJ: Princeton University Press.

Baker, S., Berninger, V. W., Bruck, M., Chapman, J., Eden, G., Elbaum, B., et al., (2002, May 21). Evidence-based research on Reading Recovery. [A letter sent to educational policymakers regarding the effectiveness of Reading Recovery.] Retrieved May 21, 2002, from http://www.educationnews.org/Reading Recoveryisnotsuccessful.htm

Barnes, N. (2001, April 25). What makes research useful? A look at school-based inquiry in small schools. *Education Week,* 40, 42.

Barnett, W. S. (1996). Economics of school reform: Three promising models. In H. F. Ladd (Ed.), *Holding schools accountable: Performance-based reform in education* (pp. 299-326). Washington, DC: Brookings Institution.

Bartell, E. (1968). *Costs and benefits of Catholic elementary and secondary schools.* Notre Dame, IN: Notre Dame University Press.

Berliner, D. C., & Casanova, U. (1993). *Putting research to work in your school.* New York: Scholastic.

Bloom, H., Ham, S., Kagehiro, S., Melton, L., O'Brien, J., Rock, J., & Doolittle, F. (2001). *Evaluating the Accelerated Schools Program: A look at its early implementation and impact on student achievement in eight schools.* New York: Manpower Development Research Corporation.

Boaz, D., & Barrett, R. M. (1996). *What would a school voucher buy? The real cost of private schools* (Cato Briefing Paper No. 25). Washington, DC: Cato Institute.

Bogdan, R., & Biklen, S. N. (1998). *Qualitative research for education: An introduction to theory and methods.* Boston: Allyn & Bacon.

Boozer, M., & Rouse, C. (1995). *Intraschool variation in class size: Patterns and implications* (Working Paper No. 5144). Cambridge, MA: National Bureau of Economic Research.

Boruch, R. (1997). *Randomized experiments for planning and evaluation: A practical guide.* Thousand Oaks, CA: Sage.

Boruch, R., De Moya, D., & Snyder, B. (2002). The importance of randomized field trials in education and related areas. In F. Mosteller & R. F. Boruch (Eds.). *Evidence matters: Randomized trials in education research* (pp. 50-79). Washington, DC: Brookings Institution.

Bray, J. N., Lee, J., Smith, L. L. & Yorks, L. (2002). *Collaborative inquiry in practice.* Thousand Oaks, CA: Sage.

Brewer, D. J., Krop, C., Gill, B. P., & Reichardt, R. (1999). Estimating the cost of national class size reductions under different policy alternatives. *Educational Evaluation and Policy Analysis, 21*(2), 179-192.

Brookings Institution. (1999, December 8). Can we make education policy on the basis of evidence? What constitutes high quality education research and how can it be incorporated into policymaking? In *Proceedings of a Brookings Press Forum.* Washington, DC: Brookings Institution.

Brooks, A., & Watkins, K. E. (1994). A new era for action technologies: A look at the issues. In A. Brooks & K. E. Watkins (Eds.), *The emerging power of action inquiry technologies* (pp. 5-16). San Francisco: Jossey-Bass.

Bruce, D. (1969). (Ed.). *My brimful book: Favorite poems of childhood, Mother Goose rhymes, and animal stories.* New York: Platt & Munk.

Bryk, A. S., Lee, V. E., & Holland, P. B. (1993). *Catholic schools and the common good.* Cambridge, MA: Harvard University Press.

California Department of Education. (1987). *Caught in the middle.* Sacramento, CA: CDE.

Campbell Collaboration. (2001). *Frequently asked questions about The Campbell Collaboration.* Retrieved March 23, 2002, from http://campbell.gse.upenn.edu/c2-FAQ.htm

Campbell, D. T. (1957). Factors relevant to the validity of experiments in social settings. *Psychological Bulletin, 54,* 297-312.

Campbell, D. T., & Stanley, J. C. (1963). *Experimental and quasi-experimental designs for research.* Chicago: Rand McNally.

Carbo, M. (1988). Debunking the great phonics myth. *Phi Delta Kappan, 70,* 226-240.

Carbo, M. (1996). Whole language or phonics? Use both. *Education Digest, 61,* 60-64.

Carnegie Corporation. (1989). *Turning points: Preparing American youth for the 21st century.* Washington, DC: Carnegie Council on Adolescent Development.

Carr, W., & Kemmis, S. (1986). *Becoming critical: Education, knowledge, and action research.* London: Falmer.

Carroll, L. (1946). *Alice's adventures in wonderland and through the looking glass.* New York: Grossett & Dunlap.

Chall, J. S. (1967). *Learning to read: The great debate.* New York: McGraw-Hill.

Chall, J. S. (1989). Learning to read: The great debate 20 years later—A response to "Debunking the Great Phonics Myth." *Phi Delta Kappan, 70,* 521-537.

Chubb, J. E., & Moe, T. M. (1990). *Politics, markets, and America's schools.* Washington, DC: Brookings Institution.

Clay, M. M. (1985). *The early detection of reading difficulties* (3rd ed.). Auckland, New Zealand: Heinemann.

Clune, W. H. (2002). Methodological strength and policy usefulness of cost-effectiveness research. In H. M. Levin & P. J. McEwan (Eds.), *Cost-effectiveness and educational policy: 2002, yearbook of the American Education Finance Association* (pp. 55-68). Larchmont, NY: Eye on Education.

Coleman, J. S., Campbell, E. Q., Hobson, C. J., McPartland, J., Mood, A. M., Weinfeld, F. D., & York, R. L. (1966). *Equality of educational opportunity* (Office of Education Publication No. OE-38001). Washington, DC: Government Printing Office.

Coleman, J. S., Hoffer, T., & Kilgore, S. (1982). *High school achievement: Public, Catholic, and private schools compared.* New York: Basic Books.

Coles, G. S. (1997, April 2). Phonics findings discounted as part of flawed research [Letter to the editor]. *Education Week,* p. 45.

Comer School Development Program. (2002, February 14). Retrieved May 29, 2002, from Yale University, Yale Child Study Center Web Site http://www.med.yale.edu/comer/

Cook, D. R., & LaFleur, N. K. (1975). *A guide to educational research.* Boston: Allyn & Bacon.

Cook, T. D. (1999). *Considering the major arguments against random assignment: An analysis of the intellectual culture surrounding evaluation in American schools of education.* Unpublished manuscript, Northwestern University.

Cook, T. D., & Campbell, D. T. (1979). *Quasi-experimentation: Design and analysis issues for field settings.* Chicago: Rand McNally.

Cook, T. D., Habib, F. N., Phillips, M., Settersten, R. A., Shagle, S. C., & Degirmencioglu, S. M. (1999). Comer's School Development Program in Prince George's County, Maryland: A theory-based evaluation. *American Educational Research Journal, 36*(3), 543-597.

Cook, T. D., Murphy, R. F., & Hunt, H. D. (2000). Comer's School Development Program in Chicago: A theory-based evaluation. *American Educational Research Journal, 37*(2), 535-597.

Cooper, H., & Hedges, L. V. (Eds.). (1994). *The handbook of research synthesis.* New York: Russell Sage Foundation.

Covey, S. (1990). *The 7 habits of highly effective people: Powerful lessons in personal change.* New York: Fireside.

Cronbach, L. J. (1975). Beyond two disciplines of scientific psychology. *American Psychologist, 30,* 116-127.

Cunningham, J. B. (1993). *Action research and organizational development.* Westport, CT: Praeger.

Dewey, J. (1929). *The quest for certainty.* New York: Minton, Balch.

Dewey, J. (1933). *How we think* (Rev. ed.). Lexington, MA: Heath.

Donald, A. (2002). A practical guide to evidence-based medicine. *Medscape Psychiatry & Mental Health eJournal, 7*(2). Retrieved May 28, 2002, from http://www.medscape.com/viewarticle/430709

Dorn, R. (1995). The changing roles of principals and staff members. *Wingspan, 10*(2), 7-10).

DuFour, R. (2000). Data puts a face on shared vision. *Journal of Staff Development, 21*(1), 71-72.

DuFour, R., & Eaker, R. (1998). *Professional learning communities at work: Best practices for enhancing student achievement.* Bloomington, IN: National Educational Service.

Dyer, P. (1992). Reading Recovery: A cost-effectiveness and educational outcomes analysis. *ERS Spectrum, 10,* 10-19.

Editorial. (2002, March 20). *USA Today,* p. 14A.

Edmondson, A. (2001, June 19). Watson kills all reform models for city schools. *The Memphis Commercial Appeal.* Retrieved May 30, 2002, from http://nl12.newsbank.com

Ehri, L. C., Nunes, S. R., Stahl, S. A., & Willows, D. (2001). Systematic phonics instruction helps students learn to read: Evidence from the National Reading Panel's meta-analysis. *Review of Educational Research, 71*(3), 393-447.

Elbaum, B., Vaughn, S., Hughes, M. T., & Moody, S. W. (2000). How effective are one-to-one tutoring programs in reading for elementary students at-risk for reading failure? A meta-analysis of the intervention research. *Journal of Educational Psychology, 92,* 605-619.

Establish CSR Program Bill of 1996, Cal. S.B. 1777 (1996). Retrieved December 15, 2002, from   http://www.cde.ca.gov/classsize/legis/sb_1777.htm

Evans, T. L. P. (1996). *I can read deze books: A quantitative comparison of the Reading Recovery* program and a small-group intervention. Unpublished doctoral dissertation. Auburn University, Auburn, Alabama.

Evans, W. N., & Schwab, R. M. (1995). Finishing high school and starting college: Do Catholic schools makes a difference? *Quarterly Journal of Economics, 110(4), 941-974.*

Fetterman, D. M. (1982). Ibsen's baths: Reactivity and insensitivity. *Educational Evaluation and Policy Analysis, 4,* 261-279.

Filstead, W. (1970). *Qualitative methodology.* Chicago: Markham.

Fine, M. (1991). *Framing dropouts: Notes on the politics of an urban high school.* Albany, NY: State University of New York Press.

Fleischer, C. (1995). *Composing teacher-research: A prosaic history.* Albany: State University of New York Press.

Foorman, B. R., Fletcher, J. M., Francis, D. J., & Schatschneider, C. (2000). Response: Misrepresentation of research by other researchers. *Educational Research, 29*(6), 27-37.

Foorman, B. R., Fletcher, J. M., Francis, D. J., & Schatschneider, C., & Mehta, P. (1998). The role of instruction in learning to read: Preventing reading failure in at-risk children. *Journal of Educational Psychology, 90*(1), 37-55.

Freire, P. (1993). *Pedagogy of the oppressed* (rev. 20th anniv. ed.). New York: Continuum. (Original work published in 1970)

Friedman, M. (1955). The role of government in education. In R. A. Solo (Ed.), *Economics and the public interest* (pp. 123-144). New Brunswick, NJ: Rutgers University Press.

Gage, N. L. (1989). The paradigm wars and their aftermath: A "historical" sketch of research on teaching since 1989. *Teachers College Record, 91*(2), 135-156.

Gamoran, A. (1996). Student achievement in public magnet, public comprehensive, and private city high schools. *Educational Evaluation and Policy Analysis, 18*(1), pp. 1-18.

Gaskins, I. W. (1998). There's more to teaching at-risk and delayed readers than good reading instruction. *Reading Teacher, 51*(7), 534-547.

Gaskins, I. W., Downer, M. A., Anderson, R. C., Cunningham, P. M., Gaskins, R. W., & Schommer, M. (1988). A metacognitive approach to phonics: Using what you know to decode what you don't know. *Remedial and Special Education, 9*(1), 36-41.

Gaskins, I. W., Ehri, L. C., Cress, C., O'Hara, C., & Donnelly, K. (1997a). Analyzing words and making discoveries about the alphabetic system: Activities for beginning readers. *Language Arts, 74,* 172-184.

Gaskins, I. W., Ehri, L. C., Cress, C., O'Hara, C., & Donnelly, K. (1997b). Procedures for word learning: Making discoveries about words. *The Reading Teacher, 50*(4), 312-327).

Gaskins, I. W., & Elliot, T. T. (1991). *Implementing cognitive strategy instruction across the school: The Benchmark manual for teachers.* Cambridge, MA: Brookline.

Gilbert, M. (1991). *Churchill: A life.* New York: Henry Holt.

Greaney, K. T., Tunmer, W. E., & Chapman, J. W. (1997). Effects of rime-based orthographic analogy training on the word recognition skills of children with reading disability. *Journal of Educational Psychology, 89,* 645-651.

Greenberg, D., & Shroder, M. (1997). *The digest of social experiments* (2nd ed.). Washington, DC: Urban Institute Press.

Greene, J. P., Peterson, P. E., & Du, J. (1998). School choice in Milwaukee: A randomized experiment. In P. E. Peterson & B. C. Hassel (Eds.), *Learning from school choice* (pp. 335-356). Washington, DC: Brookings Institution.

Greenleaf, C. (1999, April). *Apprenticing adolescent readers to academic literacy.* Paper presented at the annual meeting of the American Educational Research Association, Montreal.

Greenwald, R., Hedges, L. V., & Laine, R. D. (1996). The effect of school resources on student achievement. *Review of Educational Research, 66*(3), 361-396.

Griliches, Z. (1985). Data and econometricians—the uneasy alliance. *American Economic Review, 75*(2), 196-200.

Grissmer, D. (1999). Class size effects: Assessing the evidence, its policy implications, and future research agenda. *Educational Evaluation and Policy Analysis, 21*(2), 231-248.

Grissmer, D. (2002). Cost-effectiveness and cost-benefit analysis: The effect of targeting interventions. In H. M. Levin & P. J. McEwan (Eds.), *Cost-effectiveness and educational policy: 2002, yearbook of the American Education Finance Association* (pp. 97-110). Larchmont, NY: Eye on Education.

Grundy, S. (1982). Three modes of action research. *Curriculum Perspectives, 2*(3), 23-34.

Guryan, J. (2001). *Does money matter? Regression-discontinuity estimates from education finance reform in Massachusetts* (Working Paper No. 8269). Cambridge, MA: National Bureau of Economic Research.

Hale, C. R. (2000). What is activist research? *Items and Issues, 2*(1-2), 13.

Hanushek, E. A. (1986). The economics of schooling: Production and efficiency in public schools. *Journal of Economic Literature, 24*(3), 1141-1177.

Hanushek, E. A. (1997). Assessing the effect of school resources on student performance: An update. *Educational Evaluation and Policy Analysis, 19*(2), 141-164.

Hanushek, E. A. (1999). Some findings from an independent investigation of the Tennessee STAR experiment and from other investigations of class size effects. *Educational Evaluation and Policy Analysis, 21*(2), 143-163.

Harman, W. W. (1990). Shifting context for executive behavior: Signs of change and revaluation. In S. Srivastva, D. L. Cooperrider, and Associates (Eds.), *Appreciative management and leadership: The power of positive thought and action in organizations* (pp. 37-54). San Francisco: Jossey-Bass.

Harris, D. (2002). Identifying optimal class sizes and teacher salaries. In H. M. Levin & P. J. McEwan (Eds.), *Cost-effectiveness and educational policy: 2002, yearbook of the American Education Finance Association* (pp. 177-191). Larchmont, NY: Eye on Education.

Haycock, K., & Ames, N. (2000, July 24-25). Where are we now? Taking stock of middle grades education. In *Proceedings of the National Conference on Curriculum, Instruction, and Assessment in the Middle Grades: Linking Research and Practice* (pp. 49-77). Washington, DC: National Educational Research Policy and Priorities Board, U.S. Department of Education.

Heron, J. (1981). Experiential research methodology. In P. Reason & J. Rowan (Eds.), *Human inquiry* (pp. 153-166). Chichester, UK: Wiley.

Hiebert, E. H. (1994). Reading Recovery in the United States: What difference does it make to an age cohort? *Educational Researcher, 23*(9), 15-25.

Howell, W. G., Wolf, P. J., Campbell, D. E., & Peterson, P. E. (2002). School vouchers and academic performance: Results from three randomized field trials. *Journal of Policy Analysis and Management, 21*(2), 191-217.

Hoxby, C. M. (1998). What do America's "traditional" forms of school choice teach us about school choice reforms? *Federal Reserve Bank of New York Economic Policy Review, 4*(1), 47-59.

Illig, D. C. (1996). Reducing class size: A review of the literature and options for consideration. Retrieved June 11, 2002, from http://www.library.ca.gov/CRB/clssz/clssiz.html#RTFToC13

Interagency Education Research Initiative. (2002). Retrieved May 23, 2002, from http://www.ed.gov/offices/OERI/IERI/index.html

Jacobson, L. (2001, Feb. 28). Research: Sizing up small classes. *Education Week.* Retrieved April 23, 2002, from http://www.edweek.com/ew/ewstory.cfm?slug=24classsize.h20

Johnston, R. C. (1996, August 7). Calif. Budget allows for smaller classes. *Education Week.* Retrieved October 2, 2002 from http://www.edweek.com

Jones, E. M., Gottfredson, G. D., & Gottfredson, D. C. (1997). Success for some: An evaluation of a Success for All program. *Evaluation Review, 21*(6), 643-670.

Jordan, H., Mendro, R., & Weerasinghe, D. (1997, July). Teacher effects on longitudinal student achievement. Paper presented at the CREATE Annual Meeting, Indianapolis, IN.

Kaestle, C. F. (1993). The awful reputation of education research. *Educational Researcher, 22*(1), 26-31.

King, J. A. (1994). Meeting the needs of at-risk students: A cost analysis of three models. *Educational Evaluation and Policy Analysis, 16*, 1-19.

King, G., Keohane, R. D., & Verba, S. (1994). *Designing social inquiry: Scientific inference in qualitative research.* Princeton, NJ: Princeton University Press.

Krueger, A. B. (1999). Experimental estimates of education production functions. *Quarterly Journal of Economics, 114*(2), 497-532.

Krueger, A. B. (2000, October). Understanding the magnitude and effect of class size on student achievement (Working Paper No. 121, Economic Policy Institute). Retrieved May 27, 2002, from http://www.epinet.org/Workingpapers/classsize.html

Krueger, A. B., & Whitmore, D. M. (2001). The effect of attending a small class in the early grades on college-test taking and middle school test results: Evidence from Project STAR. *Economic Journal, 111*(468), 1-28.

Lagemann, E. C. (2000). *An elusive science: The troubling history of education research.* Chicago: University of Chicago Press.

Lagemann, E. C. (2002, January 24). Useable knowledge in education: A memorandum for the Spencer Foundation Board of Directors. Retrieved March 13, 2002, from http://www. spencer.org/publications/usable_knowledge_report_ecl_a.htm

Lagemann, E. C. & Shulman, L. S. (Eds.). (1999). *Issues in education research: Problems and possibilities.* San Francisco: Jossey-Bass.

Levin, H. M. (1975). Cost-effectiveness in evaluation research. In M. Guttentag & E. Struening (Eds.), *Handbook of evaluation research* (Vol. 2, pp. 89-122). Beverly Hills, CA: Sage.

Levin, H. M. (1991). The economics of educational choice. *Economics of Education Review, 10*(2), 137-158.

Levin, H. M. (1998). Educational vouchers: Effectiveness, choice, and costs. *Journal of Policy Analysis and Management, 17*(3), 373-391.

Levin, H. M. (2002). Issues in designing cost-effectiveness comparison of whole-school reforms. In H. M. Levin & P. J. McEwan (Eds.), *Cost-effectiveness and educational policy: 2002, yearbook of the American Education Finance Association* (pp. 71-96). Larchmont, NY: Eye on Education.

Levin, H. M., & Driver, C. E. (1997). Costs of an educational voucher system. *Education Economics, 5*(3), 265-283.

Levin, H. M., Glass, G. V., & Meister, G. R. (1987). Cost-effectiveness of computer assisted instruction. *Evaluation Review, 11*(1), 50-72.

Levin, H. M., & McEwan, P. J. (2001). *Cost-effectiveness analysis: Methods and applications* (2nd ed.). Thousand Oaks, CA: Sage.

Levin, H. M., & McEwan, P. J. (Eds.). (2002). *Cost-effectiveness and educational policy: 2002, yearbook of the American Education Finance Association.* Larchmont, NY: Eye on Education.

Lewin, K. (1946). Action research and minority problems. *Journal of Social Issues 2*(4), 34-46.

Lewis-Beck, M. S. (1980). *Applied regression: An introduction* (Quantitative Applications in the Social Sciences, No. 22). Newbury Park, CA: Sage.

Lindamood, C., & Lindamood, P. (1984). *Auditory discrimination in depth.* San Luis Obispo, CA: Gander.

Lindblom, C. E., & Cohen, D. K. (1979). *Usable knowledge: Social science and social problem solving.* New Haven, CT: Yale University Press.

Lipsitz, J. (1984). *Successful schools for young adolescents.* New Brunswick, NJ: Transaction.

Masse, L. N., & Barnett, W. S. (2002). A benefit-cost analysis of the Abecedarian Early Childhood Intervention. In H. M. Levin & P. J. McEwan (Eds.), *Cost-effectiveness and educational policy: 2002, yearbook of the American Education Finance Association* (pp. 157-176). Larchmont, NY: Eye on Education.

Mathes, P. G., & J. K. Torgesen, J. K. (1997). A call for equity in reading instruction for all students: A response to Allington and Woodside-Jiron, (p. 6). *Educational Researcher, 29*(6), 4-14.

Mayer, D. P., Peterson, P. E., Myers, D. E., Tuttle, C. C., & Howell, W. G. (2002). School choice in New York City after three years: An evaluation of the School Choice Scholarships Program (Report 8404-045). *Mathematica Policy Research.* Retrieved May 25, 2002, from http://www.mathematica-mpr.com/PDFs/nycfull.pdf

McEwan, E. K. (2002). *Teach them all to read: Catching the kids who fall through the cracks.* Thousand Oaks, CA: Corwin.

McEwan, P. J. (2000). The potential impact of large-scale voucher programs. *Review of Educational Research, 70*(2), 103-149.

McEwan, P. J. (2002). Are cost-effectiveness methods used correctly? In H. M. Levin & P. J. McEwan (Eds.), *Cost effectiveness and educational policy: 2002 Yearbook of the American Educational Finance Association* (pp. 37-53). Larchmont, NY: Eye on Education.

McKechnie, J. L. (Ed.). (1983). *Webster's new universal unabridged dictionary* (2nd ed.). New York: Simon & Schuster.

McLaren, P. (1998). *Life in schools: an introduction to critical pedagogy in the foundations of education.* New York: Longman.

Miller, D. W. (1999, August 6). The black hole of education research. *Chronicle of Higher Education,* A17-18.

Millsap, M. A., Chase, A., Obeidallah, D., Perez-Smith, A., Brigham, N., & Johnson, K. (2000). *Evaluation of Detroit's Comer Schools and Families Initiative: Final report.* Cambridge, MA: Abt.

Moe, T. M. (Ed.). (1995). *Private vouchers.* Stanford, CA: Hoover Institution.

Molnar, A., Smith, P., Zahorik, J., Palmer, A., Halbach, A., & Ehrle, K. (1999). Evaluating the SAGE Program: A pilot program in targeted pupil-teacher reduction. *Educational Evaluation and Policy Analysis, 21*(2), 165-177.

Mosteller, F. (1995). The Tennessee study of class size in the early school grades. *The Future of Children, 5*(2), 113-127.

Mosteller, F., & Boruch, R. (Eds.). (2002). *Evidence matters: Randomized trials in education research.* Washington, DC: Brookings Institution.

National Center for Accelerated Schools. (2002a). *General information.* Retrieved April 23, 2002, from http://www.acceleratedschools.net/

National Center for Accelerated Schools. (2002b). *General information.* Retrieved June 15, 2002, from http://www.acceleratedschools.net/main_gen.htm

National Center for Education Statistics. (2001, January 24). *NAEP 1988 reading report card. National and state highlights.* Retrieved May 29, 2001 from http://nces.ed.gov/nationsreportcard/reading/stureadmore.asp

National Center for Education Statistics. (2002a). *High school and beyond.* Retrieved May 28, 2002, from http://nces.ed.gov/surveys/hsb/

National Center for Education Statistics. (2002b). *National Education Longitudinal Study (NELS).* Retrieved May 28, 2002, from http://nces.ed.gov/surveys/nels88/

National Clearinghouse for Comprehensive School Reform. (2002, May 24). *Home page.* Retrieved June 1, 2002, from http://www.goodschools.gwu.edu

National Educational Research Policy and Priorities Board. (2000a). *A blueprint for progress in American education* (A White Paper). Washington, DC: Author.

National Educational Research Policy and Priorities Board. (2000b). *Proceedings of the National Conference on Curriculum, Instruction, and Assessment in the Middle Grades: Linking Research and Practice,* July 24-25, 2000. Washington, DC: Author. Retrieved May 28, 2002, from http://www.ed.gov/offices

National Educational Research Policy and Priorities Board. (2002). *Mission statement.* Retrieved May 28, 2002, from http://www.ed.gov/offices/

National Forum to Accelerate Middle Grades Reform (2002). *Schools to watch: Selection criteria.* Retrieved on May 28, 2002, from http://www.mgforum.org/criteria.asp

National Middle School Association. (1982). *This we believe.* Columbus, OH: Author.

National Reading Panel. (2000). *Report of the National Reading Panel: Teaching children to read: An evidence-based assessment of the scientific research literature on reading and its implications for reading instruction. Reports of the Subgroups.* Rockville, MD: National Institute of Child Health and Human Development.

National Science Foundation. (2002). *NSF creation and mission.* Retrieved May 31, 2002, from http://www.nsf.gov/home/ about/creation.htm

Neal, D. (1998). What have we learned about the benefits of private schooling? *Federal Reserve Bank of New York Economic Policy Review, 4*(1), 79-86.

No Child Left Behind Act of 2002, Pub. L. No. 107-110 115 Stat.1425, H. R. 1 (2002). Retrieved May 28, 2002, from http://www.ed.gov.legislation/ESEA02/

Noblit, G. E., & Hare, D. W., (1988). *Meta-ethnography: Synthesizing qualitative studies.* Thousand Oaks, CA: Sage.

Northwest Regional Educational Laboratory. (2001). *The catalog of school reform models.* Retrieved April, 23, 2001 from http://www.nwrel.org/scpd/ catalog/modellist.asp

Nye, B., Hedges, L. V., & Konstantopoulos, S. (1999). The long-term effects of small classes: A five-year follow-up of the Tennessee class size experiment. *Educational Evaluation and Policy Analysis, 21*(2), 127-142.

Olson, L. (1996, Sept. 4). New studies on private choice contradict each other. *Education Week.* Retrieved May 28, 2002, from http://www.edweek.org/ew/vol-16/01choice.h16

Olson, L., & Viadero, D. (2002, January 30). Law mandates scientific base for research. *Education Week, 1,* 14-15.

Orr, L. L. (1999). *Social experiments: Evaluating public programs with experimental methods.* Thousand Oaks, CA: Sage.

Patton, M. Q. (1986). *Utilization-focused evaluation.* Thousand Oaks, CA: Sage.

Patton, M. Q. (2002). *Qualitative research & evaluation methods* (3rd ed.). Thousand Oaks, CA: Sage.

Peters, T., & Waterman, R. H. (1982). *In search of excellence: Lessons from America's best-run companies.* New York: Harper & Row.

Phillips, D. C. (2000). *The expanded social scientist's bestiary: A guide to fabled threats to, and defenses of, naturalistic social science.* Lanham, MD: Rowman & Littlefield.

Pilgreen, J. L. (2000). *The SSR handbook: How to organize and manage a sustained silent reading program.* Portsmouth, NH: Boyton/Cook.

Policy Studies Associates, Inc. (2002). *A validation report on READ 180: A print and electronic adaptive intervention program, grades 4-8.* Washington, DC: Author.

Public Agenda. (2002). *Reality check 2002.* New York: Author.

Pressley, M., Burkell, J., Cariglia-Bull, T., Lysynchuk, L., McGoldrick, J. A., Schneider, B., Snyder, B., Symons, S., & Woloshyn, V. E. (1995). *Cognitive strategy instruction that really improves children's academic performance.* Cambridge, MA: Brookline.

Ravitch, D. (1998, December 16). What if research really mattered? *Education Week.* Retrieved February 25, 2002, from http://www. edweek.com

Reading Recovery Council of North America. (2002a). *Reading Recovery facts and figures (U.S. 1984-1999).* Retrieved May 28, 2002, from http://www. readingrecovery.org/sections/reading/ facts.asp

Reading Recovery Council of North America (2002b). *The cost-benefits of Reading Recovery.* Retrieved May 28, 2002, from http://www.readingrecovery.org

Revans, R. (1982). What is action learning? *Journal of Management Development, 1*(3), 64-75.

Rice, J. K. (1997). Cost analysis in education: Paradox and possibility. *Educational Evaluation and Policy Analysis, 19*(4), 309-317.

Rouse, C. E. (1998). Private school vouchers and student achievement: An evaluation of the Milwaukee parental choice program. *Quarterly Journal of Economics, 113*(2), 553-602.

Ruffini, S. (1992). *Assessment of Success for All school years 1988-1991.* Unpublished report. Baltimore: Baltimore City Public Schools, Department of Research and Evaluation.

Sanford, N. (1981). A model for action research. In P. Reason & J. Rowan (Eds.), *Human inquiry* (pp. 173-181). Chichester, UK: Wiley.

Santa, C. M. (1986). Content reading in secondary school. In J. Orasanu. (Ed.), *Reading comprehension: From research to practice* (pp. 303-317). Hillsdale, NJ: Lawrence Erlbaum.

Sarason, S. B. (1996). *Revisiting "The Culture of the School and the Problem of Change."* New York: Teachers College Press.

Schmoker, M. (2001). *The results fieldbook: Practical strategies from dramatically improved schools.* Alexandria, VA: Association for Supervision and Curriculum Development.

Schoenbach R., Greenleaf, C., Cziko, C., & Hurwitz, L. (1999). *Reading for understanding: A guide to improving reading in middle and high school classrooms.* San Francisco: Jossey-Bass.

Scholastic. (n.d.). *READ180: Proven intervention that turns lives around* (Brochure). New York: Author.

Schwandt, T. A. (2001). *Dictionary of qualitative inquiry* (2nd ed.). Thousand Oaks, CA: Sage.

Shadish, W. R., Cook, T. D., & Campbell, D. T. (2002). *Experimental and quasi-experimental designs for generalized causal inference.* Boston: Houghton Mifflin.

Shaker, P., & Heilman, E. E. (2002). Advocacy versus authority—Silencing the education professoriate. *Policy Perspectives, 3*(1), 1-6.

Shavelson, R. J., & Towne, L. (Eds.). (2002). *Scientific inquiry in education.* Washington, DC: National Academy Press.

Silverman, D. (2001). *Interpreting qualitative data.* London: Sage.

Slavin, R. E., & Madden, N. A. (1995, April). *Effects of Success for All on the achievement of English language learners.* Paper presented at the annual meeting of the American Educational Research Association, San Francisco.

Slavin, R. E., & Madden, N. A. (1999). *Success for All/Roots & Wings: Summary of research on achievement outcomes* (Report No. 41). Baltimore: Johns Hopkins University, Success for All Foundation.

Slavin, R. E, & Madden, N. A. (2001). *One million children: Success for All.* Thousand Oaks, CA: Corwin.

Slavin, R. E., Madden, N. E., Dolan, L., J., & Wasik, B. A. (1996). *Every child, every school: Success for all.* Thousand Oaks, CA: Corwin.

Smith, M. L., & Glass, G. V. (1987). *Research and evaluation in education and the social sciences.* Englewood Cliffs, NJ: Prentice Hall.

Snow, C. E. (2001). Knowing what we know: Children, teachers, researchers. *Educational Researcher, 30*(7), 3-9.

Snow, C. E. Burns, M. W., & Griffin, P. (Eds.). (1998). *Preventing reading difficulties in young children.* Washington, DC: National Academy Press, Committee on the Prevention of Reading Difficulties in Young Children, Commission on Behavioral and Social Sciences and Education, National Research Council.

Spindler, G. D. (1982). *Doing the ethnography of schooling: Educational anthropology in action.* New York: Holt, Rinehart, & Winston.

Srivastva, S., Fry, R. E., & Cooperrider, D. L. (1990). Introduction: The call for executive appreciation. In S. Srivastva, D. L. Cooperrider, and Associates (Eds.), *Appreciative management and leadership: The power of positive thought and action in organizations* (pp. 1-33). San Francisco: Jossey-Bass.

Stecher, B. M., & Bornstedt, G. W. (2002). *Class size reduction in California: Summary findings from 1999-00 and 2000-01* (Technical Report, CSR Research Consortium). Retrieved May 28, 2002, from http://www.classize.org/techreport/index-01.htm

Stokes, D. E. (1997). *Pasteur's quadrant: Basic science and technological innovation.* Washington, DC: Brookings Institution.

Strategic Education Research Partnership. (2002). *Current BBCSSE (Behavioral, Cognitive, Sensory Science, and Education) Projects.* Retrieved November 22, 2002, from http://www7.nationalacademies.org

Success for All Foundation. (2002). *Our history.* Retrieved May 28, 2002, from http://www.successforallNet/about/history.htm

Taylor, B. M., Anderson, R. C., Au, K. H., Raphael, T. E. (2000). Discretion in the translation of research to policy: A case from beginning reading. *Educational Researcher, 29*(6), 16-26.

ten Have, P. (1998) *Doing conversation analysis: A practical guide.* London: Sage.

Torbert, W. R., (1981). Why education research has been so uneducational: The case for a new model of social science based on collaborative inquiry. In P. Reason (Ed.), *Human inquiry in action: Developments in new paradigm research* (pp. 141-151). London: Sage.

Torbert, W. R. (1987). *Managing the corporate dream: Restructuring for long-term success.* Homewood, IL: Dow Jones-Irwin.

Torbert, W. R. (1991). *The power of balance.* Newbury Park, CA: Sage.

Torgesen, J. K., Wagner, R. K., Rashotte, C. A., Rose, E., Lindamood, P., & Conway, T. (1999). Preventing reading failure in young children with phonological processing difficulties: Group and individual responses to instruction. *Journal of Educational Psychology, 91*(4), 579-593.

Urdegar, S. (1998). *Evaluation of the Success for All Programs, 1997-1998.* Unpublished report. Miami Public Schools, Miami, FL.

Urdegar, S. (1999, August 10). Success for All is unethical. Letter to the Editor. *Wall Street Journal,* 21A

Urquiola, M. (2000). *Identifying class size effects in developing countries: Evidence from rural schools in Bolivia.* Unpublished manuscript, Cornell University.

U.S. Department of Education. (2002, February 6). *The use of scientifically based research in education* (A Working Group Conference). Washington, DC: Author.

Venezky, R. (1998). An alternative perspective on Success for All. In K. K. Wong (Ed.), *Advances in educational policy: Perspectives on the social functions of school* (Vol. 4, pp. 57-78). Greenwich, CT: JAI.

Viadero, D. (2001, January 10). Panel to define scientific rigor in schools research. *Education Week,* 16.

Viadero, D. (2002, April 3) Campbell Collaboration seeks to firm up 'soft sciences.' *Education Week,* 8.

Walker, M. H. (1996). What research really says. *Principal, 74*(4), 41.

West, E. G. (1967). Tom Paine's voucher scheme for public education. *Southern Economic Journal, 33,* 378-382.

"What Works" Clearinghouse. (2002). *"What works" clearinghouse.* Retrieved May 28, 2002, from http://www.whitehouse.gov/infocus/education/teachers/sect-4.pdf

Witte, J. F. (1992). Private versus public school achievement: Are there findings that should affect the educational choice debate? *Economics of Education Review,* 11(4), 371-394.

Witte, J. F. (1998). The Milwaukee voucher experiment. *Educational Evaluation and Policy Analysis, 20*(4), 229-251.

Wolcott, H. F. (1973). *The man in the principal's office: An ethnography.* New York: Holt, Rinehart & Winston.

Wood, E., Wolosyn, V. E., & Willoughby, T. (Eds.). (1995). *Cognitive strategy instruction for middle and high schools.* Cambridge, MA: Brookline.

Wooden, J. (with Jamison, S.). (1997). *Wooden: A lifetime of observations and reflections on and off the court.* Chicago: Contemporary Books.

Zahorik, J., Molnar, A., Ehrle, K., & Halbach, A. (2000). Smaller classes, better teaching? Effective teaching in reduced-size classes. In S. W. M. Laine & J. G. Ward (Eds.), *Using what we know: A review of the research on implementing class-size reduction initiatives for state and local policymakers* (pp. 53-73). Oak Brook, IL: North Central Regional Educational Laboratory.

Zeichner, K. M., & Gore, J. M. (1995). Using action research as a vehicle for student teacher reflection: A social reconstructionist approach. In S. E. Noffke & R. B. Stevenson (Eds.), *Educational action research: Becoming practically critical* (pp. 13-30). New York: Teachers College Press.

Zemelman, S., Daniels, H., & Hyde, A. (1998). *Best practices: New standards for teaching and learning in America's schools.* Portsmouth, NH: Heinemann.

Index